SOCIETY IN AMERICA

SOCIETY IN AMERICA

Harriet Martineau

Edited, Abridged, and with an Introduction by
Seymour Martin Lipset

Transaction Publishers
New Brunswick (U.S.A.) and London (U.K.)

Second printing 1994
Transaction Edition 1981

Copyright © 1962 by Seymour Martin Lipset, published by Anchor Books, Doubleday & Co.

Library of Congress Catalog Number: 80-27647
ISBN: 0-87855-420-3 (cloth); 0-87855-853-5 (paper)
Printed in the United States of America

Library of Congress Cataloging in Publication Data

Martineau, Harriet, 1802-1875.
    Society in America.

    (Social science classics)
    Reprint of the 1962 ed. published by Anchor Books, Garden City, N.Y., which was issued as Doubleday anchor original, A302.
    Bibliography: p.
    1. United States—Social life and customs—1783-1865. 2. United States—Economic conditions—To 1865. 3. United States/Politics and government—1815-1861. 4. United States—Description and travel—1783-1848. 5. Martineau, Harriet, 1802-1876. I. Lipset, Seymour Martin. II. Title. III. Series.
[E165.M393   1981]   973   80-27647
ISBN 0-87855-420-3
ISBN 0-87855-853-5 (pbk.)

Harriet Martineau's America

SEYMOUR MARTIN LIPSET

AMERICANS today have forgotten, if they ever knew, the meaning the United States once held for the world. To the nineteenth century European, America was a land of promises. To the penniless worker and peasant, it was the land to which they might someday emigrate. There, in a country without kings or nobility, they might live as free and equal men, with the actual possibility of gaining a decent economic and social position. To the intellectuals, the politically concerned, the rulers, and the rebels, America was both a reality and a symbol. It was a democratic republic permeated by equality in social relations. To the conservative and to the radical, it proved that such republics could survive.

This image of a new society brought thousands of "travelers," men and women of middle- and upper-class background who came to observe how the new revolutionary system worked. The intellectuals returned home to inform their compatriots through articles and books about America. These writings, the "foreign-traveler" literature, have always commanded attention both in their home countries and in America.[1]

[1] For a discussion of the meaning of America to different sections of British opinion in the mid-nineteenth century, see

The foreign-traveler literature constitutes a treasure-trove for students of American society. In a sense, these works were the first massive effort to apply sociology's conceptual framework to the study of a complex society. The problem that interested everyone, foreigners and natives alike, was not America's political history, but its sociology. What were the factors involved in the development and operation of this unique social structure? The classic writings about European nations have been distinctly historical in character. England and France, for example, have been seen as products of their history. Men write of England from the Conquest to the present trying to explain the nation's development in terms of particular historical events. The same is true for France. But the United States in a certain sense has been a country without a history, without great men. The open frontier, the absence of primogeniture, egalitarian social relations, a common school system, mass production, immigration, social mobility, a heterogeneous nonestablished church, and the like are the factors given predominance in explaining America's evolution. The travelers' books contain chapter headings that read like sections of contemporary anthropological treatises on exotic peoples, religion, the place of women, children, politics, land-tenure, and so forth. The Europeans came to America from societies that retained strong elements of a feudal caste-ridden past. They were constantly struck by the differences between comparable institutions at home and in America. Explicitly or implicitly they attempted to explain the causes and the consequences of these variations. For the most part these writers employed what has come to be known as the comparative approach in sociological analysis. They treated different societies and their components as units of analysis and

Henry Pelling, *America and the British Left* (London: Adam and Charles Black, 1956), esp. pp. 1–4. For other countries see David Hecht, *Russian Radicals Look to America 1825–1894* (Cambridge: Harvard University Press, 1947); and Halvdan Koht, *The American Spirit in Europe, a Survey of Transatlantic Influences* (Philadelphia: University of Pennsylvania Press, 1949).

generalized about causal relations within social systems. Alexis de Tocqueville, perhaps the most brilliant of them, credited the comparative method with the success of his *Democracy in America.*

> In my work on America . . . though I seldom mention France, I did not write a page without thinking of her, and placing her as it were before me. . . . I believe that this perpetual silent reference to France was a principal cause of the book's success.[2]

Methodological self-consciousness also characterized the work of Harriet Martineau, whose major treatise on American society is reprinted here. On shipboard in 1834, on her way to a two-year intensive study of American society, she wrote the first draft of what later became a volume of instructions to travelers seeking to study foreign cultures, *How to Observe Manners and Morals.*[3] This volume is, perhaps, the first book on the methodology of social research in the then still unborn disciplines of sociology and anthropology. Martineau[*] realized that the study of social systems was a separate scientific discipline, and called it the "science of morals and manners." As her most recent biographer has written, "for years she had been preaching sociology without the name."[4]

[2] See his letter to Kergorlay (19 October, 1843) in *Memoir, Letters and Remains of Alexis de Tocqueville* (Boston: Ticknor and Fields, 1862), vol. I, p. 342.

[3] (London: Charles Knight and Co., 1838). This book appeared after *Society in America.* She elaborated and rewrote her shipboard draft subsequent to her stay in the United States.

[*] In deference to what I am certain would have been Harriet Martineau's wishes, I refer to her here as Martineau rather than Miss Martineau. She was a militant crusader for female equality.

[4] R. K. Webb, *Harriet Martineau, A Radical Victorian* (New York: Columbia University Press, 1960), p. 308. She was ultimately to become the first person to introduce sociology into England, since in 1851 after reading the founding treatise of sociology, Auguste Comte's *Positive Philosophy,* she undertook the task of publishing a condensed translation of his six volumes. See *The Positive Philosophy of Auguste Comte,* freely translated and condensed by Harriet Martineau (London: John Chapman, 1853), Volumes I and II.

In setting forth one of her first methodological principles, she stated: "The enlightened traveller, if he explores only one country, carries in his mind the image of all. . . ." He must learn that "every prevalent virtue or vice is a result of the particular circumstances amidst which the society exists."[5]

Perhaps the most surprising impression that emerges from a reading of Alexis de Tocqueville and Harriet Martineau, as well as of the myriad of other early nineteenth-century foreign travelers, is the congruence between their comments on American institutions and values and many of the recent major commentaries on American national character such as David Riesman's *The Lonely Crowd* and William H. Whyte's *The Organization Man*. As Riesman himself has commented, some of the major attributes that in his view define the key character traits of the mid-twentieth century American, such as other-directedness (specifically extreme sensitivity to others), were also noted by these writers:

> Yet in some respects this type [the other-directed man] is strikingly similar to *the* American, whom Tocqueville and other curious and astonished visitors from Europe, even before the Revolution, thought to be a new kind of man. Indeed, travelers' reports on America impress us with their unanimity. The American is said to be shallower, freer with his money, friendlier, more uncertain of himself and his values, more demanding of approval than the European. It all adds up to a pattern which, without stretching matters too far, resembles the kind of character that a number of social scientists have seen as developing in contemporary, highly industrialized and bureaucratic America: Fromm's "marketeer," Mills' "fixer," Arnold Green's "middle-class male child."[6]

[5] Martineau, How to Observe . . . , *op. cit.*, pp. 17, 27.
[6] David Riesman, *The Lonely Crowd* (New Haven: Yale University Press, 1950), pp. 19–20. Riesman, of course, goes on to argue that major changes have occurred.

These similarities have been noted by historians as well. Henry Steele Commager, who has used much foreign-traveler literature in his publications, has pointed to these continuities in analyzing American culture:

> We know in all outward matters America has changed profoundly in the century and a half since Independence, and that these changes have been continuous and complex; we are sometimes inclined to suppose that there have been comparable changes in the national character. This is not the conclusion to be drawn from the findings of these foreign observers. . . . To the visitors of the seventeen-seventies and the nineteen-forties, to Britons, Frenchmen, Germans, and Swedes, America *meant* much the same thing.[7]

A sociologist, Lee Coleman, also examined the writings dealing with "the American way" in four different periods—before the Civil War, from the Civil War to World War I, from the war to the Great Depression, and during the 1930's—and compiled a list of traits mentioned by the various observers. He reported that "when the lists for each of the four time periods were compared, no important differences between the traits mentioned by modern observers and those writing in the earlier periods of American history were discovered."[8]

Harriet Martineau's *Society in America* is one of the most important of the early efforts to describe and account for these seemingly constant aspects of American society.

[7] *America in Perspective, The United States Through Foreign Eyes* (New York: Mentor Books, 1947), pp. x–xi.

[8] Lee Coleman, "What is America? A Study of Alleged American Traits," *Social Forces*, 19 (1941), 492–499. A detailed examination of the evidence drawn from the writings of foreigners concerning the effective continuity of major elements in the American value system may be found in S. M. Lipset, "A Changing American Character?" in S. M. Lipset and Leo Lowenthal, eds., *Culture and Social Character* (New York: The Free Press of Glencoe, 1961), pp. 136–171; see also S. M. Lipset, "Stability in the Midst of Change," *The Social Welfare Forum, 1959* (New York: Columbia University Press, 1959), pp. 14–38. I have drawn on my previous work for this essay.

A source of much controversy in both Britain and America, it played a major role in forming English opinion, particularly among the liberal left of her day. Charles Dickens, although not in this category, described it as the best book written on the United States. Based on a two-year stay from 1834–1836, it is replete with vivid descriptions of life at the time, analyses of various institutions and patterns of behavior, and a considerable amount of what even to her contemporaries was annoying moralizing about diverse subjects. A careful reading of *Society in America* reveals a relatively integrated analytic portrait of the America of Andrew Jackson's day, one that offers much to those interested in the factors underlying the so-called American national character. Since the basic conceptual framework of the book is never explicitly laid out, I will try to do so here.

SOCIETY IN AMERICA

At the center of Harriet Martineau's study of American society was the assumption that the country's basic moral values were a major factor in determining its institutional structure. Where the central value system and the institutional reality were in conflict the values engendered a strong force towards bringing the practices into line— though she recognized that changes in other institutions, particularly the economic and the political, could greatly affect the value system. In emphasizing the value system as a causal agent, Martineau was an early precursor of one of the major sociological orientations, an approach that attempts to analyze the effect of values on structure and change. Max Weber, perhaps the most influential in this line of inquiry, demonstrated the relationship between economic development and moral beliefs. He showed that a basic prerequisite to the rise of capitalism in Western Europe was the independent emergence of a particular religious ethos. The Calvinist ethic led men to behave in ways that facilitated the accumulation of investment capital and promoted a deep commitment to sustained work.[9] Talcott Parsons, one of the foremost theorists in modern sociology, has elaborated on Weber's approach, and made values the central component in his conceptual framework for the study of total social systems.[10]

Perhaps the most influential work on an American social problem, *An American Dilemma,* Gunnar Myrdal's study of race relations, approached the analysis of American society in almost identical terms to those used by Harriet Martineau a century earlier. Myrdal, a Swedish sociologist and economist, assumed that the United States could be understood as reflecting "the ever-raging conflict between on one hand, the valuations preserved on the general plane which we shall call the 'American Creed,' where the American thinks, talks, and acts under the influence of high national and Christian precepts, and, on the other hand, the valuations on specific planes of individual and group living, where personal and local interests; economic, social and sexual jealousies; considerations of community prestige and conformity; group prejudice against particular persons or types of people; and all sorts of miscellaneous wants, impulses, and habits dominate his outlook."[11] And Myrdal sought to show how the belief in the "American Creed" of equality has served as a major force for actual changes in the position of the Negro.

Society in America also began with the assumption that the American Creed as set down in the Declaration of Independence, the belief in "human equality," in the "obligation of human justice," and in the right of the whole people to be self-governing, is the key to the understanding

[9] Max Weber, *The Protestant Ethic and the Spirit of Capitalism* (New York: Charles Scribner's Sons, 1958); see Talcott Parsons, *The Structure of Social Action* (New York: McGraw-Hill, 1937), pp. 500–588; and Reinhard Bendix, Max Weber, *An Intellectual Portrait* (New York: Doubleday, 1960), pp. 71–102, for detailed discussions of Weber's analysis of the relationship between values and economic development.

[10] Talcott Parsons, *op. cit.;* see also *Structure and Process in Modern Societies* (Glencoe: The Free Press, 1960), pp. 98–169.

[11] *An American Dilemma* (New York: Harper and Brothers, 1944), p. xliii.

of the way in which American society has developed. Thus the student of America was obliged to specify the way in which the norms implicit in the core values determined the structure of institutions. He had also to note the sources of deviations from the values and the way in which the strains between basic values and institutional practices were handled. As we have seen, explicit in both Martineau's approach and Myrdal's is the assumption that such strains constitute a principal cause of social change. Both argued that those Americans who believed in equalitarian democracy in all spheres possessed a great weapon, since complete social equality and democracy are the country's legitimate moral tradition.

The reality of equalitarianism in Jacksonian America impressed itself deeply on Harriet Martineau:

[I]n America . . . the English insolence of class to class, of individuals towards each other, is not even conceived of, except in the one highly disgraceful instance of people of colour. Nothing in American civilisation struck me so forcibly and so pleasureably as the invariable respect paid to man, as man. Perhaps no Englishman can become so fully aware, without going to America, of the atmosphere of insolence in which he dwells; of the taint of contempt which affects all the intercourses of his world.

Although Martineau was admittedly a biased observer, she wanted to believe that an egalitarian democracy could work—her reports on such behavior are abundantly reiterated by almost all foreign commentators, among them many conservatives and aristocrats.[12] Thus, as if echoing her emphasis on the "insolence" of the English privileged towards those whom they regarded as their inferiors, the

[12] A detailed summary of the writings of English commentators before the Civil War states: "Most prominent of the many impressions that Britons took back with them was the aggressive equalitarianism of the people." Max Berger, *The British Traveller in America* (New York: Columbia University Press, 1943), pp. 54–55.

conservative Anthony Trollope complained in 1860 that in America "the man to whose service one is entitled answers one with determined insolence."[13]

But equalitarianism in social relations did not mean the absence of hierarchy, or of competition. Rather, if anything, the very absence of fixed class lines placed pressure on *all* as the burden of success lay with the individual himself. As Martineau put it: "In a country where the whole course is open to every one; where in theory, everything must be obtained by merit, men have the strongest stimulus to exert their powers, and try what they can achieve. . . . [This social pressure] can lead to ill-considered enterprise. This is an evil sometimes to the individual, but not to society." In this comment, she affirmed a similar generalization by Tocqueville that by destroying aristocracy, Americans "have opened the door to universal competition."[14]

The emphasis on success intertwined with the absence of aristocratic norms not only may have destructive consequences for individuals by tempting them to try to succeed by illegitimate or untried means, but it may also lead other Americans to excuse immoral methods of attaining

[13] Anthony Trollope, *North America* (New York: Alfred A. Knopf, 1951), p. 77. His mother, Frances Trollope, who visited America shortly before Harriet Martineau, complained about the "coarse familiarity, untempered by any shadow of respect which is assumed by the grossest and lowest in their intercourse with the highest and most refined." *Domestic Manners of the Americans* (London: Whittaker, Treacher and Co., 1832), p. 109. A survey of the opinions of Europeans who visited the United States around the turn of the twentieth century provides further evidence of this spirit and practice of egalitarianism: "Some foreign observers found the arrogance of American workers [towards their superiors] intolerable." Robert W. Smuts, *European Impressions of the American Worker* (New York: King's Crown Press, 1953), p. 7.

[14] Alexis de Tocqueville, *Democracy in America* (New York: Vintage Books, 1959), II, p. 146. And the study of late nineteenth and early twentieth-century commentors cited earlier indicates that many of them concluded that "social and economic democracy in America, far from mitigating competition for social status, intensified it." Smuts, *op. cit.*, p. 13.

success.[15] For example, she suggested that in America, bankrupts usually do not "pay their old debts when they rise again. This laxity is favoured by the circumstances of the community, which require the industry of all its members . . . [F]ew things are more disgraceful in American society than the carelessness with which speculators are allowed to game with other people's funds, and, after ruining those who put trust in them, to lift up their heads in all places. . . ." A decade later, Charles Dickens was to make the same analysis of the behavior of Americans, pointing out that they cared not about the "merits of a broken speculation, or a bankruptcy, or of a successful scoundrel," but rather saw pecuniary success as evidence of cleverness.[16]

This stress on equality also failed to eliminate the factors that pressed men to try to establish hereditary classes. And the very moral force that denied the legitimacy of hereditary privileged strata operated to create an upper class more "vulgar" in its behavior and outlook than those in societies where aristocracy was part of the established value system. In her chapter on "caste" Martineau discussed the attempts to create a socially exclusive "aristocracy." As she analyzed the sources of this behavior:

> Caste is no more likely to become obsolete in a republic than among the Hindoos themselves. The distinctive characteristics may vary; but there will be ranks, and *tenacity of rank* wherever there is society. . . .

> It is not to be supposed that the mere circumstance of living in a republic will ever eradicate that kind of self-love which takes the form of family pride. . . . *This species of exclusiveness exists wherever there are families.*

> Wherever the appearance of a conventional aristocracy exists in America, it must arise from wealth. . . .

[15] This analysis replete in the writings of many nineteenth-century travelers has been elaborated by Robert K. Merton as a special case of his means-ends typology. See "Social Structure and Anomie" in his *Social Theory and Social Structure* (Glencoe: The Free Press, 1957), esp. pp. 167–169.

[16] Charles Dickens, *American Notes and Pictures from Italy* (London: Oxford University Press, 1957), pp. 245–246.

An aristocracy of mere wealth is vulgar everywhere. In a republic it is vulgar in the extreme.

. . . I imagine that the English who have complained the most copiously of the vulgarity of American manners have done so from . . . their intercourse with the Americans having been confined to those who consider themselves the aristocracy of the United States; the wealthy and showy citizens of the Atlantic ports.

. . . I was told a great deal about "the first people in Boston:" which is perhaps as aristocratic, vain, and vulgar a city, as described by its own "first people," as any in the world.

. . . [T]he spirit of caste . . . flourishes in a society which on Sunday and holidays professes to have abjured it. It is true that the people of New England have put away duelling; but the feelings which used to vent themselves by the practice of duelling are cherished by the members of the conventional aristocracy. . . .

The children are such faithful reflectors of this spirit as to leave no doubt of its existence, even amidst the nicest operations of cant. Gentlemen may disguise their aristocratic aspirations under sighs for the depressed state of literature and science; supposing that wealth and leisure are the constituents of literature; and station the proximate cause of science. . . . The ladies may conceal their selfish pride of caste, even from themselves, under pretensions to superior delicacy and refinement. But the children use no such disguises. *Out they come with what they have learned at home.* A school-girl told me what a delightful "set" she belonged to at her school; how comfortable they all were once, without any sets, till several grocers' daughters began to come in, as their fathers grew rich; and it became necessary for the higher girls to consider what they should do, and to form themselves into sets. . . .

In Philadelphia I was much in society. Some of my hospitable acquaintances lived in Chesnut Street, some in Arch Street, and many in other places. When I had been a few weeks in the city, I found to my surprise that some of the ladies who were my admiration had not only never seen or heard of other beautiful young ladies whom I admired quite as much, but never would see or hear of them. . . . One person told me . . . that the mutual ignorance was from the fathers of the Arch Street ladies having made their fortunes, while the Chesnut Street ladies owed theirs to their grandfathers.

The phenomenon of a class of self-conscious "vulgar" "exclusives" who must always "find their aims 'impossible,'" undermined by the social values, has also been commented on by many other foreign observers as inherent in a society that stressed equality. They have noted that precisely as a result of the emphasis on equality and opportunity, *Americans have been more status-conscious than those who lived in the more aristocratic societies of Europe.*[17] In effect, what Harriet Martineau and others have suggested is that the American upper strata have always behaved basically like *parvenues.*[18]

The efforts to sustain a hereditary upper class in the United States were inhibited by two main factors: (1) the institutionalized inheritance system that led the wealthy to distribute their wealth among many heirs; and (2) the antagonism to high status endemic in the egalitarian value system that served to strengthen those forces in the political arena fighting to reduce the privileges of wealth and high position.[19] Thus Martineau noted:

[17] For further detail see my two articles referred to earlier.

[18] See Dixon Wecter, *The Saga of American Society* (New York: Charles Scribner's Sons, 1937), esp. p. 137. James Bryce reported that America was more exclusive than Britain in that a self-made "millionaire has a better and easier social career open to him in England, than in America." *The American Commonwealth* (New York: The Macmillan Co., 1911), II, p. 815.

[19] The thesis that the chief values of the society determine basic structural elements has been advanced by Henry Nash Smith. He has argued that the frontier movement in American history has in large measure reflected an effort to sustain "the Myth of the Garden," the image of the ideal society being one

The popular feeling is so strong against transmitting large estates, and favouring one child, that nobody attempts to do it. The rare endeavours made by persons of feudal prepossessions to perpetuate this vicious custom, have been all happily frustrated. Much ridicule was occasioned by the manœuvres of one such testator, who provided for the portions of a large estate reverting periodically. . . .

This remote approach to an equalisation of property is, as far as it goes, an improvement upon the state of affairs in the Old World. . . .[20]

The pressure to equalize property and prevent the cumulation of large family fortunes and a distinct aristocratic class has been reinforced in more recent times by the passage of progressive tax legislation, which both limits total earnings and also severely taxes large estates. The probable passage of such legislation by democratic governments has always been feared by the conservatives and the wealthy in all societies for, as Martineau pointed out, one of their "most painful apprehensions seems to be that the poorer will heavily tax the richer members of society; the rich being always a small class. If it be true . . . that rulers in general are prone to use their power for selfish purposes, there remains the alternative, whether the poor shall over-tax the rich, or whether the rich shall over-tax the poor. . . ." And she recognized that politics in the United States,

of independent family farmers. And, according to Smith, Great Plains farmers supported legislation to limit farms to the relatively small 160 acre homestead unit rather than adapting to the requirements of farming in an arid region. Such farming would have dictated much larger units similar to what emerged in Australia. *Virgin Land: The American West as Symbol and Myth* (Cambridge: Harvard University Press, 1950), esp. pp. 195–200.

[20] Tocqueville too noted that under the American "law of inheritance, the death of each owner brings about a revolution in property; not only do his possessions change hands, but their very nature is altered, since they are parceled into shares, which become smaller and smaller at each division." This serves to disperse both family and fortunes. *Op. cit.*, I, pp. 50.

despite the lack of ideological clarity, reflected this ever-present class conflict.[21] As she put it:

> The vagueness of the antagonism between the two parties is for some time perplexing to the traveller in America; and he does not know whether to be amazed or amused at the apparent triviality of the circumstances which arouse the strongest party emotions. After a while, a body comes out of the mystery, and he grasps a substantial cause of dissension. . . .

> In the United States, as elsewhere, there are and have always been, two parties in politics. . . . As long as men continue as differently organised as they now are, there will be two parties . . . an aristocracy and a democracy. . . . Men who have gained wealth, whose hope is fulfilled, and who fear loss by change, are naturally of the aristocratic [party]. . . . [The democratic party] will include all those who have the most to gain and least to lose.

This perception of the meaning of American politics by a left-wing English woman was almost identical with that reported by the more conservative French aristocrat, Tocqueville, written about the same time:

> To a stranger all the domestic controversies of the Americans at first appear to be incomprehensible or puerile. . . . But when he comes to study the secret propensities that govern the factions of America, he easily perceives that the greater part of them are more or less connected with one or the other of those two great divisions which always existed in free communities. The deeper we penetrate into the inmost thought of these parties, the more we perceive that the object of the one is to limit and that of the other to extend the

[21] For a review of the evidence which on the whole sustains the thesis that the two party struggle in the United States has always reflected divisions based on class divisions see S. M. Lipset, *Political Man. The Social Bases of Politics* (New York: Doubleday, 1960), pp. 285–309.

authority of the people . . . they are the main points and soul of every faction in the United States.[22]

As a self-proclaimed radical, Harriet Martineau did not hide her sympathies. To her it was clear (as of 1837 following Jackson's two terms in office) "that the Democratic Party has achieved everything that has been achieved since the United States' constitution began to work." Consequently since democracy meant the power of the more popularly based party "it is no wonder that there is panic in many hearts, and that I heard from so many tongues of the desolations of the 'leveling spirit,' and the approaching ruin of political institutions." Popular antagonism to great wealth and privilege did not mean, however, as the wealthy feared, the endangering of the institutions of private property. She argued that a value system that included a commitment to equality of opportunity meant, for some time to come, greater rather than lesser belief in the integrity of property. "There is . . . as great a horror in America as everywhere else of the despotism that would equalise property arbitrarily. . . . Such aggression upon property can never take place . . . where the Declaration of Independence claims for every one, with life and liberty, the pursuit of happiness in his own way. There will be no attacks on property in the United States." And Tocqueville also commented: "I know of no country . . . where a profounder contempt is expressed for the theory of the permanent equality of property."[23]

During the age of Jackson, foreign visitors heard from the wealthy among whom they moved that the tyranny of the majority was the great threat to the republic, that the ignorant mass would be susceptible to the appeals of demagogues and would support policies destructive of liberty. Harriet Martineau, like American Jacksonians, would not admit that such a danger was more to be deplored or feared than the evils existing in the dictatorial or Oligarchic European societies, which depressed the poor in order to maintain the privileges of the wealthy. She

[22] Tocqueville, op. cit., I, pp. 185–186.
[23] Ibid., I, p. 53.

maintained that in America the spread of education, political experience, and economic opportunity would invest its lower classes with sufficient maturity and stake in a democratic polity to enable them to resist such appeals. However, she acknowledged that even in America, "there is much ignorance; so much as to be an ever-present peril."

But the United States had already found a way of reducing this danger when it rejected the European system of concentrating power in the hands of one central government. As she put it: "If the general government managed everything, the public service would soon become the privilege of a certain class, or a number of classes of men, as is seen to be the case elsewhere."[24] Harriet Martineau joined the many commentators who have seen in the federal system one of the most salient safeguards of democracy: "It is inevitable that there will be some who fear the too great strength of the state governments, as there will be many who have the same fear about the general government. Instead of seeing in this any cause for dismay, or even regret, the impartial observer will recognise in the mutual watchfulness the best security that the case admits of for the general and state governments preserving their due relation to one another."

If Harriet Martineau and Alexis de Tocqueville, coming from different nations and reflecting varying political outlooks, agreed on many questions about the nature of Jacksonian America, there is one glaring contradiction in their testimony and analysis. Tocqueville saw American democracy sustained by high levels of political participation by the bulk of its citizenry:

> [T]he political activity that pervades the United States must be seen in order to be understood. . . .
>
> To take a hand in the regulation of society and to discuss it is his biggest concern and so to speak, the

[24] The Federalists, who most feared popular rule, sought to increase the central power, while their more populist-oriented opponents had fought for strong local government, and a division of powers that placed an ultimate limit on the tyranny of a national majority.

only pleasure an American knows. This feeling pervades the most trifling habits of life; even the women frequently attend public meetings and listen to political harangues. . . .[25]

But where Tocqueville saw intense participation both in politics and voluntary organizations, Harriet Martineau was impressed by the political indifference of Americans and devoted a separate section to "Apathy in Citizenship." She reported that various individuals had told her they did not vote, and she cited comments from different people complaining about the general low state of political interest in the country. Interestingly enough, the best known of later British travelers in America, James Bryce, who first visited here in 1870, agreed more with Martineau than with Tocqueville. He too complained about the disinterest of Americans and noted: "The citizen has little time to think about political problems. Engrossing all the working hours, his avocation leaves him only stray moments for this fundamental duty. . . . It astonished me in 1870 and 1881 to find how small a part politics played in conversation among the best educated classes and generally in cities."[26]

It is difficult to evaluate these opposing portraits of Jacksonian Americans by Tocqueville and Martineau. At that time, women, Negroes, and in some states the very poor, were barred from the polls. A recent study of voting participation points out that: "In spite of Tocqueville's impression that a very large number of Americans were immersed in politics, . . . [the available statistical] data show the limitations of this interpretation. Only 10 to 12 per cent of the population voted in the presidential elections of the 1830's, which, to be sure, is certainly more than the percentage voting in France from 1815 to February 1848. But only thirteen years after the first edition of *Democracy in America* appeared in Paris, French elections (1848) were attracting 64 per cent and, in one case, 84 per cent of the electorate to the polls—and the electorate

[25] Tocqueville, *op. cit.*, I, pp. 259–260.
[26] Bryce, *op. cit.*, II, p. 291.

included all male citizens twenty-one and over in possession of civil rights."[27]

If we examine the sources of political apathy in Harriet Martineau's account, we come to a key aspect of her analysis of American traits, conformism or the concern for the opinions of others.

> There is another cause for the reluctance to vote which is complained of by the best friends of the people; but is almost too humbling and painful to discuss. Some are afraid to vote! . . .

> The fear of opinion sometimes takes the form of an almost insane dread of responsibility.

This constant anxiety about the opinions of others reduced the propensity of Americans to speak their minds on politics, and even of some of them to vote in an age where the secret ballot was not an attribute of the political process. For Martineau, political indifference was a special case of the American's fear of being different, a fear that permeated every aspect of his life.

> [Americans] may travel over the world, and find no society but their own which will submit to the restraint of perpetual caution, and reference to the opinions of others. They may travel over the whole world, and find no country but their own where the very children beware of getting into scrapes, and talk of the effect of actions upon people's minds; where the youth of society determine in silence what opinions they shall bring forward, and what avow only in the family circle; where women write miserable letters, almost universally be-

[27] Robert Lane, *Political Life* (Glencoe: The Free Press, 1959), pp. 17–18. See also Lee Benson, "Research Problems in American Political Historiography," in Mirra Komarovsky, ed., *Common Frontiers of the Social Sciences* (Glencoe: The Free Press, 1957), pp. 148–155, for a discussion of the problems involved in drawing conclusions about participation in the Jackson elections. Benson states that in 1824, 350,000 votes were cast out of a population of nearly 11,000,000, while in 1828, there were 1,150,000 voters among 12,250,000 inhabitants.

cause it is a settled matter that it is unsafe to commit oneself on paper; and where elderly people seem to lack almost universally that faith in principles which inspires a free expression of them at any time, and under all circumstances. . . .

I doubt whether they can even conceive of a state of society, of its ease and comfort, where no man fears his neighbour, and it is no evil to be responsible for one's opinions: where men, knowing how undiscernible consequences are, and how harmless they must be to the upright, abide them without fear, and do not perplex themselves with calculating what is incalculable.

In describing the American of the 1830's as other-directed, as constantly adjusting his behavior to please others, Harriet Martineau is in agreement with Tocqueville, who commented:

I know of no country in which there is so little independence of mind and real freedom of discussion as in America. . . .

In that immense crowd which throngs the avenues to power in the United States, I found very few men who displayed that manly candor and masculine independence of opinion which frequently distinguished the Americans in former times. . . . It seems, at first sight, as if all the minds of the Americans were formed on one model, so accurately do they follow the same route.[28]

James Bryce also argued, consistent with his analysis of politically apathetic Americans, that "self-distrust, a despondency, a disposition to fall into line, to acquiesce in the dominant opinion" inheres in the society. This "tendency to acquiescence and submission" is not to be "confounded with the tyranny of the majority . . . [it] does not imply any compulsion exerted by the majority," in the sense discussed by Tocqueville. Rather Bryce, like Harriet Martineau, described what he felt to be a basic psychologi-

[28] Tocqueville, *op. cit.*, I, pp. 273, 277.

cal trait of Americans, their "fatalism," which involved a "loss of resisting power, a diminished sense of personal responsibility, and of the duty to battle for one's own opinions."[29]

Many other foreign travelers commented on the other-directedness of the American national character in much the same vein. Another contemporary of Harriet Martineau and Alexis de Tocqueville, the prodemocratic German aristocrat, Francis Grund, described Jacksonian Americans in these terms: "Nothing can excite the contempt of an educated European more than the continual fears and apprehensions in which even the 'most enlightened citizens' of the United States seem to live with regard to their next neighbors, lest their actions, principles, opinions and beliefs should be condemned by their fellow creatures."[30]

This propensity towards conformism and its consequent effect of reducing interest and involvement in politics was seen by these nineteenth-century foreign travelers as another concomitant of the very egalitarian values that they regarded as the Americans' most positive trait, their de-emphasis of fixed class lines. It may be argued that in a situation of "status anarchy," where people are encouraged to struggle upward, but in which no clearly defined reference points mark their arrival, and where success in achieving and retaining high status is determined by the good opinion of others, caution and regard for others' good opinion is natural. Seldom secure in their status, Americans are sensitive to the judgments of others in a way that those who live in a more status-bound society do not have to be. As Harriet Martineau said: "Where . . . honour [that is, status] is to be derived from present human opinion, there must be fear, ever present, and perpetually exciting to or withholding from action." And she reported that a friend of hers ascribed the reluctance of good men to engage in politics "to the want of protection from his neighbours to

[29] *Op. cit.*, II, p. 352.

[30] *Aristocracy in America* (New York: Harper Torch Books, 1959), p. 162. For further citations and discussion see my article, "A Changing American Character?", *op. cit.*

which a man is exposed from the want of caste."[31] She noted a significant difference in the behavior of the upper classes in the South and the North in this regard. The South, which manifestly approved of caste lines between whites and Negroes, maintained more explicit class lines among the white community. Upper-class Southerners behaved much more like the privileged Europeans, while in the more democratic and egalitarian North, the wealthy were forced constantly to demonstrate their claim to high status through "ostentation" and were much more inhibited in their public discourse.

> In the north [as contrasted with the south] there can be little vanity of retinue, as retinue is not to be had: but there is, instead of it, much ostentation of wealth, in the commercial cities. It is here that the aristocracy form and collect; and, as has been said before, the aristocratic is universally the fearing . . . party. The fear of opinion takes many forms. There is fear of vulgarity, fear of responsibility; and above all, fear of singularity. There is something more displeasing, at the first view, in the caution of the Yankees than in the recklessness of the cavalier race of the south. . . .

> The Americans of the northern States are, from education and habit, so accustomed to the caution of which I speak, as to be unaware of its extent and singularity. They think themselves injured by the remarks which strangers make upon it, and by the ridicule with which it is treated by their own countrymen who have travelled abroad.

[31] In a strikingly similar comment written 60 years later, James Muirhead, then editor of the American *Baedeker*, stated that "the Briton's indifference to criticism," as compared with the American's is linked to the fact that "England is still the stronghold of the obsolescent institution of caste, that it frankly and even brutally asserts the essential inequality of man. . . . Social adaptability is not his [the Briton's] foible. He accepts the conventionality of his class and wears it as an impenetrable armor." *America, the Land of Contrasts: A Briton's View of his American Kin* (London: Lemson, Wolffe and Company, 1898), p. 91.

Again, one may find similar comments by other visitors to Jacksonian America. Francis Grund suggested that the ambiguous class structure of an egalitarian society made status-striving tantamount to conformity:

> Society in America . . . is characterized by a spirit of exclusiveness and persecution unknown in any other country. Its gradations not being regulated according to rank and title, selfishness and conceit are its principal elements. . . . What man is there in this city [New York] that dares to be independent, at the risk of being considered bad company? And who can venture to infringe upon a single rule of society? . . .

> This habit of conforming to each other's opinions, and the penalty set upon every transgression of that kind, are sufficient to prevent a man from wearing a coat cut in a different fashion, or a shirt collar no longer *a la mode,* or, in fact, to do, say, or appear anything which could render him unpopular among a certain set. In no other place, I believe, is there such a stress laid upon "saving appearances."[32]

The consequences of American equalitarianism that Martineau found distasteful were not limited to conformism in opinions or status-seeking ostentation.

> [T]he most prominent of their bad habits [is] . . . flattery. . . . Its prevalence is so great as to tempt one to call it a necessary result. There is no getting out of the way of it. A gentleman, who was a depraved schoolboy, a fiendish husband, father, and slave-owner, whose reputation for brutality was as extensive as the country, was eulogised in the newspapers at his death. Every book that comes out is exalted to the skies. The public orators flatter the people; the people flatter the orators. Clergymen praise their flocks; and the flocks stand amazed at the excellence of their clergymen. Sunday-school teachers admire their pupils; and the scholars magnify their teachers. As to guests, especially from

[32] *Op. cit.*, pp. 52, 157.

abroad, hospitality requires that some dark corner should be provided in every room where they may look when their own praises are being told to their own faces.

The intimate connection between other-directedness, flattery, and egalitarian values suggested by these comments recalls the same connection perceived by Plato with almost identical examples in *The Republic*, written two millenniums before the birth of the United States:

> [In a democracy, the father] accustoms himself to become like his child and to fear his sons. . . . Metic [resident alien] is like citizen and citizen like metic, and stranger like both. . . . The schoolmaster fears and flatters his pupils. . . . The young act like their seniors, and compete with them in speech and action, while the old men condescend to the young and become triumphs of versatility and wit, imitating their juniors in order to avoid the appearance of being sour or despotic.[33]

As Plato noted, and Harriet Martineau testified, democratic man is deeply imbued with the desire to accommodate to others, which results in kindness and generosity in personal relations and in a reluctance to offend. Martineau commented also on this much more positive side of the concern for others inherent in democracy:

> The manners of Americans are the best I ever saw; . . . but I speak now of more than usually meets the eye of a stranger; of the family manners, which travellers have rarely leisure or opportunity to observe. . . .
>
> They have been called the most good-tempered people in the world: and I think they must be so. . . . I imagine that the practice of forbearance requisite in a republic is answerable for this pleasant peculiarity. If the moral independence of some, of many, sinks under this equal pressure from all sides, it is no little set-off against such an evil that the outbreaks of domestic tyranny are thereby restrained; and that the respect for mutual rights

[33] Plato, *The Republic*, ed. by Ernest Rhys (London: J. M. Dent and Co., 1935), pp. 200 ff.

which citizens have perpetually enforced upon them abroad, comes thence to be observed towards the weak and unresisting in the privacy of home.

The strength of republican principles, that is equalitarianism, respect and concern for others, was seen by Harriet Martineau as necessarily linked to the internal structure of the family, the major socialization institution. She commented that the "freedom of manners in children of which so much complaint has been made by observers . . . is a necessary fact. Till the United States ceases to be republican . . . the children there will continue as free and easy and as important as they are. For my own part, I delight in American children; . . . the independence and fearlessness of children were a perpetual charm in my eyes."[34] In attempting to explain the practices that produced such mature and free children, she linked them directly to the over-all value system of the society:

They [American parents] do not lay aside their democratic principles in [their relations with children] . . . more than in others, because they happen to have almost unlimited power in their own hands. They watch and guard: they remove stumbling-blocks: they manifest approbation and disapprobation: they express wishes, but, at the same time, study the wishes of their little people: they leave as much as possible to natural retribution: they impose no opinions, and quarrel with none: in short, they exercise the tenderest friendship without presuming upon it.[35]

[34] Her comments on children coincided with those of most British and French visitors. See Max Berger, op. cit., pp. 83–84, Wecter, op. cit., pp. 191–192. Both cite many comments, some dating from Revolutionary times, concerning the independence of American youth.
[35] An American educator H. Humphrey wrote in his book, Domestic Education, published in 1840, as follows: "The opinion seems to be gaining ground, in some respectable and influential quarters, that punishments are rarely if ever necessary family government. It is said, that if parents would begin early, and cultivate the social affections of their children and enlighten their understanding, and bring the whole force of moral influence to bear . . . there would be no need of resorting to pun-

Martineau also perceived a causal connection between childhood socialization practices stressing love, approbation, and respect for children as equals, and the development of adult personalities characterized by good temper and impressed with the importance of kindly relations with others. In this analysis, she clearly foreshadowed later developments in psychology that have emphasized the significance of early child-parent relations in the formation of personality, as well as various contemporary efforts to relate attributes of national character to child-rearing practices. As she put it:

> One reason of the pleasure with which I regarded the freedom of American children was that I took it as a sign that the most tremendous suffering perhaps of human life is probably lessened, if not obviated, there:— the misery of concealed doubts and fears, and heavy solitary troubles—the misery which makes the early years of a shy child a fearful purgatory. Yet purgatory is not the word: for this misery purges no sins, while it originates many. I have a strong suspicion that the faults of temper so prevalent where parental authority is strong, and where children are made as insignificant as they can be made, and the excellence of temper in America, are attributable to the different management of childhood in the one article of freedom. There is no doubt that many children are irrecoverably depressed and unnerved for want of being convinced that anybody cares for them. They nourish doubts, they harbour fears and suspicions, and carry within them prejudices and errors, for want of its occurring to them to ask questions; and though they may outgrow these defects and errors, they never recover from them. Unexplained and inexplicable obstacles are thrown in the way of their filial duty,—obstacles which not even the strongest conscientiousness can overcome with grace: the vigour of the spirit is prostrated, or perverted into wilfulness: the calmness of self-

ishments." Cited in Arthur W. Calhoun, *A Social History of the American Family from Colonial Times to the Present* (Cleveland: The Arthur H. Clark Co., 1918), II, pp. 63–64.

respect is forfeited, and so is the repose of a loving faith in others. In short, the temper is ruined, and the life is spoiled; and all from the parents not having made friends of their children from the beginning.[36]

Not only did the child-oriented American family and its child-rearing practices seem unique to the visitors from abroad, the other major institution devoted to instilling and perpetuating societal values, religion, also struck them as having distinctively American overtones. The United States, though lacking an established church, was a strongly religious country. Max Berger summarized the reports of various pre-Civil War English travelers who: "pointed to the fact that America, though still largely a primitive country, had as many churches as the British Isles, that religious assemblages were being held at one place or another practically all the time; that large donations were constantly being made for religious purposes. America, they concluded, was basically a very religious country . . . Church services were always crowded on Sundays. . . ."[37] Tocqueville, too, observed that "there is no country in the world where the Christian religion retains a greater influence over the souls of men than in America."[38]

To the liberal Unitarian Harriet Martineau, the pervasiveness of organized Christianity in the then most revolutionary society in the world was not necessarily testimony to the genuine religiosity of the society. She suspected that it might be another example of the conformism of Americans, of their fear publicly to avow dissident views such as atheism. As she wrote:

> [The uniform public support for religion] is the first striking fact which presents itself. . . . If there were no constraint,—no social reward or penalty,—such an ap-

[36] Arthur Calhoun cites an 1848 American magazine addressed to mothers that stated: "no child is ever improved by scolding: but always injured. . . . No cause is so active for evil among children as their mother's impatience." *Ibid.*, pp. 169–170.

[37] *Op. cit.*, pp. 133–134.

[38] *Op. cit.*, I, p. 314.

proach to uniformity of profession could not exist as is seen in the United States. In a society where speculation and profession were left perfectly free . . . there would be many speculative (though probably extremely few practical) atheists: there would be an adoption by many of the principles of natural religion, otherwise than in and through Christianity. . . . There are many ways of professing Christianity in the United States: but there are few, very few men, whether speculative or thoughtless . . . who do not carefully profess Christianity, in some form or other. This, as men are made, is unnatural.

But though she cited many examples to illustrate the pervasiveness of religious affiliation and church attendance, she did not conclude that the majority of Americans firmly believed in traditional revealed religion. Rather, their behavior demonstrated that they did not permit religion to influence their day-to-day life. In fact, she felt many Americans assumed that normal people were not concerned with religion outside of church.

One circumstance struck me throughout the country. Almost as often as the conversation between myself and any other person on religious subjects became intimate and earnest, I was met by the supposition that *I was a convert*. It was the same in other instances: wherever there was a strong interest in the Christian religion, conversion to a particular profession of it was confidently supposed. *This fact speaks volumes.*

Other travelers also testified to the propensity of Americans to scorn irreligion, while revealing their lack of deep religious commitment in unconcern for the doctrinal content and practices of various denominations. Tocqueville commented that in no other country is Christianity "clothed with fewer forms, figures, and observances than in the United States, or where it presents more distinct, simple, and general notions to the mind. Although the Christians of America are divided into a multitude of sects, they look upon their religion in the same light."[39] Anthony Trollope,

[39] *Op. cit.*, II, p. 28.

too, noted that although disbelief was frowned upon, little real concern was shown for the content of a man's creed. He commented that fathers believed "that a young lad should go somewhere on a Sunday; but a sermon is a sermon. . . . Everybody is bound to have a religion, but it does not much matter what it is . . . anything will do. But it is expected of him that he shall place himself under some flag. . . ."[40]

In large measure, much of what Harriet Martineau liked and disliked about American society—its egalitarianism and its seeking after place, its philanthropy and its concern for the feelings of others, its propensity to flatter and conform—could be traced to attributes of a radical democracy. Some major aspects of the society, however, violated major tenets of egalitarianism: slavery in the South and discrimination against free Negroes in the North, the inferior social and legal position of women, and discrimination against certain groups of recent immigrants. Since such practices violated fundamental values, she felt certain that in time the struggle of liberal Americans to abolish them would succeed. In her writings she did her best to fight these evils. Her chapters on slavery are an eloquent answer to those who contended that slavery though morally obnoxious did not result in severe maltreatment of the slaves. The picture she presented of the way in which slaves were dehumanized, family life made impossible, and morality ignored, infuriated the apologists for the peculiar Southern institution. Recent historical research has abundantly validated her powers of observation.[41]

She accepted none of the arguments concerning the in-

[40] *Op. cit.*, pp. 278–281. On this point generally in American history see Carl L. Becker, *Everyman His Own Historian* (New York: Appleton-Century-Crofts, Inc., 1935), pp. 21–22. I have discussed the evidence concerning the general religiosity of Americans, as well as their propensity to ignore the content of religion in "Religion in America," *Columbia University Forum*, II (1959), pp. 17–21.

[41] See Stanley Elkins, *Slavery* (Chicago: University of Chicago Press, 1959) for a detailed analysis of the extent to which American slaveowners outdid those in other societies in their maltreatment of their human property.

herent inferiority of the Negro. In both the North and the South she found examples of Negroes who, given the opportunity, demonstrated real abilities. This proved to her that the Negro like other men was capable of the highest human attainments. Moreover, she pointed out in a comment, which has obvious contemporary reference, that the white Southerner had need to believe in the ignorant-yet-happy Negro, for any evidence that the Negro was a man like other men placed the dominant race under an unbearable load of guilt, a guilt they then displaced by even greater hatred of those whom they oppressed:

> I was frequently told of the "endearing relation" subsisting between master and slaves. . . . As long as the slave remains ignorant, docile, and contented, he is taken good care of, humoured, and spoken of with a contemptuous, compassionate kindness. But from the moment he exhibits the attributes of a rational being,—from the moment his intellect seems likely to come into the most distinct competition with that of whites, the most deadly hatred springs up;—not in the black, but in his oppressors. It is an old truth that *we hate those whom we have injured.* Never was it more clear than in this case.

The abolitionists were her heroes in American society. They alone, though still a small minority, stood up against the opprobrium of polite society in the North, and even against physical violence. And Harriet Martineau chose to identify publically with their cause, though this act led many Northerners who had welcomed her, and whom she regarded as friends, to turn on her.[42]

Slavery would end with the triumph of the abolitionists,

[42] After her return to England, she continued her close interest and co-operation with the work of the American abolitionists. During the Civil War, she devoted much of her energy to writing articles explaining and defending the position of the North. A leading Liberal politician, W. E. Forster "said that Harriet Martineau alone was keeping England straight in regard to America." See Vera Wheatley, *The Life and Work of Harriet Martineau* (London: Secker and Warburg, 1957), p. 374.

though she recognized that it would be a bitter struggle. Discrimination against the immigrants also would decline with their economic integration into the society. She believed that much of the ill-feeling against them resulted from their being poor and exhibiting the characteristic traits of the very poor.

In discussing the position of women in the United States, Martineau drew a parallel with that of the Negroes, a parallel that a century later was to be elaborated by Gunnar Myrdal in his analysis of the American Negro problem. Both Harriet Martineau and Gunnar Myrdal called attention to the similar arguments used to justify a denial of rights to each group.[43] Supporters of both white and male supremacy have argued that Negroes and women are happier without responsibility, their basic temperaments do not fit them for various important tasks, they benefit greatly from the protection of the more powerful group, and they prefer their inferior position. To Harriet Martineau these were simply the rationales employed by the privileged to justify their position, and in the case of women they represented the preservation of outmoded doctrines and practices inherited from feudal and aristocratic society. The position of women differed from that of Negro slaves, however, in that they had much more opportunity to fight for their own freedom. Martineau urged, in words predating a similar statement by Karl Marx, that: "The progression or emancipation of any class usually, if not always, takes place through the efforts of individuals of that class: and so it must be here." Women must take the struggle for equal rights into their own hands, they must fight to make the principles of the Declaration of Independence applicable to all, not just to white men.

Events have borne out Harriet Martineau's expectations about the end of slavery, about the improvement in the social and economic position of those of recent immigrant background, and about the position of women. There is

[43] See Gunnar Myrdal, *op. cit.*, Vol. II, Appendix 5, "A Parallel to the Negro Problem," pp. 1073–1078. In this discussion, Myrdal cites Martineau's original discussion as well as various Southern replies to it.

still, however, one further institutional change that she pre-
dicted would result from the pressures to fulfill the imminent logic of equalitarianism; that was the creation of a
co-operative commonwealth or a socialist society. She did
not use these words and only cursorily suggested it, but
it is clear that in her opinion the institution of private property fundamentally conflicted with American values and
would eventuate in an overt collision between them in the
distant future. As she wrote:

> There is, as there ought to be, as great a horror in
> America as everywhere else of the despotism that would
> equalise property arbitrarily. . . .
>
> But it appears to me inevitable that there will be a
> general agreement, sooner or later, on a better principle
> of property than that under which all are restless. . . .
>
> In America the . . . democratic principles of their
> social arrangements, operating already to such an equal-
> isation of property as has never before been witnessed,
> are favourable to changes which are indeed necessary
> to the full carrying out of the principles adopted. When
> the people become tired of their universal servitude to
> worldly anxiety,—when they have fully meditated and
> discussed the fact . . . that the largest proportion of
> human faults bear a relation to selfish possession; that
> the most formidable classes of disease are caused by
> over or under toil, and by anxiety of mind; they will be
> ready for the inquiry whether this tremendous incubus
> be indeed irremovable; and whether any difficulties at-
> tending its removal can be comparable to the evils it
> inflicts. . . .
>
> [Americans] will only for a time be able to resist the
> convictions which the working of republican principles
> will force upon them, that there is no way to securing
> perfect social liberty on democratic principles but by
> community of property.

Harriet Martineau's conviction that a socialist society
would some day emerge in America was not unique among

nineteenth-century foreign visitors, though it was a minority viewpoint. Karl Marx drew some of his assumptions about the political potential of the working class, of their inherent drive to abolish property distinctions, from reading this literature, particularly Thomas Hamilton's *Men and Manners in America,* but also the works of Tocqueville and Beaumont. He concluded in some of his early writings that the American social and political structure would evolve into a socialist society.[44]

Clearly these anticipations about a socialist future are still far from approaching reality. History has, in fact, seemingly validated Harriet Martineau's perception cited earlier that "aggression upon property can never take place . . . where the Declaration of Independence claims for every one, with life and liberty, the pursuit of happiness in his own way." This belief that the incorporation of all classes into the body politic in America would reduce prospects for a lower-class-based radical movement has been elaborated in one of the most remarkable efforts to account for the failure of socialism in this country, that advanced by the socialist writer Leon Samson in the early 1930's.[45] He attributed this failure to the entire agreement of the basic values of Americanism with those of socialism. Samson in a sense validated the position of those like Harriet Martineau who have urged that American values are basically radical. He cited statements from various leading Americans, including many arch conservatives and capitalists such as Herbert Hoover and Andrew Mellon, and from socialist thinkers, such as Marx, Engels, and Lenin, which

[44] His main writings on the subject are in "On the Jewish Question," in Karl Marx, *Selected Essays* (New York: H. J. Stenning, 1926). I am indebted to an as yet unpublished paper by Lewis Feuer, "The North American Origin of Marx's Socialism," for calling these important American influences upon Marx to my attention.

[45] Leon Samson, *Toward a United Front: A Philosophy for American Workers* (New York: Farrar and Rinehart, Inc., 1933). See also Sidney Hook, "The Philosophical Basis of Marxian Socialism in the United States," in D. D. Egbert and S. Persons, eds., *Socialism and American Life* (Princeton: Princeton University Press, 1952), pp. 450–451.

indicated that, apart from property arrangements, they completely agreed about the nature of the good society, about its social relationships, need for equality of opportunity, work orientation, and style of life. Samson's thesis is that Americans never supported socialism because it seemed to offer them in the guise of a European ideology and language what they already had. The appeal of socialism to the European underprivileged, he suggested, has been that this movement incorporated in its ideology the values subsumed in the Declaration of Independence.

These then are some of the major theses and arguments presented in *Society in America*. While recognized as a research resource for historians and other students of nineteenth-century America, it has long deserved to be rediscovered by the general reader. Sociologists in particular owe Harriet Martineau some attention for, as I noted earlier, she belongs in the annals of those who carved out a niche for a science of society. Moreover, she was one of the first to apply explicitly a sociological approach to comparative analysis, a discipline that she suggested "is, perhaps, the least cultivated, the least definite, the least ascertained in itself, and the most difficult in application."[46] She argued that: "The observer of Men and Manners stands as much in need of intellectual preparation as any other student. . . . Of the large number of tourists who annually sail from our ports, there is probably not one who would dream of pretending to make observations on any subject of physical inquiry, of which he did not understand the principles. . . . But few, or none, make the same avowal about the morals and manners of a nation. Every man seems to imagine that he can understand men at a glance."[47]

Her methodological treatise testifies to the considerable sophistication that she brought to this inquiry. She noted that an observer or interviewer must always be self-conscious about both his biases and his roles. "There are two parties to the work of observation in Morals and Manners

[46] *How to Observe Manners and Morals, op. cit.,* p. 3.
[47] *Ibid.,* p. 2.

—the observer and the observed."[48] She was also sensitive to the problem of sampling bias:

> [The traveler] must seek intercourse with all classes of the society he visits,—not only the rich and the poor, but those who may be classed by profession, pursuit, habits of mind, and turn of manners. He must converse with young men and maidens, old men and children, beggars and savans, postillions and potentates. . . .

> The chief reason why the discourse of individuals, apart from the observation of classes of fact, is almost purely deceptive as to morals, is that the traveller can see no more than one in fifty thousand of the people, and has no security that those he meets are a sample of the whole. This difficulty does not interfere with one very important advantage which he may obtain from conversation,—knowledge of and light upon particular questions.[49]

Since the lone observer can never interview a representative sample of a population, he should concentrate his research efforts on what he can systematically study, the operation of institutions.

> The Institutions of a nation,—political, religious, or social,—put evidence into the observer's hands as to its capabilities and wants which the study of individuals could not yield in a life-time. . . . Thus also must Manners be judged of, since there never was a society yet . . . which did not include a variety of manners. General indications must be looked for, instead of generalisations being framed from the manners of individuals. In cities, do social meetings abound? and what is their purpose and character? Are they more religious, political, or festive? If religious, have they more the character of Passion Week at Rome, or of a camp-meeting in Ohio? . . . Are women there? In what proportions. . . . In country towns, how is the imitation of the me-

[48] *Ibid.*, p. 11.
[49] *Ibid.*, pp. 222, 226.

tropolis carried on? . . . In the villages, what are the
popular amusements? . . . There is as wide a difference
among the humbler classes of various countries as among
their superiors in rank. . . . The manners of the great
body of professional men must indicate much of the
requisitions of the society they serve.—So, also, must
every circumstance concerned with the service of society
. . . testify to the desires and habits, and therefore to
the manners of a community, better than the conversation of any individual in the society can do.[50]

In rejecting the study of individual opinion as feasible in
her day because of the lack of techniques to deal with
the problem of securing a representative sample, Martineau
did not rule out the scientific study of the "Philosophy of
Mind," that is, psychology. She suggested instead of seeking to construct philosophical systems that comprehend
mental behavior but are "sadly liable to be puffed away in
dark vapour with the first breeze of reality," that those interested should try the "experimental method." More specifically, she urged that the blind and the deaf presented
students of the mind with a natural experiment, making it
possible to test out some of the theories advanced by different philosophical schools. "Let the . . . speculations be
pursued with all vigour: but if there are joined with these
a close and unwearied study of the phenomena of the
minds of persons deficient in a sense, and especially of
those precluded from the full sense of language, the world
might fairly look for an advance in the science of the Mind
equal to that which medical science owes to pathology."
To those who wonder why such a sophisticated analyst
has been allowed to linger for so long in the obscurity of
nineteenth-century editions, the answer must be that the
blame rests with Harriet Martineau herself. The first edition of *Society in America* ran to well over 800 pages. But
what is worse, as R. K. Webb has suggested in his recent
biography, it is "badly constructed and at times tedious."[51]
Harriet Martineau was afflicted with many ills, but writ-

---

[50] *Ibid.*, pp. 64–66.
[51] *Op. cit.*, p. 157.

er's block was not one of them. She once turned out nine volumes in two years, and in her lifetime wrote close to fifty books.[52] The original version of *Society in America* reflects some of the weaknesses of a writer who could put everything in her mind quickly onto paper. In editing it, I have tried to remain faithful to the longer work, but I have been concerned, at the same time, with eliminating much of what has made it tedious to some readers. The present edition contains about one half of the text.

Perhaps the best justification for condensing a book such as this was presented by Harriet Martineau in her Preface to her translation and condensation of Auguste Comte's *Positive Philosophy.* She pointed out that "M. Comte's work, in its original form, does no justice to its importance. . . . M. Comte's style is singular. It is at the same time rich and diffuse. . . . [I]t is overloaded with words. His scrupulous honesty leads him to guard his enunciations with epithets so constantly repeated that . . . they become wearisome . . . and lose their effect by constant repetition. . . . [I]t appeared to me worthwhile to condense his work, if I undertook nothing more, in order to divest it of the disadvantages arising from redundancy alone. My belief is that thus, if nothing more were done, it might be brought before the minds of many who would be deterred from the study of it by its bulk."[53]

One wonders what Harriet Martineau would have thought of the America of today. In many ways, many of her analyses and predictions have been validated by contemporary sociological analyses. On the other hand, the institution of private property appears to be as strong as ever and many of the morals and manners she disliked remain. I would hazard the guess that she would be as optimistic as ever. She would see in the continuing strength of the American Creed, in the reforms attained since her death, evidence that America still offered hope to the

[52] An excellent detailed bibliography may be found in Joseph B. Rivlin, *Harriet Martineau. A Bibliography of Her Separately Printed Books* (New York: The New York Public Library, 1947).

[53] *Op. cit.,* p. 4.

world, provided there remained a resolute group of radicals willing to risk antagonizing public opinion in order to fight for more pervasive equality, thus bringing ever increasing harmony between America's values and its reality. This struggle would take the form of a continuing fight against large-scale capitalism. For she argued: "[E]normous private wealth is inconsistent with the spirit of republicanism. Wealth is power; and large amounts of power ought not to rest in the hands of individuals."

FURTHER REFERENCES

Since an excellent recent biography about Harriet Martineau is available, as well as a detailed *Autobiography,* and various other works about her, including a comprehensive bibliography of her writings, I have not discussed her life and publications here. Those who are interested in reading further are referred to the following books and articles:

Theodora Bosanquet, *Harriet Martineau, An Essay in Comprehension* (London: F. Etchells and H. Macdonald, 1927).

Maria W. Chapman, *Memorials of Harriet Martineau* and *Harriet Martineau's Autobiography* (Boston: James R. Osgood and Co., 1877).

Janet C. Courtney, "Harriet Martineau," *Freethinkers of the Nineteenth Century* (New York: E. P. Dutton and Co., 1920), pp. 198–239.

F. Fenwick Miller, *Harriet Martineau* (London: W. H. Allen and Co., 1889).

John C. Nevill, *Harriet Martineau* (London: Frederick Muller, 1943).

Una Pope-Hennessy, "Harriet Martineau," *Three Englishwomen in America* (London: Ernest Benn Limited, 1929), pp. 211–304.

Narola E. Rivenburg, *Harriet Martineau. An Example of Victorian Conflict* (Philadelphia: privately printed, 1932).

Joseph B. Rivlin, *Harriet Martineau. A Bibliography of Her Separately Printed Books* (New York: The New York Public Library, 1947).

R. K. Webb, *Harriet Martineau, A Radical Victorian* (New York: Columbia University Press, 1960).

Vera Wheatley, *The Life and Work of Harriet Martineau* (London: Secker and Warburg, 1957).

CONTENTS

SOCIETY IN AMERICA

Introduction

"To seize a character, even that of one man, in its life and secret mechanism, requires a philosopher; to delineate it with truth and impressiveness is work for a poet. How then shall one or two sleek clerical tutors, with here and there a tedium-stricken esquire, or speculative half-pay captain, give us views on such a subject? How shall a man, to whom all characters of individual men are like sealed books, of which he sees only the title and the covers, decipher from his four-wheeled vehicle, and depict to us, the character of a nation? He courageously depicts his own optical delusions; notes this to be incomprehensible, that other to be insignificant; much to be good, much to be bad, and most of all indifferent; and so, with a few flowing strokes, completes a picture, which, though it may not resemble any possible object, his countrymen are to take for a national portrait. Nor is the fraud so readily detected: for the character of a people has such a complexity of aspect, that even the honest observer knows not always, not perhaps after long inspection, what to determine regarding it. From his, only accidental, point of view, the figure stands before him like the tracings on veined marble,—a mass of mere random lines, and tints, and entangled strokes, out of which a lively fancy may shape almost *any* image. But the image he brings with him is always the readiest; this is tried; it answers as well as another; and a second voucher now testifies its correctness. Thus each, in confident tones, though it be with a secret misgiving, repeats his precursor; the hundred-times-repeated comes in the end to be believed; the foreign nation is now once for all understood, decided on, and registered accordingly; and dunce the thousandth writes of it like dunce the first."

Edinburgh Review, No. xlvi. p. 309.

THIS passage cannot but strike upon the heart of any traveller who meditates giving to the world an account of the foreign country he has visited. It is the mirror held up before his face; and he inevitably feels himself, for the moment, "dunce the thousandth." For my own part, I felt the truth contained in this picture so strongly, before I was acquainted with the passage itself, that I had again and again put away the idea of saying one word in print on the condition of society in the United States. Whenever I encountered half-a-dozen irreconcilable, but respectable opinions on a single point of political doctrine; whenever half-a-dozen fair-seeming versions of a single fact were offered to me; whenever the glow of pleasure at obtaining, by some trivial accident, a piece of important knowledge passed into a throb of pain at the thought of how much must remain concealed where a casual glimpse disclosed so much; whenever I felt how I, with my pittance of knowledge and amidst my glimmerings of conviction, was at the mercy of unmanageable circumstances, wafted now here and now there, by the currents of opinion, like one surveying a continent from a balloon, with only starlight above him,—I was tempted to decline the task of generalising at all from what I saw and heard. In the intervals, however, I felt that this would be wrong. Men will never arrive at a knowledge of each other, if those who have the opportunity of foreign observation refuse to relate what they think they have learned; or even to lay before others the materials from which they themselves hesitate to construct a theory, or draw large conclusions.

In seeking for methods by which I might communicate what I have observed in my travels, without offering any pretension to teach the English, or judge the Americans, two expedients occurred to me; both of which I have adopted. One is, to compare the existing state of society in America with the principles on which it is professedly founded; thus testing Institutions, Morals, and Manners by an indisputable, instead of an arbitrary standard, and securing to myself the same point of view with my readers of both nations.

In working according to this method, my principal dangers are two. I am in danger of not fully apprehending the principles on which society in the United States is founded; and of erring in the application to these of the facts which came under my notice. In the last respect, I am utterly hopeless of my own accuracy. It is in the highest degree improbable that my scanty gleanings in the wide field of American society should present a precisely fair sample of the whole. I can only explain that I have spared no pains to discover the truth, in both divisions of my task; and invite correction, in all errors of fact. This I earnestly do; holding myself, of course, an equal judge with others on matters of opinion.

My readers, on their part, will bear in mind that, in showing discrepancies between an actual condition and a pure and noble theory of society, I am not finding fault with the Americans, as for falling behind the English, or the French, or any other nation. I decline the office of censor altogether. I dare not undertake it. Nor will my readers, I trust, regard the subject otherwise than as a compound of philosophy and fact. If we can all, for once, allay our personal feelings, dismiss our too great regard to mutual opinion, and put praise and blame as nearly as possible out of the question, more that is advantageous to us may perhaps be learned than by any invidious comparisons and proud judgments that were ever instituted and pronounced.

The other method by which I propose to lessen my own responsibility, is to enable my readers to judge for themselves, better than I can for them, what my testimony is worth. For this purpose, I offer a brief account of my travels, with dates in full; and a report of the principal means I enjoyed of obtaining a knowledge of the country.

At the close of a long work which I completed in 1834, it was thought desirable that I should travel for two years. I determined to go to the United States, chiefly because I felt a strong curiosity to witness the actual working of republican institutions; and partly because the circumstance of the language being the same as my own is very important to one who, like myself, is too deaf to enjoy anything like an average opportunity of obtaining correct knowledge, where intercourse is carried on in a foreign language. I went with a mind, I believe, as nearly as possible unprejudiced about America, with a strong disposition to admire democratic institutions, but an entire ignorance how far the people of the United States lived up to, or fell below, their own theory. I had read whatever I could lay hold of that had been written about them; but was unable to satisfy myself that, after all, I understood anything whatever of their condition. As to knowledge of them, my mind was nearly a blank: as to opinion of their state, I did not carry the germ of one.

I landed at New York on the 19th of September, 1834: paid a short visit the next week to Paterson, in New Jersey, to see the cotton factories there, and the falls of the Passaic; and passed through New York again on my way to stay with some friends on the banks of the Hudson, and at Stockbridge, Massachusetts. On the 6th of October, I joined some companions at Albany, with whom I travelled through the State of New York, seeing Trenton Falls, Auburn, and Buffalo, to the Falls of Niagara. Here I remained nearly a week; then, after spending a few days at Buffalo, I embarked on Lake Erie, landing in the back of Pennsylvania, and travelling down through Meadville to Pittsburgh, spending a few days at each place. Then, over the Alleghenies to Northumberland, on the fork of the Susquehanna, the abode of Priestley after his exile, and his burial place. I arrived at Northumberland on the 11th of October, and left it, after visiting some villages in the neighbourhood, on the 17th, for Philadelphia, where I remained nearly six weeks, having very extensive intercourses with its various society. My stay at Baltimore was three weeks, and at Washington five. Congress was at that time in session, and I enjoyed peculiar opportunities of witnessing the proceedings of the Supreme Court and both houses of Congress. I was acquainted with almost every eminent senator and representative, both on the administration and opposition sides; and was on friendly and intimate terms with some of the judges of the Supreme Court. I enjoyed the hospitality of the President, and of several of the heads of departments: and was, like everybody else, in society from morning till night of every day; as the custom is at Washington. One day was devoted to a visit to Mount Vernon, the abode and burial-place of Washington.

On the 18th of February I arrived at Montpelier, the seat of Mr. and Mrs. Madison, with whom I spent two days, which were wholly occupied with rapid conversation; Mr. Madison's share of which, various and beautiful to a remarkable degree, will never be forgotten by me. His clear reports of the principles and history of the Constitution of the United States, his insight into the condition, his speculations on the prospects of nations, his wise playfulness, his placid contemplation of present affairs, his abundant household anecdotes of Washington, Franklin, and Jefferson, were incalculably valuable and exceedingly delightful to me.

The intercourse which I had with Chief Justice Marshall was of the same character, though not nearly so copious. Nothing in either delighted me more than their hearty admiration of each other, notwithstanding some wide differences in their political views. They are both gone; and I now deeply feel what a privilege it is to have known them.

From Mr. Madison's I proceeded to Charlottesville, and passed two days amidst the hospitalities of the Professors of Jefferson's University, and their families. I was astonished to learn that this institution had never before been visited by a British traveller. I can only be sorry for British travellers who have missed the pleasure. A few days more were given to Richmond, where the Virginia legislature was in session; and then ensued a long wintry journey through North and South Carolina to Charleston, occupying from the 2nd to the 11th of March. The hospitalities of Charleston are renowned; and I enjoyed them in their perfection for a fortnight; and then a renewal of the same kind of pleasures at Columbia, South Carolina, for ten days. I traversed the southern States, staying three days at Augusta,

Georgia, and nearly a fortnight in and near Montgomery, Alabama; descending next the Alabama river to Mobile. After a short stay there, and a residence of ten days at New Orleans, I went up the Mississippi and Ohio to the mouth of the Cumberland river, which I ascended to Nashville, Tennessee. I visited the Mammoth Cave in Kentucky, and spent three weeks at Lexington. I descended the Ohio to Cincinnati; and after staying there ten days, ascended the river again, landing in Virginia, visiting the Hawk's Nest, Sulphur Springs, Natural Bridge, and Weyer's Cave, arriving at New York again on the 14th of July, 1835. The autumn was spent among the villages and smaller towns of Massachusetts, in a visit to Dr. Channing in Rhode Island, and in an excursion to the mountains of New Hampshire and Vermont. The winter was passed in Boston, with the exception of a trip to Plymouth, for "Forefather's Day." In the Spring I spent seven weeks in New York; and a month in a farmhouse at Stockbridge, Massachusetts; making an excursion, meanwhile, to Saratoga and Lake George. My last journey was with a party of friends, far into the west, visiting Niagara again, proceeding by Lake Erie to Detroit, and across the territory of Michigan. We swept round the southern extremity of Lake Michigan to Chicago: went a long day's journey down into the prairies, back to Chicago, and by the Lakes Michigan, Huron, and St. Clair to Detroit, visiting Mackinaw by the way. We landed from Lake Erie at Cleveland, Ohio, on the 13th of July; and travelled through the interior of Ohio till we joined the river at Beaver. We visited Rapp's Settlement at Economy, on the Ohio, and returned to New York from Pittsburgh, by the canal route through Pennsylvania, and the railroad over the Alleghenies. I sailed from New York for England on the 1st of August, 1836, having then been absent just two years.

In the course of this tour, I visited almost every kind of institution. The prisons of Auburn, Philadelphia, and Nashville: the insane and other hospitals of almost every considerable place: the literary and scientific institutions; the factories of the north; the plantations of the south; the farms of the west. I lived in houses which might be called palaces, in log-houses, and in a farm-house. I travelled much in wagons, as well as stages; also on horseback, and in some of the best and worst of steamboats. I saw weddings, and christenings; the gatherings of the richer at watering places, and of the humbler at country festivals. I was present at orations, at land sales, and in the slave market. I was in frequent attendance on the Supreme Court and the Senate; and witnessed some of the proceedings of state legislatures. Above all, I was received into the bosom of many families, not as a stranger, but as a daughter or a sister. I am qualified, if any one is, to testify to the virtues and the peace of the homes of the United States; and let it not be thought a breach of confidence, if I should be found occasionally to have spoken of these out of the fulness of my heart.

It would be nearly impossible to relate whom I knew, during my travels. Nearly every eminent man in politics, science and literature, and almost every distinguished woman, would grace my list. I have respected and beloved friends of each political party; and of nearly every religious denomination; among slave-holders, colonizationists, and abolitionists; among farmers, lawyers, merchants, professors, and clergy. I travelled among several tribes of Indians; and spent months in the southern States, with negroes ever at my heels.

Such were my means of information. With regard to my power of making use of them, I have but a few words to say.

It has been frequently mentioned to me that my being a woman was one disadvantage; and my being previously heard of, another. In this I do not agree.

I am sure, I have seen much more of domestic life than could possibly have been exhibited to any gentleman travelling through the country. The nursery, the boudoir, the kitchen, are all excellent schools in which to learn the morals and manners of a people: and, as for public and professional affairs,—those may always gain full information upon such matters, who really feel an interest in them,— be they men or women. No people in the world can be more frank, confiding and affectionate, or more skilful and liberal in communicating information, than I have ever found the Americans to be. I never asked in vain; and I seldom had to ask at all; so carefully were my inquiries anticipated, and my aims so completely understood. I doubt whether a single fact that I wished to learn, or any doctrine that I desired to comprehend, was ever kept from me because I was a woman.

As for the other objection, I can only state my belief, that my friends and I found personal acquaintance so much pleasanter than any previous knowledge by hearsay, that we always forgot that we had heard of each other before. It would be preposterous to suppose that, received as I was into intimate confidence, any false appearances could be kept up on account of any preconceptions that could have been entertained of me.

I laboured under only one peculiar disadvantage, that I am aware of; but that one is incalculable. I mean my deafness. This does not endanger the accuracy of my information, I believe, as far as it goes; because I carry a trumpet of remarkable fidelity; an instrument, moreover, which seems to exert some winning power, by which I gain more in *tête-à-têtes* than is given to people who hear general conversation. Probably its charm consists in the new feeling which it imparts of ease and privacy in conversing with a deaf person. However this may be, I can hardly imagine fuller revelations to be made in household intercourse than my trumpet brought to me. But I am aware that there is no estimating the loss, in a foreign country, from not hearing the casual conversation of all kinds of people, in the streets, stages, hotels, &c. I am aware that the lights which are thus gathered up by the traveller for himself are often far more valuable than the most elaborate accounts of things offered to him with an express design. This was my peculiar disadvantage. It could not be helped; and it cannot be explained away. I mention it, that the value of my testimony may be lowered according to the supposed worth of this circumstance.

Much is often said about the delicacy to be observed, in the act of revealing the history of one's travels, towards the hosts and other friends of the traveller who have reposed confidence in him. The rule seems to me a very plain one, which reconciles truth, honour and utility. My rule is to speak of the public acts of public persons, precisely as if I had known them only in their public character. This may be sometimes difficult, and sometimes painful, to the writer; but it leaves no just cause of complaint to any one else. Moreover, I hold it allowable and necessary to make use of opinions and facts offered in fire-side confidence, as long as no clue is offered by which they may be traced back to any particular fire-side. If any of my American friends should find in this book traces of old conversations and incidents, let them keep their own counsel, and be assured that the conversation and facts remain private between them and me. Thus far, all is safe; and further than this, no honourable person would wish to go.

This is not the place in which to speak of my obligations or of my friendships. Those who know best what I have in my heart to say meet me here under a new relation. In these pages, we meet as writer and readers. I would only entreat them to bear this distinction in mind, and not to measure my attachment to themselves by anything this book may contain about their country and their nation. The bond which unites us bears no relation to clime, birth-place, or institutions. In as far as our friendship is faithful, we are fellow-citizens of another and a better country than theirs or mine.

I. Politics

_____

"...... Those unalterable relations which Providence has ordained that everything should bear to every other. These relations, which are truth itself, the foundation of virtue, and consequently, the only measures of happiness, should be likewise the only measures by which we should direct our reasoning. To these we should conform in good earnest, and not think to force nature, and the whole order of her system, by a compliance with our pride and folly, to conform to our artificial regulations. It is by a conformity to this method we owe the discovery of the few truths we know, and the little liberty and rational happiness we enjoy."

Burke

Mr. Madison remarked to me, that the United States had been "useful in proving things before held impossible." Of such proofs, he adduced several. Others, which he did not mention, have since occurred to me; and, among them, the pursuit of the *à priori* method in forming a constitution:— the *à priori* method, as it is styled by its enemies, though its advocates, with more reason, call it the inductive method. Till the formation of the government of the United States, it had been generally supposed, and it is so still by the majority of the old world that a sound theory of government can be constructed only out of the experience of man in governments; the experience mankind has had of despotisms, oligarchies, and the mixtures of these with small portions of democracy. But the essential condition of the fidelity of the inductive method is, that all the elements of experience should be included. If, in this particular problem, of the true theory of government, we take all experience of government, and leave out all experience of man, except in his hitherto governing or governed state, we shall never reach a philosophical conclusion. The true application of the inductive method here is to test a theory of government deduced from the principles of human nature, by the results of all governments of which mankind has had experience. No narrower basis will serve for such an induction. Such a method of finding a good theory of government was considered impossible, till the United States "proved" it.

This proof can never be invalidated by anything that can now happen in the United States. It is common to say "Wait; these are early days. The experiment will fail yet." The experiment of the particular constitution of the United States may fail; but the great principle which, whether successfully or not, it strives to embody,—the capacity of mankind for self-government,—is established for ever. It has, as Mr. Madison said, proved a thing previously held impossible. If a revolution were to take place to-morrow in the United States, it remains an historical fact that, for half a century, a people has been self-governed; and, till it can be proved that the self-government is the cause of the instability, no revolution, or series of revolutions, can tarnish the lustre, any more than they can impair the soundness of the principle that mankind are capable of self-government. The United States have indeed been useful in proving these two things, before held impossible; the finding a true theory of government, by reasoning from the principles of human nature, as well as from the experience of governments; and the capacity of mankind for self-government.

It seems strange that while politics are unquestionably a branch of moral science, bearing no other relation than to the duty and happiness of man, the great principles of his nature should have been neglected by politicians—with the exception of his love of power and desire of gain,—till a set of men assembled in the State House at Philadelphia, in the eighteenth century, and there throned a legitimate political philosophy in the place of a deposed king. The *rationale* of all preceding governments had been, "men love power, therefore there must be punishments for rulers who, having already much, would seize more. Men desire gain; therefore there must be punishments for those, rulers or ruled, who would appropriate the gains of others." The *rationale* of the new and "impossible" government is "that all men are created equal; that they are endowed by their Creator with certain inalienable rights; that among them are life, liberty, and the pursuit of happiness; that to secure those rights, governments are instituted among men, deriving their just powers from the consent of the governed."* This last recognizes, over and above what the former admits, the great principles of indefeasible rights; human equality in relation to these; and the obligation of universal justice.

These, then, are the principles which the statesmen in the State House at Philadelphia announced as the soul of their embryo institutions; and the rule through which they were to work was no less than that golden one which seems to have been, by some unhappy chance, omitted in the bibles of other statesmen—"Do unto others as ye would that they should do unto you." Perhaps it may be reserved for their country to prove yet one more impossible thing— that men can live by the rule which their Maker has given them to live by.

Politics are morals, all the world over; that is, politics universally implicate the duty and happiness of man. Every branch of morals is, and ought to be considered, a universal concern. Under despotic governments, there is a pretension, more or less sincere, on the part of the rulers, to moral regards; but from these the bulk of the people are, by common consent, cut off.

The same is the case of the unrepresented under governments which are not called despotic. According to the principles professed by the United States, there is there

* Declaration of Independence.

a rectification of this mighty error—a correction of this grand oversight. In that self-governing nation, all are held to have an equal interest in the principles of its institutions, and to be bound in equal duty to watch their workings. Politics there are universal duty. None are exempted from obligation but the unrepresented; and they, in theory, are none. However various may be the tribes of inhabitants in those States, whatever part of the world may have been their birth-place, or that of their fathers, however broken may be their language, however noble or servile their employments, however exalted or despised their state, all are declared to be bound together by equal political obligation, as firmly as under any other law of personal or social duty. The president, the senator, the governor, may take upon himself some additional responsibility, as the physician and lawyer do in other departments of office; but they are under precisely the same political obligation as the German settler, whose axe echoes through the lonely forest; and the Southern planter, who is occupied with his hospitalities; and the New England merchant, whose thoughts are on the sea; and the Irishman, in his shanty on the canal-bank; and the negro, hoeing cotton in the hot field, or basking away his sabbath on the shore of the Mississippi. Genius, knowledge, wealth, may in other affairs set a man above his fellows; but not in this. Weakness, ignorance, poverty may exempt a man from other obligations; but not from this. The theory of the government of the United States has grasped and embodied the mighty principle, that politics are morals;—that is, a matter of universal and equal concern. We shall have to see whether this principle is fully acted out.

Implicated with this is the theory, that the majority will be in the right, both as to the choice of principles which are to govern particular cases, and the agents who are to work them. This theory, obviously just as it appears, as long as it is applied to matters of universal and equal concern, cannot be set aside without overthrowing all with which it is involved. We shall have to see, also, whether this principle is effectually carried out.

II. Parties

"For these are the men that, when they have played their parts,
and had their exits, must step out, and give the moral of their
scenes, and deliver unto posterity an inventory of their virtues
and vices."

Sir Thomas Browne

THE first gentleman who greeted me on my arrival in the
United States, a few minutes after I had landed, informed
me without delay, that I had arrived at an unhappy crisis;
that the institutions of the country would be in ruins before
my return to England; that the levelling spirit was desolat-
ing society; and that the United States were on the verge
of a military despotism. This was so very like what I had
been accustomed to hear at home, from time to time, since
my childhood, that I was not quite so much alarmed as I
might have been without such prior experience. It was
amusing too to find America so veritably the daughter of
England.

I looked around me carefully, in all my travels, till I
reached Washington, but could see no signs of despotism;
even less of military. Except the officers and cadets at
West Point, and some militia on a training day at Sauger-
ties, higher up on the Hudson, I saw nothing that could be
called military; and officers, cadets, and militia, appeared
all perfectly innocent of any design to seize upon the government. At Washington, I ventured to ask an explanation

from one of the most honoured statesmen now living; who told me, with a smile, that the country had been in "a crisis" for fifty years past; and would be for fifty years to come.

This information was my comfort, from day to day, till I became sufficiently acquainted with the country to need such support no longer. Mournful predictions, like that I have quoted, were made so often, that it was easy to learn how they originated.

In the United States, as elsewhere, there are, and have always been, two parties in politics, whom it is difficult to distinguish on paper, by a statement of their principles, but whose course of action may, in any given case, be pretty confidently anticipated. It is remarkable how nearly their positive statements of political doctrine agree, while they differ in almost every possible application of their common principles. Close and continued observation of their agreements and differences is necessary before the British traveller can fully comprehend their mutual relation.

As long as men continue as differently organized as they now are, there will be two parties under every government. Even if their outward fortunes could be absolutely equalised, there would be, from individual constitution alone, an aristocracy and a democracy in every land. The fearful by nature would compose an aristocracy, the hopeful by nature a democracy, were all other causes of divergence done away. When to these constitutional differences are added all those outward circumstances which go to increase the fear and the hope, the mutual misunderstandings of parties are no longer to be wondered at. Men who have gained wealth, whose hope is fulfilled, and who fear loss by change, are naturally of the aristocratic class. So are men of learning, who, unconsciously identifying learning and wisdom, fear the elevation of the ignorant to a station like their own. So are men of talent, who, having gained the power which is the fit recompense of achievement, dread the having to yield it to numbers instead of desert. So are many more who feel the almost universal fear of having to part with educational prejudices, with doctrines with which honoured teachers nourished the pride of youth, and prepossessions inwoven with all that has been to them most pure, lofty, and graceful. Out of these a large aristocratic class must everywhere be formed.

Out of the hopeful,—the rising, not the risen,—the aspiring, not the satisfied,—must a still larger class be everywhere formed. It will include all who have most to gain and least to lose; and most of those who, in the present state of education, have gained their knowledge from actual life, rather than, or as well as, from books. It will include the adventurers of society, and also the philanthropists. It will include, moreover,—an accession small in number, but inestimable in power,—the men of genius. It is characteristic of genius to be hopeful and aspiring. It is characteristic of genius to break up the artificial arrangements of conventionalism, and to view mankind in true perspective, in their gradations of inherent rather than of adventitious worth. Genius is therefore essentially democratic, and has always been so, whatever titles its gifted ones may have worn, or on whatever subjects they may have exercised their gifts. To whatever extent men of genius have been aristocratic, they have been so in spite of their genius, not in consistency with it. The instances are so few, and their deviations from the democratic principle so small, that men of genius must be considered as included in the democratic class.

Genius being rare, and its claims but tardily allowed by those who have attained greatness by other means, it seems as if the weight of influence possessed by the aristocratic party,—by that party which, generally speaking, includes the wealth, learning, and talents of the country,—must overpower all opposition. If this is found not to be the case, if it be found that the Democratic party has achieved everything that has been achieved since the United States' constitution began to work, it is no wonder that there is panic in many hearts, and that I heard from so many tongues of the desolations of the "levelling spirit," and the approaching ruin of political institutions.

These classes may be distinguished in another way. The description which Jefferson gave of the Federal and Re-

publican parties of 1799 applies to the Federal and Democratic parties of this day, and to the aristocratic and
democratic parties of every time and country. "One," says
Jefferson, "fears most the ignorance of the people; the
other, the selfishness of rulers independent of them."

There is much reason in both these fears. The unrea-
sonableness of party lies in entertaining the one fear, and
not the other. No argument is needed to prove that rulers
are prone to selfishness and narrowness of views: and no
one can have witnessed the injuries that the poor suffer in
old countries,—the education of hardship and insult that
furnishes them with their only knowledge of the highest
classes, without being convinced that their ignorance is to
be feared;—their ignorance, not so much of books as of liberty and law. In old countries, the question remains open
whether the many should, on account of their ignorance,
be kept still in a state of political servitude, as some declare; or whether they should be gradually prepared for
political freedom, as others think, by an amelioration of
their condition, and by being educated in schools; or
whether, as yet others maintain, the exercise of political
rights and duties be not the only possible political education. In the New World, no such question remains to be
debated. It has no large, degraded, injured, dangerous
(white) class who can afford the slightest pretence for a
panic-cry about agrarianism. With the exception of the
foreign paupers on the seaboard, and those who are
steeped in sensual vice, neither of which classes can be
politically dangerous, there are none who have not the
same interest in the security of property as the richest
merchant of Salem, or planter of Louisiana. Law and order
are as important to the man who holds land for the subsistence of his family, or who earns wages that he may
have land of his own to die upon, as to any member of the
president's cabinet.

Nor is there much more to fear from the ignorance of
the bulk of the people in the United States, than from
their poverty. It is too true that there is much ignorance;
so much as to be an ever-present peril. Though, as a whole,
the nation is, probably, better informed than any other

entire nation, it cannot be denied that their knowledge is
far inferior to what their safety and their virtue require.
No one who has observed society in America will question
the existence or the evil of ignorance there: but neither
will he question that such real knowledge as they have is
pretty fairly shared among them.

The vagueness of the antagonism between the two parties is for some time perplexing to the traveller in America;
and he does not know whether to be most amazed or
amused at the apparent triviality of the circumstances
which arouse the strongest party emotions. After a while,
a body comes out of the mystery, and he grasps a substantial cause of dissension. From the day when the first
constitution was formed, there have been alarmists, who
talk of a "crisis:" and from the day when the second began
its operations, the alarm has, very naturally, taken its subject matter from the failure of the first. The first general
government came to a stand through weakness. The entire
nation kept itself in order till a new one was formed and
set to work. As soon as the danger was over, and the nation
proved, by the last possible test, duly convinced of the
advantages of public order, the timid party took fright
lest the general government should still not be strong
enough; and this tendency, of course, set the hopeful party
to watch lest it should be made too strong. The panic and
antagonism were at their height in 1799.* A fearful col-

* Jefferson writes, September, 1798, "The most long-sighted
politician could not, seven years ago, have imagined that the
people of this wide extended country could have been en-
veloped in such delusion, and made so much afraid of themselves and their own power, as to surrender it spontaneously to
those who are manœuvring them into a form of government,
the principal branches of which may be beyond their control."
Again, March, 1801:—"You have understood that the revolutionary movements in Europe had, by industry and artifice,
been wrought into objects of terror in this country, and had
really involved a great portion of our well-meaning citizens in
a panic which was perfectly unaccountable, and during the
prevalence of which they were led to support measures the
most insane. They are now pretty thoroughly recovered from it,
and sensible of the mischief which was done, and preparing
to be done, had their minds continued a little longer under

lision of parties took place, which ended in the establishment of the hopeful policy, which has continued, with few interruptions, since. The executive patronage was retrenched, taxes were taken off, the people were re-assured, and all is, as yet, safe. While the leaders of the old Federal party retired to their Essex junto, and elsewhere, to sigh for monarchy, and yearn towards England, the greater number threw off their fears, and joined the Republican party. There are now very few left to profess the politics of the old Federalists. I met with only two who openly avowed their desire for a monarchy; and not many more who prophesied one. But there still is a Federal party, and there ever will be. It is as inevitable that there will be always some who will fear the too great strength of the state governments, as that there will be many who will have the same fear about the general government. Instead of seeing in this any cause for dismay, or even regret, the impartial observer will recognise in this mutual watchfulness the best security that the case admits of for the general and state governments preserving their due relation to one another. No government ever yet worked both well and indisputably. A pure despotism works (apparently) indisputably; but the bulk of its subjects will not allow that it works well, while it wrings their heads from their shoulders, or their earnings from their hands. The government of the United States is disputed at every step of its workings: but the bulk of the people declare that it works well, while every man is his own security for his life and property.

The extreme panic of the old Federal party is accounted for, and almost justified, when we remember, not only that the commerce of England had penetrated every part of the country, and that great pecuniary interests were therefore everywhere supposed to be at stake; but that republicanism, like that which now exists in America, was a thing unheard of—an idea only half-developed in the minds of

that derangement. The recovery bids fair to be complete, and to obliterate entirely the line of party division, which had been so strongly drawn."—*Jefferson's Correspondence,* vol. iii. pp. 401, 457.

those who were to live under it. Wisdom may spring, full-formed and accomplished, from the head of a god, but not from the brains of men. The Americans of the Revolution looked round upon the republics of the world, tested them by the principles of human nature, found them republican in nothing but the name, and produced something, more democratic than any of them; but not democratic enough for the circumstances which were in the course of arising. They saw that in Holland the people had nothing to do with the erection of the supreme power; that in Poland (which was called a republic in their day) the people were oppressed by an incubus of monarchy and aristocracy, at once, in their most aggravated forms; and that in Venice a small body of hereditary nobles exercised a stern sway. They planned something far transcending in democracy any republic yet heard of; and they are not to be wondered at, or blamed, if, when their work was done, they feared they had gone too far. They had done much in preparing the way for the second birth of their republic in 1789, and for a third in 1801, when the republicans came into power; and from which date, free government in the United States may be said to have started on its course.

Advantageous, therefore, as it may be, that the present Federal party should be perpetually on the watch against the encroachments of the state governments,—useful as their incessant recurrence to the first practices, as well as principles, of the constitution may be,—it would be for their comfort to remember, that the elasticity of their institutions is a perpetual safeguard; and, also, that the silent influence of the Federal head of their republics has a sedative effect which its framers themselves did not anticipate. If they compare the fickleness and turbulence of very small republics,—Rhode Island, for instance,—with the tranquillity of the largest, or of the confederated number, it is obvious that the existence of a federal head keeps down more quarrels than ever appear.

When the views of the present apprehensive Federal party are closely looked into, they appear to be inconsistent with one or more of the primary principles of the constitution which we have stated. "The majority are right." Any fears of the majority are inconsistent with this maxim, and were always felt by me to be so, from the time I entered the country till I left it.

One sunny October morning I was taking a drive, with my party, along the shores of the pretty Owasco Lake, in New York state, and conversing on the condition of the country with a gentleman who thought the political prospect less bright than the landscape. I had been less than three weeks in the country, and was in a state of something like awe at the prevalence of, not only external competence, but intellectual ability. The striking effect upon a stranger of witnessing, for the first time, the absence of poverty, of gross ignorance, of all servility, of all insolence of manner, cannot be exaggerated in description. I had seen every man in the towns an independent citizen; every man in the country a land-owner. I had seen that the villages had their newspapers, the factory girls their libraries. I had witnessed the controversies between candidates for office on some difficult subjects, of which the people were to be the judges. With all these things in my mind, and with every evidence of prosperity about me in the comfortable homesteads which every turn in the road, and every reach of the lake, brought into view, I was thrown into a painful amazement by being told that the grand question of the time was "whether the people should be encouraged to govern themselves, or whether the wise should save them from themselves." The confusion of inconsistencies was here so great as to defy argument: the patronage among equals that was implied; the assumption as to who were the wise; and the conclusion that all the rest must be foolish. This one sentence seemed to be the most extraordinary combination that could proceed from the lips of a republican.

The expressions of fear vary according to the pursuits, or habits of mind of those who entertain them: but all are inconsistent with the theory that the majority are right. One fears the influence in the national councils of the "Tartar population" of the west, observing that men retrograde in civilisation when thinly settled in a fruitful country. But the representatives from these regions will be few while they are thinly settled, and will be in the minority when in the wrong. When these representatives become numerous, from the thick settlement of those regions, their character will have ceased to become Tartar-like and formidable: even supposing that a Tartar-like character could co-exist with the commerce of the Mississippi. Another tells me that the State has been, again and again, "on a lee shore, and a flaw has blown it off, and postponed the danger; but this cannot go on for ever." The fact here is true; and it would seem to lead to a directly contrary inference. "The flaw" is the will of the majority, which might be better indicated by a figure of something more stable. "The majority is right." It has thus far preserved the safety of the state; and this is the best ground for supposing that it will continue to be a safeguard.

One of the most painful apprehensions seems to be that the poorer will heavily tax the richer members of society; the rich being always a small class. If it be true, as all parties appear to suppose, that rulers in general are prone to use their power for selfish purposes, there remains the alternative, whether the poor shall over-tax the rich, or whether the rich shall over-tax the poor: and, if one of these evils were necessary, few would doubt which would be the least. A friend in the South, while eulogizing to me the state of society there, spoke with compassion of his northern fellow citizens, who were exposed to the risks of "a perpetual struggle between pauperism and property." To which a northern friend replied, that it is true that there is a perpetual struggle everywhere between pauperism and property. The question is, which succeeds. In the United States, the prospect is that each will succeed. Paupers may obtain what they want, and proprietors will keep that which they have. As a mere matter of convenience, it is shorter and easier to obtain property by enterprise and labour in the United States, than by pulling down the wealthy. Even the most desponding do not consider the case as very urgent, at present. I asked one of my wealthy friends, who was predicting that in thirty years his children would be living under a despotism, why he did not remove. "Where," said he, with a countenance of perplexity, "could I be better off?"—which appeared to me a truly reasonable question.

In a country, the fundamental principle of whose politics is, that its "rulers derive their just powers from the consent of the governed," it is clear that there can be no narrowing of the suffrage. However earnestly some may desire this, no one hopes it. But it does not follow that the apprehensive minority has nothing left but discontent. The enlightenment of society remains not only matter for hope, but for achievement. The prudent speak of the benefits of education as a matter of policy, while the philanthropic promote it as a matter of justice. Security of person and property follows naturally upon a knowledge of rights. However the aristocracy of wealth, learning, and talent may differ among themselves, as to what is the most valuable kind of knowledge, all will agree that every kind will strengthen the bonds of society. In this direction must the aristocracy work for their own security. If they sufficiently provide the means of knowledge to the community, they may dismiss their fears, and rest assured that the great theory of their government will bear any test; and that "the majority will be in the right."

If the fears of the aristocracy are inconsistent with the theory of the government under which they live, so is much of the practice of the democracy. Their hopefulness is reasonable; their reliance on the majority is reasonable. But there are evils attendant on their practice of their true theories which may account for the propounding of worse theories by their opponents.

Learning by experience is slow work. However sure it may be, it is slow; and great is the faith and patience required by men who are in advance of a nation on a point which they feel that they could carry, if they had not to wait the pleasure of the majority. Though the majority be right in respect of the whole of politics, there is scarcely a sensible man who may not be more in the right than the majority with regard to some one point; and no allowance can be too great for the perpetual discouragement hence arising. The majority eventually wills the best;

but, in the present imperfection of knowledge, the will is long in exhibiting itself; and the ultimate demonstration often crowns a series of mistakes and failures. From this fact arises the complaint of many Federalists that the Democratic party is apt to adopt their measures, after railing both at those measures, and at the men who framed them. This is often true: and it is true that, if the people had only had the requisite knowledge, they would have done wisely to have accepted good measures from the beginning, without any railing at all. But the knowledge was wanting. The next best thing that can happen is, that which does happen: that the people learn, and act upon their learning. If they are not wise enough to adopt a good measure at first, it would be no improvement of the case that they should be too obstinate to accept it at last. The case proves only that out of ignorance come knowledge, conviction, and action; and the majority is ultimately in the right. Whenever there is less of ignorance to begin with, there will be less of the railing, which is childish enough, whether as a mere imputation, or as a reality.

The great theory presumes that the majority not only will the best measures, but choose the best men. This is far from being true in practice. In no respect, perhaps, are the people more behind their theory than in this. The noble set of public servants with which the people were blessed in their revolutionary period seems to have inspired them at first with a somewhat romantic faith in men who profess strong attachment to whatever has been erected into a glory of the nation; and, from that time to this, the Federal party has, from causes which will be here-after explained, furnished a far superior set of men to the public service than the Democratic party. I found this fact almost universally admitted by the wisest adherents of Democracy; and out of it has arisen the mournful ques-tion, whether an honest man with false political principles be not more dangerous as a ruler than an unscrupulous man with true political principles. I have heard the case put thus: "There is not yet a sufficiency of real friends of the people willing to be their servants. They must take either a somewhat better set of men whose politics they disapprove, or a somewhat worse set of men to make tools of. They take the tools, use them, and throw them away."

This fact, however, has one side as bright as the other is dark. It is certain that many corrupt public servants are supported under the belief that they are good and great men. No one can have attended assiduously on the course of public affairs at Washington, and afterwards listened to conversation in the stages, without being convinced of this. Retribution often comes sooner than it could have been looked for. Every corrupt faction breaks up, sooner or later, and character is revealed: the people let down their favourite, to hide his head, or continue to show his face, as may best suit his convenience; and forthwith choose a better man; or one believed to be better. In such cases, the evil lies in ignorance—a temporary evil; while the principle of rectification may work, for aught we can see, eternally.

Two considerations,—one of fact, another of inference, —may reassure those who are discouraged by these discrepancies between the theories of the United States' government, and the practice of the Democratic party, with regard to both measures and men. The Americans are practically acquainted with the old proverb, "What is every body's business is nobody's business." No man stirs first against an abuse which is no more his than other people's. The abuse goes on till it begins to overbear law and liberty. Then the multitude arises, in the strength of the law, and crushes the abuse. Sufficient confirmation of this will occur to any one who has known the State histories of the Union for the last twenty years, and will not be wholly contradicted by the condition of certain affairs there which now present a bad aspect. Past experience sanctions the hope that when these bad affairs have grown a little worse, they will be suddenly and completely redressed.

The other ground of hope of which I spoke as being inferential, arises out of the imaginative political character of the Americans. They have not yet grown old in the ways of the world. Their immediate fathers have done such a deed as the world never saw; and the children have not yet passed out of the intoxication of success. With far less of

vanity and presumption than might have been looked for
from their youth among the nations, with an extraordinary
amount of shrewdness and practical talent shared among
individuals, the American people are as imaginative as any
nation I happen to have heard or read of. They reminded
me every day of the Irish. The frank, confiding character
of their private intercourses, the generous nature of their
mutual services, the quickness and dexterity of their doings,
their fertility of resource, their proneness to be run away
with by a notion, into any extreme of absurdity—in all this,
and in everything but their deficiency of moral independence, (for which a difference of circumstances will fully
account,) they resemble the Irish. I regard the American
people as a great embryo poet: now moody, now wild,
but bringing out results of absolute good sense: restless and
wayward in action, but with deep peace at his heart: ex-
ulting that he has caught the true aspect of things past,
and at the depth of futurity which lies before him, wherein
to create something so magnificent as the world has
scarcely begun to dream of. There is the strongest hope
of a nation that is capable of being possessed with an idea;
and this kind of possession has been the peculiarity of the
Americans from their first day of national existence till now.

The American people have not only much to learn, and
a painful discipline to endure, but some disgraceful faults
to repent of and amend. They must give a perpetual and
earnest heed to one point; to cherish their high democratic
hope, their faith in man. The older they grow, the more
must they "reverence the dreams of their youth." They
must eschew the folly and profaneness so prevalent in the
old world, of exalting man, abstractedly and individually,
as a piece of God's creation, and despising men in the
mass. The statesman in a London theatre feels his heart
in a tumult, while a deep amen echoes through its chambers at Hamlet's adoration of humanity; but not the less,
when he goes home, does he speak slightingly, compas-
sionately, or protectingly of the masses, the population,
the canaille. He is awestruck with the grandeur of an individual spirit; but feels nothing of the grandeur of a con-
gregated million of like spirits, because they happen to be

far off. This proves nothing but the short-sightedness of such a man. Such shortness of sight afflicts some of the wisest and best men in the new world. I know of one who regards with a humble and religious reverence the three or four spirits which have their habitation under his roof, and close at hand; who begins to doubt and question, in the face of far stronger outward evidence of good, persons who are a hundred miles off; and has scarcely any faith left for those who happen to be over the sea. The true democratic hope cannot coexist with such distrust. Its basis is the unmeasured scope of humanity; and its *rationale* the truth, applicable alike to individuals and nations, that men are what they are taken for granted to be.

III. Apparatus of Government

"The true foundation of republican government is the equal right of every citizen, in his person and property, and in their management. . Try by this, as a tally, every provision of our constitution, and see if it hangs directly on the will of the people."

Jefferson

THOUGH it be true that the principles of government are to be deduced more from experience of human nature than experience of human governments, the institutions in which those principles are to be embodied must be infinitely modified by preceding circumstances. Bentham must have forgotten this when he offered, at sixty-four, to codify for several of the United States, and also for Russia. He proposed to introduce a new set of terms. These could not, from his want of local knowledge, have been very specific; and if general, what was society to do till the lawyers had done arguing? How could even a Solomon legislate, three thousand miles off, for a republic like that of Connecticut, which set out with taking its morals and politics by handfuls, out of Numbers and Deuteronomy? or for Virginia, rank with feudal prejudices and methods? or for Delaware, with its monarchical martyr spirit? or for Louisiana, compounded of Spain, France, and America? Though at the time of the framing of the constitution, the States bore a strong general resemblance in their forms of government, endless minor differences existed, mainly arising from the different tenure on which they had been held under the English crown. Some had been provinces, governed by royal commissions, according to royal convenience. Others, again, were under charter governments; ruled and altogether disposed of by political corporations. It is absurd to suppose that communities, where wide differences of customs, prejudices, and manners still exist, can be, or ought to be, brought into a state of exact conformity of institutions. Diversities, not only of old custom, but of climate, productions and genealogy, forbid it; and reason does not require it. That institutions should harmonise with the same first principles, is all that is requisite. Some, who would not go so far as to offer to codify for countries where they have not set their foot, are yet apt to ask the use of one or another institution, to which the Americans seem to be unreasonably attached. It is a sufficient general answer that institutions are rarely sudden and complete inventions. They have usually an historical origin, even when renovated by revolution. Their protracted existence, and the attachment of the people to them are strong presumptions of their having some use. If their purposes can be better attained in another way, they will surely be modified.

THE GENERAL GOVERNMENT

"WE, the people of the United States, in order to form a more perfect union, establish justice, ensure domestic tranquillity, provide for the common defence, promote the general welfare, and secure the blessings of liberty to ourselves and our posterity, do ordain and establish this Constitution for the United States of America."

So much for the authority, and the objects of this celebrated constitution, as set forth in its preamble.

Its provisions are so well known that it is needful only to indicate them. In Europe, the difficulty is to avoid supposing the state governments to be subordinate to the general. "They are co-ordinate departments of one simple and

integral whole." State government legislates and adminis-
ters in all affairs which concern its own citizens. To the
federal government are consigned all affairs which concern
citizens, as foreigners from other states, or as fellow-
citizens with all in certain specified relations.

The general objects of the instrument are easily stated;
and an apparently clear case of separation between the general and state governments drawn out upon paper. But the
application of the instrument to practice is the difficulty.

There has never been a solemn instrument drawn up yet
without leaving room for varieties of construction. There
never can be, under our present use of abstract terms; no
two men's abstractions being alike, or discoverably so. Of
course, the profession in this case is, that words are to be
taken according to their just and natural import; that there
is to be no straining; that they are to be judged of according to common sense; and so on. The old jests against
etymologists are enough to prove how far men are from
agreeing what straining is.

It was agreed that all unforeseen questions which might
arise with [for example] regard to the respective powers
of the general and state governments, should be settled by
the state governments; but then, there was an indefinite
limitation introduced in the clause, that the general government should have all powers necessary for the prosecution of such and such purposes. This vague clause has
been the occasion of the Union being shaken to its centre;
and it may be thus shaken again, before the questions arising out of it are all settled.

Even these, being open questions, are less formidable
than the compromise of the true republican principle which
is apparent in some provisions of the constitution, and in
some of the most important institutions of the country.
The northern States, which had abolished, on principle, a
far milder slavery than that of the cotton and sugar-
growing south, agreed to admit slavery in the south as a
basis for direct taxation, and for representation. They did
worse. They agreed to act in behalf of their southern
fellow-citizens in the capture and restitution of runaway
slaves, and in the defence of masters against rebellious

slaves. What bitter sorrows of conscience and of feeling this compromise has cost their children, it is impossible fully to describe. Of course, the law, being against conscience, *i.e.* the law of man coming into collision with the law of God, is constantly broken; and causes of dissension hence arise. It is impossible to estimate the evils which have proceeded from, and which will yet arise out of this guilty but "necessary" compromise.

There was difficulty in bringing the greater and smaller States into union. The smaller States could not agree to such an unequal representation as should render them liable to be swallowed up by the larger; while the larger could not consent to be reduced to an equality with the smaller. The Senate was established to afford an equal state representation; while the House of Representatives affords a fair representation of the nation in the aggregate, according to numbers. But the principle of the general government is, that it governs the entire people as one nation, and not as a league of States.

Nothing can be more striking to a stranger than the experience gained, after some residence in the United States, of the ultimate ascendency of the will of the majority—*i.e.* of the right—in defiance of all appearances to the contrary. The review of what I witnessed of this kind, in the course of two years, with regard to the conduct of Congress alone, surprises and cheers me. It is true that I see several wrongs unredressed; several wounds inflicted on the people's liberties yet unhealed; but these are cases in which the people do not yet understand what has been done; or have not yet roused themselves to show that they do.

In the Senate, the people's right of petition is invaded. Last session, it was ordained that all petitions and memorials relating to a particular subject—slavery in the District of Columbia—should be laid on the table unread, and never recurred to. Of course, the people will not long submit to this. What has been already achieved in Congress on this topic is a security that the rest will follow. When I entered the United States, there was an absolute and most ominous silence in Congress about slavery. Almost every leading man there told me in conversation that it was the grand question of all; that every member's mind was full of it; that nearly all other questions were much affected, or wholly determined by it; yet no one even alluded to it in public. Before I left, it had found its way into both houses. The houses had, in some sort, come to a vote upon it, which showed the absolute abolition strength in the House of Representatives to be forty-seven. The entering wedge having been thus far driven, it is inconceivable that the nation will allow it to be withdrawn by surrendering their right of petition.

THE EXECUTIVE

THE principle which is professed in the appointment of a chief magistrate in the United States is, that his removal is to be as easy as possible, and effected without disturbing for a moment the proceedings of government. Under the idea that this last must be impossible, some of the patriots of 1789 were opposed to the institution of the office of President altogether; and there are now some who desire that the chief magistrate should be, as nearly as possible, a cipher; that, for this purpose, his election should be annual; and that, if this cannot be, the term should continue to be four years, but without renewal. Such declare that the office was made for the man, Washington, who was wanted, to reconcile all parties. They maintain that, though it was, for a considerable time, well filled, it must become, sooner or later, dangerous to the public welfare: that it comprehends too much power for a citizen of a republic to hold, presents too high a stake, occupies too much thought, and employs too much endeavour, to the exclusion of better objects.

Some desire that the office should have a duration of six years, without renewal.

Some think so highly of the dignity of the chief magistracy, as to propose that ex-presidents should be debarred from holding lower offices. This looks too like an approximation to the monarchical principle to be, or to become, a popular way of viewing the subject. It is a proposition of the high Federalists. I was far more gratified than amused at seeing Mr. Adams daily in his seat in the House of Representatives, while the history of his administration was perpetually referred to by those who discussed the politics of the country with me. I am aware that two interpretations may be put upon the fact of an ex-president desiring a lower office. It may occur from a patriotism which finds its own dignity in the welfare of its country, or from a restless ambition to be in the public eye. In either case, it seems to be no matter for a fixed rule. The republican principle supposes every man to be at all times ready to serve his country, when called upon. The rest must be left to the character of the man, and the views of his constituents.

Others think so much more highly of the dignity of the Senate than of the executive, as to desire that senators should be ineligible for the office of President. The object here is two-fold: to exalt the Senate; and, by making half a hundred offices higher in honour than that of President, to drain off some of the eager ambition which flows in the direction of the executive function. But power is more alluring than honour; and executive offices will always be objects of choice, in preference to legislative, except with a very small class of men. Besides, the Senate is already further removed from the control of the people, than consistency with the true republican principle allows: and if the people are to be precluded from choosing their chief magistrate from among the fifty wisest men (as the senators are in theory) that the States can choose for the guardianship of their interests, the dignity of both functions would be much lowered. In theory, the people's range of choice for their chief magistrate is to extend from the vice-president's chair to the humblest abode which nestles in the rocks of their eastern coasts, or overlooks the gulf of Mexico. The honour in which the Senate is held must depend on its preserving the character, which, on the whole, it has hitherto maintained. A nobler legislative body, for power and principle, has probably never been known. Considering the number of individuals of whom it is composed, its character has, perhaps, been as remarkable as that of the noble array of Presidents, of which the United States have to boast. If, amidst its indirect mode of election, and long term of office, it should prove equally stable in principle, and flexible in its methods of progress, it may yet enjoy a long term of existence, as honourable as could be secured by any exclusion of its members from other offices in the commonwealth.

By far the greatest apprehension connected with the President's office, relates to the extent of his patronage. It was highly alarming, at first, to hear all that was said about the country being ridden with administration-officers, and office-expectants. A little arithmetic, however, proved very cheering. The most eminent alarmist I happened to converse with, stated the number of persons directly and indirectly interested in the bestowment of office by the executive, to be 150,000. No exact calculation can be made, since no one can do more than conjecture how many persons at a time are likely to be in expectation of any one office. But the above may be taken as the widest exaggeration which an honest alarmist can put forth. This class of interested persons is, after all, but a small section of the population. There is every reason to fear that official corruption is abundant under all governments: and, for some reasons which will be easily apprehended, remarkably so under the government of the United States; but, when it is considered how small a proportion of the people is, at any time, interested in office, and how many persons in office are to be, in fairness, supposed honest, the evil of executive patronage diminishes to the imagination so rapidly as to induce a suspicion that many who say the most about it are throwing a tub to the whale. The watchfulness on the executive power thus induced is a benefit which will set off against a great amount of alarm. It will assist the people to find the true mean between their allowing the President too much power over the servants who are to transact their business, and their assuming too much control over the servants who are to transact his.

Difficult as it is to resist impressions on the spot, from all that is said about the power of the executive, and the character of the President of the time, the worst alarms are derided by the event. It does not appear as if the President could work any permanent effect upon the mind and destiny of the nation. It is of great consequence to the morals and prosperity of the season, that the chief magistrate should be a man of principle, rather than expediency; a frank friend of the people, rather than their cunning flatterer; a man of sense and temper, rather than an angry bigot; a man of business, rather than a blunderer. But the term of an unworthy or incapable President is pretty sure to be the shortest; and, if permitted to serve his eight years, he can do little unless he acts, on the whole, in accordance with the mind of the people. If he has any power, it is because the people are with him: in which case, he cannot be very destructive to their interests. If he does not proceed in accordance with public sentiment, he has no power.

Washington's influence is a topic which no one is ever hardy enough to approach, in the way of measurement or specification. Within the compass of his name lies more than other words can tell of his power over men. It is Washington, the man, not the President, whose name is lovingly spoken, whose picture smiles benignly in every inhabited nook of his own congregation of republics. It is even Washington, the man, not the President, whose name is sacred above all others, to men of all political parties. It was Washington, the man, who united the votes of all parties in his presidentship, since, so far from pretending to agree with all, he took and left, without fear or favour, what convictions he could or could not adopt from each. The one impression which remains of his presidentship is its accordance with himself. Had it been, in any respect, a lower self, there would have been little left of Washington in the people now.

Adams came in by the strength of the Federal party. Supported by the slave States, and all the Federalism of the north, he had the means, if any President ever had, of leaving a strong and permanent impression on the face of affairs. He filled up his offices with Federalists. Everything during his term of office favoured the influence of the Federalists. The nation was almost beside itself with panic at the political convulsions of Europe. Yet, notwithstanding all this, and Mr. Adams's great weight of character, giving influence to his partialities, the people revealed themselves, in the choice of his successor, staunchly Republican.

Jefferson's influence was greater than that of any other President, except Washington; and the reason is, that his convictions went along with the national mind. If Jefferson, with the same love of the people, the same earnestness of temper, and grace of manners, had been in any considerable degree less democratic, he might have gone creditably through his term, and have been well spoken of now; but he would not have been the honourable means of two successors of the same principles with himself, being brought in; nor would he have lain, as he now does, at the very heart of the people. At the outset, his state-rights principle secured him the south, and his philanthropic, democratic principles, the north. He was popular, almost beyond example. His popularity could scarcely be increased; but it has never declined. The common charges against him, of irreligion, of oppression in the management of his patronage, of disrespect to his predecessors, are falling into oblivion, while his great acts remain. There is one infallible test by which to try old men who have had much to do in the world. If their power and privilege of admiration survive their knowledge of the world, they are true-hearted; and they occasion as much admiration as they enjoy. Jefferson stands this test.

His great acts are much heard of. The reduction of taxes and correction of abuses with which he began his administration; his having actually done something against slavery; his invariable decision for advocacy or opposition, in accordance with the true democratic principle, are now spoken of more frequently than things less worthy to be remembered. His influence has been greater than that of any other President since Washington, exactly in proportion to his nearer approach to the national idea of a chief magistrate.

No great change took place during the administration of his two successors, Madison and Monroe. They were strong in the strength of his principles, and of their own characters. Madison's term of office would have been memorable in history, if he had not immediately followed his friend Jefferson. Their identity of views, put into practice by Madison, with the simplest honesty and true modesty, caused less observation than the same conduct immediately succeeding a federal administration would have done. Hence the affectation, practised by some, of calling Madison a tool of Jefferson. Those who really knew Mr. Madison and his public life, will be amused at the idea of his being anybody's tool.

The reason why John Quincy Adams's administration is little notorious is somewhat of the same nature. He was a pure President; a strictly moral man. His good morality was shown in the devotion of his fine powers to the faithful conduct of evanescent circumstances. His lot was that of all good Presidents in the quiet days of the republic. He would not use his small power for harm; and possessed no very great power for political good.

General Jackson was brought into office by an overpowering majority, and after a series of strong party excitements. If ever there was a possibility of a President marking his age, for good or for evil, it would have been done during Jackson's administration. He is a man made to impress a very distinct idea of himself on all minds. He has great personal courage, much sagacity, though frequently impaired by the strength of his prejudices, violent passions, an indomitable will, and that devotion to public affairs in which no President has ever failed. He had done deeds of war which flattered the pride of the people; and in doing them, he had acquired a knowledge of the people, which has served him instead of much other knowledge in which he is deficient. Here are all the requisites for success in a tyrannical administration. Even in England, we heard rumours in 1828, and again in 1832, about the perils of the United States, under the rule of a despotic soldier. The cry revived with every one of his high-handed deeds; with every exercise of the veto,—which he has used oftener than all the other Presidents put together, —with every appointment made in defiance of the Senate;

with the removal of the deposits; with his messages of menace to the French government. Yet to what amounts the power now, at the close of his administration, of this idol of the people, this man strong in war, and subtle in council, this soldier and statesman of indomitable will, of insatiable ambition, with the resources of a huge majority at his disposal? The deeds of his administration remain to be justified in as far as they are sound, and undone if they are faulty. Meantime, he has been able to obtain only the barest majority in the Senate, the great object of his wrath: he has been unable to keep the slavery question out of Congress,—the introduction of which is by far the most remarkable event of his administration. One of the most desponding complaints I heard of his administration was, not that he had strengthened the general government—not that his government had tended to centralisation—not that he had settled any matters to his own satisfaction, and left the people to reconcile themselves to his pleasure as they best might,—but that every great question is left unsettled; that it is difficult now to tell any party by its principles; that the principles of such affairs as the currency, land, slavery, internal improvements, &c. remain to be all argued over again. Meantime, men will have reason to smile at their fears of the formidable personage, who is now descending from the presidential chair; and their enthusiasm will have cooled down to the temperature fixed by what the event will prove to have been his merits. They will discuss him by their firesides with the calmness with which men speak of things that are past; while they keep their hopes and fears to be chafed up at public meetings, while the orator points to some rising star, or to some cloud no bigger than a man's hand. Irish emigrants occasionally fight out the battle of the Boyne in the streets of Philadelphia; but native Americans bestow their apprehensions and their wrath upon things future; and their philosophy upon things past. While they do this, it will not be in the power of any President to harm them much or long.

THE STATE GOVERNMENTS

NEVER, perhaps, did statesmen begin their task of con-
stitution-making with so much aid from preceding circumstances as the great men of the Revolution. A social
neighbourhood of colonies, all suffering under colonial
grievances, and all varying in their internal government,
afforded a broad hint of the present system, and fine facilities for putting it in practice. There was much less speculation in the case than might appear from a distance; and
this fact so far takes away from the superhuman character
of the wisdom which achieved the completion of the
United States' constitution, as to bring the mind down from
its state of amazement into one of very wholesome admiration.

The state governments . . . enable the will of the majority to act with freedom and convenience. Though the
nation is but an aggregation of individuals, as regards the
general government, their division into States, for the management of their domestic affairs, precludes a vast amount
of confusion and discord. Their mutual vigilance is also a
great advantage to their interests, both within each State,
and abroad. No tyrant, or tyrannical party, can remain
unwatched and unchecked. There is, in each State, a people ready for information and complaint, when necessary;
a legislature ready for deliberation; and an executive ready
to act.

Under no other arrangement, perhaps, could the advantage be secured of every man being, in his turn, a
servant of the commonwealth. If the general government
managed everything, the public service would soon become the privilege of a certain class, or a number of classes
of men; as is seen to be the case elsewhere. The relation
and gradation of service which are now so remarkable a
feature in the United States commonwealth, could never
then happen naturally, as they now do. Whatever ex-
traneous impediments may interfere with the true working
of the theory, every citizen feels, or ought to feel, what a

glorious career may lie before him. In his country, every road to success is open to all. There are no artificial disqualifications which may not be surmounted. All *humbug*, whether of fashion and show, of sanctimoniousness, of licentiousness, or of anything else, is there destined to speedy failure and retribution. There is no hereditary humbug in the United States. If the honest, wise man, feels himself depressed below the knave, he has, if he did but know it, only to wait patiently a little while, and he will have his due.

Another . . . effect of the state governments is the facilities they afford for the correction of solecisms, the renovation of institutions as they are outgrown, and the amendment of all unsuitable arrangements. If anything wants to be rectified in any State, it can be done on the mere will of the people concerned. There is no imploring of an uninterested government at a distance.

It is amusing to look over the proceedings of the state legislatures for any one year. Maine amends her libel law, decreeing that proof of truth shall be admitted as justification. Massachusetts decrees a revision and consolidation of her laws, and the annihilation of lotteries. Rhode Island improves her quarantine regulations. Connecticut passes an act for the preservation of corn-fields from crows. Vermont decrees the protection of the dead in their graves. New York prohibits the importation of foreign convicts. New Jersey incorporates a dairy company. Pennsylvania mitigates the law which authorises imprisonment for debt. Maryland authorises a geological survey. Georgia enlarges her law of divorce. Alabama puts children, in certain circumstances, under the protection of chancery. Mississippi decrees a census. Tennessee interdicts barbecues in the neighbourhood of camp meetings. Ohio regulates the care of escheated lands. Indiana prohibits a higher rate of interest than ten per cent. Missouri authorises the conveyance of real estate by married women. And so on. It seems difficult to imagine how many abuses can reach an extreme, or be tardy of cure, where the will of the majority is not only speedily made known, but where the division of employment is so skilfully arranged that the majority

may be trusted to understand the case on which they are
to decide.

It has always appeared to me that much misapprehension is occasioned by its being supposed that the strength
of the general government lies in the number of its functions; and its weakness in the extent of its area. To me it
appears directly the reverse. A government which has the
management of all the concerns of a people, the greater
and the smaller, preserves its stability by the general interest in its more important functions. If you desire to
weaken it, you must withdraw from its guardianship the
more general and important of its affairs. If you desire to
shield it from cavil and attack, you must put the more local
and partial objects of its administration under other management. If the general government of the United States
had to manage all legislation and administration within
their boundaries, it could hardly hold together one year.
If it had only one function, essential to all, and impossible
to be otherwise fulfilled, there seems no reason why it
should not work prosperously till there are fifty States
around it, and longer. The importance of the functions of
the general government depends partly upon the universality of the interest in them; and partly upon the numbers
included under them. So far, therefore, from the enlargement of the area of the United States being perilous to the
general government, by making it "cumbrous," as many
fear, it seems to me likely to work a directly contrary effect.
A government which has to keep watch over the defence,
foreign policy, commerce, and currency, of from twenty-five to fifty small republics, is safer in the guardianship of
its subjects than if it had to manage these same affairs for
one large republic, with the additional superintendence of
its debtors, its libellers, and the crows of its corn-fields.

A brief account of the South Carolina Nullification may
exhibit the relations, and occasional enmities of the general
and states government in a clearer way than could be
done, otherwise than by a narrative of facts. This little
history shows, among many other things, that America
follows the rest of the world in quoting the constitution
as a sanction of the most opposite designs and proceedings:

what different sympathies respond to the word "patriotism;" and of how little avail is the letter of the constitution, when there is variance as to its spirit.

South Carolina . . . annulled the acts of Congress, which regarded such revenue laws as she considered contrary to general principles, and to her own interests. The President now perceived that if every State proceeded to nullify the acts of Congress, upon its own construction of the federal constitution, the general government could not be secure of its existence for a day.

The President was invited to dine at Charleston on the 4th of July, 1831; and in his answer, he thought fit to announce that he should do his duty in case of any attempt to annul the laws of the Union. The heat was rising rapidly. The nullifiers were loud in their threats, and watchful in observing the effect of those threats abroad. North Carolina repudiated the whole doctrine of Nullification: other neighbouring States showed a reluctance to sanction it.

The legislature of South Carolina, after the next election, exhibited a large majority in both houses in favour of Nullification. A convention was called at Columbia, in consequence of whose proceedings an ordinance was prepared, and speedily passed through the legislature, declaring all the acts of Congress imposing duties on imported goods, to be null and void within the state of South Carolina. The governor was empowered to call the militia into service against any opposition which might be made by the general government to this bold mode of proceeding. The entire military force of the State, and the services of volunteers, were also placed at his disposal. Arms and ammunition were ordered to be purchased.

This was too much for the President's anxiety about consistency. He ordered all the disposable military force to assemble at Charleston; sent a sloop of war to that port, to protect the federal officers in the discharge of their duties; and issued a vigorous proclamation, stating the constitutional doctrine, about the mutual relations of the general and state governments, and exhorting the citizens of South Carolina not to forfeit their allegiance. Governor Hayne issued a counter proclamation, warning the citizens of the State against being seduced from their state allegiance by the President. This was at the close of 1832.

While the South Carolina militia were training, and the munitions of war preparing, the senators and representatives of the State were wearing stern and grave faces at Washington. They would never submit to mere numbers; and would oppose force to force, till all of their small resources was spent. No one can estimate their heroism, or desperation, whichever it may be called, who has not seen the city and State which would have been the theatre of the war. The high spirit of South Carolina is of that kind which accompanies fallen, or inferior fortunes. Pride and poverty chafe the spirit. They make men look around for injury, and aggravate the sense of injury when it is real. In South Carolina, the black population outnumbers the white. The curse of slavery lies heavy on the land, and its inhabitants show the usual unwillingness of sufferers to attribute their maladies to their true cause. . . . If not a single import duty had ever been imposed, there would still have been the contrasts which they cannot endure to perceive between the thriving States of the north and their own. Now, when they see the flourishing villages of New England, they cry "We pay for all this." When the north appears to receive more favour from the general government, in its retrospective recompenses for service in war, the greater proportion of which service was rendered by the north, the south again cries, "We pay for all this." It is true that the south pays dearly; but it is for her own depression, not for others' prosperity. When I saw the face of the nullifiers' country, I was indeed amazed at their hardihood. The rich soil, watered by full streams, the fertile bottoms, superintended by the planters' mansions, with their slave quarter a little removed from the house, the fine growth of trees, and of the few patches of pasturage which are to be seen, show how flourishing this region ought to be. But its aspect is most depressing to the traveller. Roads nearly impassable in many parts, bridges carried away and not restored, lands exhausted, and dwellings forsaken, are spectacles too common in South Carolina. The young men, whose patrimony has deteriorated, migrate westward with their 'force;' selling their lands, if they can; if not, forsaking them. There are yet many plantations of unsurpassed fertility; but there are many exhausted: and it is more profitable to remove to a virgin soil than to employ slave labour in renovating the fertility of the old. There is an air of rudeness about the villages, and languor about the towns, which promise small resource in times of war and distress. And then, the wretched slave population is enough to paralyse the arm of the bravest community, and to ensure defeat to the best cause. I saw the soldiers and the preparations for war at Charleston, two years after the crisis was past. When I was to be shown the arms and ammunition, it appeared that "the gentleman that had the key was not on the premises." This showed that no immediate invasion was expected; but it was almost incredible what had been threatened with such resources. The precautionary life of the community, on account of the presence of so large a body of slaves, may be, in some sort, a training for war; but it points out the impediments to success. If South Carolina had, what some of her leading men seem to desire, a Lacedemonian government, which should make every free man a soldier, she would be farther from safety in peace, and success in war, than any quaker community, exempt from the curse of a debased and wronged servile class.

The session was within fourteen days of its close, when Mr. Clay brought in a bill which had been carefully prepared as a compromise between the contending parties. The passage of the Compromise Bill was a wise and fortunate act. Its immediate effect in honourably reconciling differences which had appeared irreconcileable, was a blessing, not only to the United States, but to the world.

Some ill effects remain,—especially in the irritation of South Carolina. There is still an air of mystery and fellowship about the leading nullifiers, and of disquiet among the Union men of Charleston. But there is cause enough for restlessness in Charleston, as I have before said; and much excuse for pique.

Meanwhile, these events have proved to thousands of republicans the mischief of compromise conveyed in vague phraseology, in so solemn an instrument as a written constitution.

In the privacy of their houses, many citizens have lamented to me, with feelings to which no name but grief can be given, that the events of 1832–3 have suggested the words "use" or "value of the Union." To an American, a calculation of the value of the Union would formerly have been as offensive, as absurd, as an estimate of the value of religion would be to a right-minded man. To Americans of this order, the Union has long been more than a matter of high utility. It has been idealised into an object of love and veneration. In answer to this *cui bono,* many have cried in their hearts, with Lear, "O reason not the need!" I was struck with the contrast in the tone of two statesmen, a chief nullifier and one of his chief opponents. The one would not disguise from me that the name of the Union had lost much of its charm in the south, since 1830. The other, in a glow, protested that he never would hear of the Union losing its charm.

There are many among the slave-holders of the south who threaten secession. Such of these as are in earnest are under the mistake into which men fall when they put everything to the hazard of one untenable object. The southern States could not exist, separately, with their present domestic institutions, in the neighbourhood of any others. They would have thousands of miles of frontier, over which their slaves would be running away, every day of the year. In case of war, they might be only too happy if their slaves did run away, instead of rising up against them at home. If it was necessary to purchase Florida because it was a retreat for runaways; if it was necessary, first to treat with Mexico for the restitution of runaways, and then to steal Texas,—the most high-handed theft of modern times; if it is necessary to pursue runaways into the northern States, and to keep magistrates and jails in perpetual requisition for the restitution of southern human property, how would the southern States manage by themselves? Only by ridding themselves of slavery; in which case, their alleged necessity of separation is superseded. As for their resources,—the shoe-business of New York State is of itself larger and more valuable than the entire commerce of Georgia,—the largest and richest of the southern States.

The mere act of separation could not be accomplished. The middle slave States, now nearly ready to discard slavery, would seize so favourable an opportunity as that afforded them by the peril of the Union. The middle free States, from Pennsylvania to the Mississippi, having everything to lose by separation, and nothing to gain, would treat the first overt act as rebellion; proceeding against it, and punishing it as such. The case is so palpable as scarcely to need even so brief a statement as this. The fact which renders such a statement worth making is, that most of those who threaten the dissolution of the Union, do it in order to divert towards this impracticable object the irritation which would otherwise, and which will, ere long, turn against the institution of slavery. The gaze of the world is fixed upon this institution. The world is shouting the one question about this anomaly which cannot be answered. The dwellers in the south would fain be unconscious of that awful gaze. They would fain not hear the reverberation of that shout. They would fain persuade themselves and others, that they are too busy in asserting their rights and their dignity as citizens of the Union, to heed the world beyond.

This self and mutual deception will prove a merely temporary evil. The natural laws which regulate communities, and the will of the majority, may be trusted to preserve the good, and to remove the bad elements from which this dissension arises. It requires no gift of prophecy to anticipate the fate of an anomaly among a self-governing people. Slavery was not always an anomaly; but it has become one. Its doom is therefore sealed; and its duration is now merely a question of time.

IV. Morals of Politics

" 'Tis he whose law is reason; who depends
Upon that law as on the best of friends;
Whence, in a state where men are tempted still
To evil for a guard against worse ill,
And what in quality or act is best,
Doth seldom on a right foundation rest,
He fixes good on good alone, and owes
To virtue every triumph that he knows."
Wordsworth

UNDER a pure despotism, the morals of politics would make but a very short chapter. Mercy in the ruler; obedience in his officers, with, perhaps, an occasional stroke of remonstrance; and taxpaying in the people, would comprehend the whole. Among a self-governing people, who profess to take human equality for their great common principle, and the golden rule for their political vow, a long chapter of many sections is required.

The morals of politics are not too familiar anywhere. The clergy are apt to leave out its topics from their list of subjects for the pulpit. Writers on morals make that chapter as brief as if they lived under the pure despotism, supposed above. An honest newspaper, here and there, or a newspaper honest for some particular occasion, and therefore uninfluential in its temporary honesty, are the only speakers on the morals of politics. The only speakers; but not the only exhibitors. Scattered here and there, through a vast reach of ages, and expanse of communities, there may be found, to bless his race, an honest statesman. Statesmen, free from the gross vices of peculation, sordid, selfish ambition, cruelty and tergiversation, are not uncommon. But the last degree of honesty has always been, and is still, considered incompatible with statesmanship. To hunger and thirst after righteousness has been naturally, as it were, supposed a disqualification for affairs; and a man, living for truth, and in a spirit of love, "pure in the last recesses of the mind," who should propose to seek truth through political action, and exercise love in the use of political influence, and refine his purity by disinfecting the political atmosphere of its corruptions, would hear it reported on every hand that he had a demon. The hour is come when dwellers in the old world should require integrity of their rulers; and dwellers in the new world, each in his turn a servant of society, should require it of each other and of themselves. The people of the United States are seeking after this, feebly and dimly. They have retained one wise saying of the fathers to whom they owe so much; that the letter of laws and constitutions is a mere instrument; with no vitality; no power to protect and bless; and that the spirit is all in all. They have been far from acting upon this with such steadiness as to show that they understand and believe it. But the saying is in their minds; and, like every other true thing that lies there, it will in time exhibit itself in the appointed mode—the will of the majority.

OFFICE

I was told that holding office is the ruin of moral independence. The case is not, however, nearly so bad as this. There is a kind of public life which does seem to injure the morals of all who enter it; but very few are affected by this. Office in a man's own neighbourhood, where his character and opinions are known, and where the honour and emolument are small, is not very seductive; and these

are the offices filled by the greater number of citizens who
serve society. The temptation to propitiate opinion becomes powerful when a citizen desires to enter the legislature, or to be the chief magistrate of the State. The peril
increases when he becomes a candidate for Congress; and
there seems to be no expectation whatever that a candidate
for the presidentship, or his partizans, should retain any
simplicity of speech, or regard to equity in the distribution
of places and promises. All this is dreadfully wrong. It
originates in a grand mistake, which cannot be rectified but
by much suffering. It is obvious that there must be mistake; for it can never be an arrangement of Providence
that men cannot serve each other in their political relations without being corrupted.

The primary mistake is in supposing that men cannot
bear to hear the truth. It has become the established
method of seeking office, not only to declare a coincidence
of opinion with the supposed majority, on the great topics
on which the candidate will have to speak and act while
in office, but to deny, or conceal, or assert anything else
which it is supposed will please the same majority. The
consequence is, that the best men are not in office. The
morally inferior who succeed, use their power for selfish
purposes, to a sufficient extent to corrupt their constituents,
in their turn. I scarcely knew, at first, how to understand
the political conversations which I heard in travelling. If a
citizen told another that A. had voted in a particular manner, the other invariably began to account for the vote.
A. had voted thus to please B., because B.'s influence was
wanted for the benefit of C., who had promised so and so
to A.'s brother, or son, or nephew, or leading section of
constituents. Those who would find the highest integrity
had better not begin their observations on office-holders,
much less on office-seekers, as a class. The office-holder
finds, too often, that it may be easier to get into office than
to have power to discharge its duties when there: and then
the temptation to subservience, to dishonest silence, is well
nigh too strong for mortal man. The office-seeker stands
committed as desiring something for which he is ready to
sacrifice his business or profession, his ease, his leisure, and

the quietness of his reputation. He stands forth as either an adventurer, a man of ambition, or of self-sacrificing patriotism. Being once thus committed, failure is mortifying, and the allurement to compromise, in order to succeed, is powerful. Once in public life, the politician is committed for ever, whether he immediately perceives this, or not. Almost every public man of my acquaintance owned to me the difficulty of retiring,—in mind, if not in presence,—after the possession of a public trust. This painful hankering is part of the price to be paid for the honours of public service: and I am disposed to think that it is almost universal; that scarcely any man knows quiet and content, from the moment of the success of his first election. The most modest men shrink from thus committing themselves. The most learned men, generally speaking, devote themselves, in preference, to professions. The most conscientious men, generally speaking, shun the snares which fatally beset public life, at present, in the United States.

A gentleman of the latter class, whose talents and character would procure him extensive and hearty support, if he desired it, told me, that he would never serve in office, because he believes it to be the destruction of moral independence: he pointed out to me three friends of his, men of remarkable talent, all in public life. "Look at them," said he, "and see what they might have been! Yet A. is a slave, B. is a slave, and C. is a worm in the dust." Too true.

Here is a grievous misfortune to the republic! My friend ascribes it to the want of protection from his neighbours, to which a man is exposed from the want of caste.

Scarcely anything that I observed in the United States caused me so much sorrow as the contemptuous estimate of the people entertained by those who were bowing the knee to be permitted to serve them. Nothing can be more disgusting than the contrast between the drawing-room gentleman, at ease among friends, and the same person courting the people, on a public occasion. The only comfort was a strong internal persuasion that the people do not like to be courted thus.

I attended a Lyceum lecture in Massachusetts. An agent

of the Colonisation Society lectured; and, when he had
done, introduced a clergyman of colour, who had just returned from Liberia, and could give an account of the
colony in its then present state. As soon as this gentleman
came forward, a party among the audience rose, and went
out, with much ostentation of noise. Mr. Wilson broke off
till he could be again heard, and then observed in a low
voice, "that would not have been done in Africa;" upon
which, there was an uproar of applause, prolonged and
renewed. All the evidence on the subject that I could collect, went to prove that the people can bear, and do prefer
to hear, the truth. It is a crime to withhold it from them;
and a double crime to substitute flattery.

The tone of the orations was the sole, but great drawback from the enjoyment of the popular festivals I witnessed. I missed the celebration of the 4th of July,—both
years; being, the first year, among the Virginia mountains,
(where the only signs of festivity which I saw, were some
slaves dressing up a marquee, in which their masters were
to feast, after having read, from the Declaration of Independence, that all men are created free and equal, and
that rulers derive their just powers from the consent of the
governed;) and the second year on the lakes, arriving at
Mackinaw too late in the evening of the great day for any
celebration that might have taken place. But I was at two
remarkable festivals, and heard two very remarkable orations. They were represented to me as fair or favourable
specimens of that kind of address; and, to judge by the
general sum of those which I read and heard, they were so.

One of the then candidates for the highest office in the
State, [Massachusetts] is renowned for his oratory. He is
one of the most accomplished scholars and gentlemen that
the country possesses. It was thought, "by his friends,"
that his interest wanted strengthening in the western part
of the State. The commemoration of an Indian catastrophe
was thought of as an occasion capable of being turned to
good electioneering purposes. I was not aware of this till
I sometime after heard it, on indisputable authority. I
should have enjoyed it much less than I did, if I had known
that the whole thing was got up, or its time and manner

chosen, for electioneering objects; that advantage was taken of the best feelings of the people for the political interest of one.

The platform from which the orator was to address the assemblage was erected under a rather shabby walnut-tree, which was rendered less picturesque by its lower branches being lopped off, for the sake of convenience. Long and deep ranges of benches were provided; and on these, with carriage cushions and warm cloaks, we found ourselves perfectly well accommodated. Nothing could be better. It was a pretty sight. The wind rustled fitfully in the old walnut-tree. The audience gathered around it were sober, quiet; some would have said dull. The girls appeared to me to be all pretty, after the fashion of American girls. Every body was well-dressed; and such a thing as ill-behaviour in any village assemblage in New England, is, I believe, unheard of.

The band arrived, leading the procession of gentlemen, and were soon called into action by the first hymn. They did their best; and, if no one of their instruments could reach the second note of the German Hymn, (the second note of three lines out of four,) it was not for want of trying.

The oration followed. I strove, as I always did, not to allow difference of taste, whether in oratory, or in anything else, to render me insensible to the merit, in its kind, of what was presented to me: but, upon this occasion, all my sympathies were baffled, and I was deeply disgusted. It mattered little what the oration was in itself, if it had only belonged in character to the speaker. If a Greenfield farmer or mechanic had spoken as he believed orators to speak, and if the failure had been complete, I might have been sorry or amused, or disappointed; but not disgusted. But here was one of the most learned and accomplished gentlemen in the country, a candidate for the highest office in the State, grimacing like a mountebank before the assemblage whose votes he desired to have, and delivering an address, which he supposed level to their taste and capacity. He spoke of the "stately tree," (the poor walnut,) and the "mighty assemblage," (a little flock in the middle

of an orchard,) and offered them shreds of tawdry sentiment, without the intermixture of one sound thought, or
simple and natural feeling, simply and naturally expressed.
It was equally an under estimate of his hearers, and a
degradation of himself.

The effect was very plain. Many, I know, were not interested, but were unwilling to say so of so renowned an
orator. All were dull; and it was easy to see that none of
the proper results of public speaking followed. These very
people are highly imaginative. Speak to them of what interests them, and they are moved with a word.

All this would be of little importance, if these orations
consisted of narrative,—or of any mere matter of fact. The
grievance lies in the prostitution of moral sentiment, the
clap-trap of praise and pathos, which is thus criminally
adventured. This is one great evil. Another, as great, both
to orators and listeners, is the mis-estimate of the people.
No insolence and meanness can surpass those of the man
of sense and taste who talks beneath himself to the people,
because he thinks it suits them.

The other festival, to which I have alluded, was the
celebration of Forefathers' Day;—of the landing of the
Pilgrims on Plymouth Rock.

The oration was by an ex-senator of the United States.
It consisted wholly of an elaboration of the transcendent
virtues of the people of New England. His manner was
more quiet than that of any other orator I heard; and I
really believe that there was less of art than of weakness
and bad taste in his choice of his mode of address. Nothing
could be imagined worse,—more discordant with the fitting
temper of the occasion,—more dangerous to the ignorant, if
such there were,—more disgusting to the wise, (as I know,
on the testimony of such,)—more unworthy of one to whom
the ear of the people was open. He told his hearers of the
superiority of their physical, intellectual, and moral constitution to that of their brethren of the middle and southern States, to that of Europeans, and all other dwellers in
the earth; a superiority which forbade their being ever
understood and appreciated by any but themselves. He
spoke especially of the intensity of the New England char-

acter, as being a hidden mystery from all but natives. He contrasted the worst circumstances of European society, (now in course of correction,) with the best of New England arrangements, and drew the obvious inferences. He excused the bigotry of the Pilgrim Fathers, their cruel persecution of the Quakers, and other such deeds, on the ground that they had come over to have the colony to themselves, and did not want interlopers. He extenuated the recent mobbing practices in New England, on the ground of their rarity and small consequences, and declared it impossible that the sons of the pilgrims should trust to violence for the maintenance of opinion. This last sentiment, the only sound one that I perceived in the oration, was loudly cheered. The whole of the rest, I rejoice to say, fell dead.

The orator was unworthy of his hearers. No man of common sense could be made to believe that any community of mortal men has ever been what the orator described the inhabitants of New England to have attained.

I am aware,—I had but too much occasion to observe,—how this practice of flattering the people from the rostrum is accounted for, and, as a matter of fact, smiled at by citizens of the United States. It is considered as a mode, inseparable from the philosophy of politics there.

I was frequently reminded by friends of what is undoubtedly very true, the great perils of office in the United States, as an excuse for the want of honesty in officials. It is perfectly true that it is ruin to a professional man without fortune, to enter public life for a time, and then be driven back into private life. I knew a senator of the United States who had served for nearly his twice six years, and who then had to begin life again, as regarded his profession. I knew a representative of the United States, a wealthy man, with a large family, who is doubting still, as he has been for a few years past, whether he shall give up commerce or public life, or go on trying to hold them both. He is rich enough to devote himself to public life; but at the very next election after he has relinquished his commercial affairs, he may be thrown out of politics. I see what temptations arise in such cases, to strain a few points, in order to remain in the public eye.

But the part for honest men to take is to expose the peril, to the end that the majority may find a remedy; and not to sanction it by yielding to it. Let the attention of the people be drawn towards the salaries of office, that they may discover whether they are too low; which is best, that adventurers of bad character should now and then get into office, because they have not reputation enough to obtain a living by other means, or that honest and intelligent men should be kept out, because the prizes of office are engrossed by more highly educated men; and whether the rewards of office are kept low by the democratic party, for the sake of putting in what their opponents call 'adventurers,' or by the aristocratic, with the hope of offices being engrossed by the men of private fortune. Let the true state of the case, according to each official's view of it, be presented to the people, rather than any countenance be given to the present dreadful practice of wheedling and flattery; and the perils of office will be, by some means, lessened.

The popular scandal against the people of the United States, that they boast intolerably of their national institutions and character, appears to me untrue: but I see how it has arisen. Foreigners, especially the English, are partly to blame for this. They enter the United States with an idea that a republic is a vulgar thing: and some take no pains to conceal their thought. To an American, nothing is more venerable than a republic. The native and the stranger set out on a misunderstanding. The English attacks, the American defends, and, perhaps, boasts. But the vain-glorious flattery of their public orators is the more abundant source of this reproach. For my own part, I remember no single instance of patriotic boasting, from man, woman, or child, except from the rostrum; but from thence there was poured enough to spoil the auditory for life, if they had been simple enough to believe what they were told. But they were not.

NEWSPAPERS

SIDE by side with the sinners of the rostrum, stand the sinners of the newspaper press. The case is clear, and needs little remark or illustration. The profligacy of newspapers, wherever they exist, is a universal complaint; and, of all newspaper presses, I never heard any one deny that the American is the worst. Of course, this depravity being so general throughout the country, it must be occasioned by some overpowering force of circumstances. The causes are various; and it is a testimony to the strength and purity of the democratic sentiment in the country, that the republic has not been overthrown by its newspapers.

While the population is so scattered as it now is, throughout the greater part of the Union, nothing is easier than to make the people know only one side of a question; few things are easier than to keep from them altogether the knowledge of any particular affair; and, worse than all, on them may easily be practised the discovery that lies may work their intended effect, before the truth can overtake them.

It is hard to tell which is worse; the wide diffusion of things that are not true, or the suppression of things that are true. It is no secret that some able personage at Washington writes letters on the politics and politicians of the general government, and sends them to the remotest corners of the Union, to appear in their newspapers; after which, they are collected in the administration newspaper at Washington, as testimonies of public opinion in the respective districts where they appear. It is no secret that the newspapers of the south keep out of their columns all information which might enlighten their readers, near and afar, as to the real state of society at home. I can testify to the *remarkable events* which occur in the southern States, unnoticed by any press, and transpiring only through accident. Two men were burned alive, without trial, by the gentlemen of Mobile, just before my arrival there; and no newspaper even alluded to the circumstance, till, many months after, a brief and obscure paragraph, in a northern journal, treated it as a matter of hearsay.

It is no secret that the systematic abuse with which the newspapers of one side assail every candidate coming forward on the other, is the cause of many honourable men, who have a regard to their reputation, being deterred from entering public life; and of the people being thus deprived of some better servants than any they have. A public man in New England gave me the history of an editor of a newspaper, who began his professional course by making an avowed distinction between telling lies in conversation and in a newspaper, where every body looks for them. Of course, he has sunk deeper and deeper in falsehood; but retribution has not yet overtaken him. My informant told me, that this editor has made some thousands of dollars by his abuse of one man; and jocosely proposed, that persons who are systematically railed at by any newspaper, should lay claim to a proportion of the profits arising out of the use of their names and characters.

The worst of it is, that the few exceptions to this depravity,—the few newspapers conducted by men of truth and superior intelligence, are not yet encouraged in proportion to their merits. It is easy to see how a youth, going into the wilds, to set up a newspaper for the neighbouring villages, should meet with support, however vicious or crude his production may be; but it is discouraging to perceive how little preference is given, in the Atlantic cities, to the best journals over the worst.

There will be no great improvement in the literary character of the American newspapers till the literature of the country has improved. Their moral character depends upon the moral taste of the people. This looks like a very severe censure. If it be so, the same censure applies elsewhere, and English morals must be held accountable for the slanders and captiousness displayed in the leading articles of British journals, and for the disgustingly jocose tone of their police reports, where crimes are treated as entertainments, and misery as a jest.

Some months before I left the United States, a man of colour was burned alive, without trial, at St. Louis, in

Missouri; a large assemblage of the "respectable" inhabitants of the city being present. No one supposed that anybody out of the State of Missouri was any further implicated with this deed, than as men have an interest in every outrage done to man. The interest which residents in other States had in this deed, was like that which an Englishman has in a man being racked in the Spanish Inquisition; or a Frenchman, in a Turk being bastinadoed at Constantinople. He is not answerable for it, or implicated in it, as a fellow-citizen; and he speaks his humane reprobation as a fellow-man. Certain American citizens, out of Missouri, contrived, however, to implicate themselves in the responsibility for this awful outrage, which, one would have thought, any man would have been thankful to avoid. The majority of newspaper editors made themselves parties to the act, by refusing, from fear, to reprobate it. The state of the case was this, as described to me by some inhabitants of St. Louis. The gentlemen of the press in that city dared not reprobate the outrage, for fear of the consequences from the murderers. They merely announced the deed, as a thing to be regretted, and recommended that the veil of oblivion should be drawn over the affair. Their hope was widely different from their recommendation. They hoped that the newspapers throughout the Union would raise such a chorus of execration as would annihilate the power of the executioners. But the newspapers of the Union were afraid to comment upon the affair, because they saw that the St. Louis editors were afraid. The really respectable inhabitants of that disgraced city were thrown almost into despair by this dastardly silence, and believed all security of life and property in their State to be at an end. A few journals were honest enough to thunder the truth in the ears of the people; and the people awoke to perceive how their editors had involved themselves in this crime, by a virtual acquiescence,—like the unfaithful mastiff, if such a creature there be, which slinks away from its master's door, to allow a passage to a menacing thief. The influence of the will of the awakening people is already seen in the improved vigour in the tone of the newspapers against outrage. On occasion of the more recent riots at Cincinnati, the editorial silence has been broken by many voices.

There is a spirited newspaper at Louisville which has done its duty well, on occasions when it required some courage to do it; informing the Cincinnati people of the meanness of their conduct in repressing the expression of opinion, lest it should injure the commerce between Ohio and Kentucky; and also, justifying Judge Shaw of Massachusetts, against the outcries of the South, for a judgment he lately gave in favour of the release of a slave, voluntarily carried into a free State. Two New York papers, the New York American and the Evening Post, have gained themselves honour by intrepidity of the same kind, and by the comparative moderation and friendliness of their spirit. I hope that there may be many more, and that their number may be perpetually on the increase.

APATHY IN CITIZENSHIP

IN England the idea of an American citizen is of one who is always talking politics, canvassing, bustling about to make proselytes abroad, buried in newspapers at home, and hurrying to vote on election days.

There is another side to the object. A learned professor of a western college told me abundance of English news, but declared himself ignorant of everything that had passed in the home portion of the political world. He never took any interest in politics. What would be the use of his disturbing himself? How far does one man's vote go? He does more good by showing himself above such affairs.

A clergyman in the north was anxious to assure me that elections are merely personal matters, and do not affect the happiness of the people. It matters not to him, for instance, who is in office, and what party in politics is uppermost: life goes on the same to him. This gentleman had probably never heard of the old lady who said that she did not care what revolutions happened, as long as she had her roast chicken, and her little game at cards. But that old lady did not live in a republic, or perhaps even she

might have perceived that there would have been no security for roast chickens and cards, if all were to neglect
political action but those who want political power and
profit. In a democracy, every man is supposed to be his
own security for life and property: and, if a man devolves
his political charge upon others, he must lay his accounts
for not being so well taken care of as he might be.

A member of Congress gave me instances of what would
have been the modifications of certain public affairs, but
for the apathy of the minority about the use of their suffrage. If citizens regulate their exertions by the probabilities of immediate success, instead of by their faith in their
own convictions, it is indeed no wonder if the minority
leave everything to their adversaries; but this is not the
way for men to show themselves worthy of the possession
of political rights.

A public man told me that it would be a great point
gained, if every citizen could be induced to vote, at least
once a year. So far is it from being true that all Americans
are the bustling politicians the English have been apt to
suppose. If such political bustle should be absurd, the
actual apathy is something worse.

There is another cause for the reluctance to vote which
is complained of by the best friends of the people; but it
is almost too humbling and painful to be discussed. Some
are afraid to vote!

There is not, in the United States, as with us, a system
of intimidation exercised by the rich over the poor. In the
country, there are no landlords and tenants at will. In the
towns, the tradesmen do not stand in need of the patronage
of the rich. Though they vote by ballot, and any man who
chooses it may vote secretly, (and many do upon occasion,) there is rarely any need of such protection. If the
educated and principled men of the community, as they
are esteemed, fall back into idleness and silence, when the
time comes for a struggle for principles, and there is a
danger of disappointing expectations, and hurting feelings,
their country has little to thank them for. They are the
men from whom the open discharge of duty is looked for;

they are the men who should show that political obligation is above private regards.

The fear of opinion sometimes takes the form of an almost insane dread of responsibility. There are occasions when public men, unable to judge for themselves of particular classes of circumstances, are obliged to ask advice of their friends and supporters. Happy he who obtains a full and true answer from any one! The chances against this are in proportion to the importance of the case. The illustrative details which might be given,—showing the general uniformity, with particular diversity, of the conduct of the advisers,—would be amusing if they were not too sad.

It is felt, and understood, in the United States, that their near future in politics is indiscernible. Odd, unexpected circumstances, determining the present, are perpetually turning up. Almost every man has his convictions as to what the state of affairs will be, in the gross, a century hence. Scarcely any man will venture a conjecture as to what will have happened next spring. This is the very condition, if the people could but see it, for the exercise of faith in principles.

ALLEGIANCE TO LAW

It is notorious that there is a remarkable failure in this department of political morals among certain parties in the United States. The mobbing events of the last few years are celebrated; the abolition riots in New York and Boston; the burning of the Charleston Convent; the bank riots at Baltimore; the burning of the mails at Charleston; the hangings by Lynch-law at Vickesburgh; the burning alive of a man of colour at St. Louis; the subsequent proceedings there towards the students of Marion College; and the abolition riots at Cincinnati. Here is a fearful list!

The first question that arises is, who has done these things? Whose hands have lighted green fagots round a living man? and strung up a dozen or twenty citizens on the same gallows? and fired and razed houses; and sent a company of trembling nuns flying for their lives at midnight? Here is evidence enough of ignorance,—of desperate, brutal ignorance. Whose ignorance?

In Europe, the instantaneous and natural persuasion of men who hear the tidings is, that the lowest classes in America have risen against the higher. In Europe, desperate, brutal ignorance is the deepest curse in the cursed life of the pauper and the serf. In Europe, mobbing is usually the outbreak of exasperated misery against laws which oppress, and an aristocracy which insults humanity. Europeans, therefore, naturally assume that the gentry of the United States are the sinned against, and the poor the sinners, in their social disturbances. They draw conclusions against popular government, and suppose it proved that universal suffrage dissolves society into chaos. They picture to themselves a rabble of ragged, desperate workmen, with torches in their hands; while the gentry look on in dismay, or tremble within their houses.

It is not so. I was informed, twenty times over, by gentlemen, that the Boston mob of last year was wholly composed of gentlemen. The only working man in it was the truckman who saved the victim. They were the gentlemen of St. Louis who burned the black man, and banished the students of Marion College. They were the gentlemen of Cincinnati who denounced the abolitionists, and raised the persecution against them. They were the magistrates and gentry of Vickesburgh who hanged way-farers, gamblers, and slaves in a long row. They were the gentlemen of Charleston who broke open the Post Office, and violated its sacred function, to the insult and injury of the whole country.

One complete narrative of a riot, for the fidelity of which I can vouch, will expose the truth of the case better than a list of deeds of horror which happened beyond my sight. It is least revolting, too, to treat of a case whose terror lies in its existence, more than in its consequences. The actors in the riot, which it was my fortune to understand, were scarcely less guilty than if they had bathed their hands in blood; but it is easier to examine, undisturbed by passion, the case of those whose hands are, to the outward eye, clean.

A very few years ago, certain citizens in New England began to discover that the planters of the south were making white slaves in the north, nearly as successfully as they were propagating black slavery in the territories of the south and west. Charleston and Boston were affectionate friends in old times, and are so still, notwithstanding the hard words that passed between them in nullification days: that is, the merchants and professional men of Boston are fond of Charleston, on account of their commercial relations. This attachment has been carried to such an extreme as to be almost fatal to the liberties of some of the best citizens of the northern city. They found their brothers dismissed from their pastoral charges, their sons expelled from colleges, their friends excluded from professorships, and themselves debarred from literary and social privileges, if they happened to entertain and express opinions unfavourable to the peculiar domestic institution by which Charleston declares it to be her intention to abide. Such is the plea of those citizens of Boston who have formed associations for the purpose of opposing, by moral influence, an institution which they feel to be inconsistent with the first principles of morals and politics. For a considerable time before my visit to that part of the country, they had encountered petty persecutions of almost every conceivable kind. There is no law in Massachusetts by which the free expression of opinion on moral subjects is punishable. I heard many regret the absence of such law. Everything was done that could be done to make up for its absence. Books on any subject, written by persons who avow by association their bad opinion of slavery, are not purchased: clergymen are no longer invited to preach: the proprietors of public rooms will not let them to members of such associations; and the churches are shut against them. Their notices of public meetings are torn in the pulpits, while all notices of other public meetings are read. The newspapers pour contempt and wrath upon them in one continued stream. Bad practices are imputed to them, and their denial is drowned in clamour. As a single instance of this last; I was told so universally in the south and west that the abolitionists of Boston and New York were in the habit of sending incendiary tracts among the slaves, that it never occurred to me to doubt the fact; though I was struck with surprise at never being able to find any one who had seen any one who had actually seen one of these tracts. Nor did it occur to me that as slaves cannot read, verbal messages would be more to the purpose of all parties, as being more effectual and more prudent. Mr. Madison made the charge, so did Mr. Clay, so did Mr. Calhoun, so did every slave-holder and merchant with whom I conversed. I chose afterwards to hear the other side of the whole question; and I found, to my amazement, that this charge was wholly groundless. No Abolition Society of New York or Massachusetts has ever sent any anti-slavery paper south of Washington, except the circulars, addressed to public officers in the States, which were burnt at Charleston. The abolitionists of Boston have been denying this charge ever since it was first made, and offering evidence of its groundlessness; yet the calumny is persisted in, and, no doubt, honestly believed, to this hour, throughout the south, whither the voice of the condemned, stifled by their fellow-citizens, cannot reach.

Only mortal things, however, can be really suffocated; and there has never yet been an instance of a murder of opinion. There seemed, in 1835, so much danger of the abolitionists making themselves heard, that an emphatic contradiction was got up, it was hoped in good time.

The abolitionists had been, they believe illegally, denied by the city authority the use of Faneuil Hall; (called, in memory of revolutionary days, the "Cradle of Liberty"). Certain merchants and lawyers of Boston held a meeting there, in August, 1835, for the purpose of reprobating the meetings of the abolitionists, and denouncing their measures, while approving of their principles. The less that is said of this meeting,—the deepest of all the disgraces of Boston,—the better. It bears its character in its face. Its avowed object was to put down the expression of opinion by opprobrium, in the absence of gag laws. Of the fifteen hundred who signed the requisition for this meeting, there are many, especially among the younger and more thoughtless, who have long repented of the deed. Some signed in anger; some in fear; many in mistake; and of each of these there are some who would fain, if it were possible, efface their signatures with their blood.

It is an invariable fact, and recognized as such, that meetings held to supply the deficiency of gag laws are the prelude to the violence which supplies the deficiency of executioners under such laws. Every meeting held to denounce opinion is followed by a mob. This was so well understood in the present case that the abolitionists were warned that if they met again publicly, they would be answerable for the disorders that might ensue. The abolitionists pleaded that this was like making the rich man answerable for the crime of the thief who robbed him, on the ground that if the honest man had not been rich, the thief would not have been tempted to rob him. The abolitionists also perceived how liberty of opinion and of speech depended on their conduct in this crisis; and they resolved to yield to no threats of illegal violence; but to hold their legal meeting, pursuant to advertisement, for the despatch of their usual business. One remarkable feature of the case was that this heavy responsibility rested upon women. It was a ladies' meeting that was in question. Upon consultation, the ladies agreed that they should never have sought the perilous duty of defending liberty of opinion and speech at the last crisis; but, as such a service seemed manifestly appointed to them, the women were ready.

On the 21st of October, they met, pursuant to advertisement, at the office of their association, No. 46, Washington Street. Twenty-five reached their room, by going three-quarters of an hour before the appointed time. Five more made their way up with difficulty through the crowd. A hundred more were turned back by the mob.

They knew that a hand-bill had been circulated on the Exchange, and posted on the City Hall, and throughout the city, the day before, which declared that Thompson, the abolitionist, was to address them; and invited the citizens, under promise of pecuniary reward, to "snake

Thompson out, and bring him to the tar-kettle before dark." The ladies had been warned that they would be killed, "as sure as fate," if they showed themselves on their own premises that day. They therefore informed the mayor that they expected to be attacked. The reply of the city marshal was, "You give us a great deal of trouble."

The committee-room was surrounded, and gazed into by a howling, shrieking mob of gentlemen, while the twenty-five ladies sat perfectly still, awaiting the striking of the clock. When it struck, they opened their meeting. They were questioned as to whether Thompson was there in disguise; to which they made no reply.

They began, as usual, with prayer; the mob shouting "Hurra! here comes Judge Lynch!" Before they had done, the partition gave way, and the gentlemen hurled missiles at the lady who was presiding. The secretary having risen, and begun to read her report, rendered inaudible by the uproar, the mayor entered, and insisted upon their going home, to save their lives. The purpose of their meeting was answered: they had asserted their principle; and they now passed out, two and two, amidst the execration of some thousands of gentlemen;—persons who had silver shrines to protect. The ladies, to the number of fifty, walked to the house of one of their members, and were presently struck to the heart by the news that Garrison was in the hands of the mob. Garrison is the chief apostle of abolition in the United States. He had escorted his wife to the meeting; and, after offering to address the ladies, and being refused, out of regard to his safety, had left the room, and, as they supposed, the premises. He was, however, in the house when the ladies left it. He was hunted for by the mob; dragged from behind some planks where he had taken refuge, and conveyed into the street. Here his hat was trampled under-foot, and brick-bats were aimed at his bare head; a rope was tied round him, and thus he was dragged through the streets. His young wife saw all this. Her exclamation was, "I think my husband will be true to his principles. I am sure my husband will not deny his principles." Her confidence was just. Garrison never denies his principles.

He was saved by a stout truckman, who, with his bludgeon, made his way into the crowd, as if to attack the victim. He protected the bare head, and pushed on towards a station house, whence the mayor's officers issued, and pulled in Garrison, who was afterwards put into a coach. The mob tried to upset the coach, and throw down the horses; but the driver laid about him with his whip, and the constables with their staves, and Garrison was safely lodged in jail: for protection; for he had committed no offence.

Before the mayor ascended the stairs to dismiss the ladies, he had done a very remarkable deed;—he had given permission to two gentlemen to pull down and destroy the anti-slavery sign, bearing the inscription, "Anti-Slavery Office,"—which had hung for two years, as signs do hang before public offices in Boston. The plea of the mayor is, that he hoped the rage of the mob would thus be appeased: that is, he gave them leave to break the laws in one way, lest they should in another. The citizens followed up this deed of the mayor with one no less remarkable. They elected these two rioters members of the State legislature, by a large majority, within ten days.

I passed through the mob some time after it had begun to assemble. I asked my fellow-passengers in the stage what it meant. They supposed it was a busy foreign-post day, and that this occasioned an assemblage of gentlemen about the post-office. They pointed out to me that there were none but gentlemen. We were passing through from Salem, fifteen miles north of Boston, to Providence, Rhode Island; and were therefore uninformed of the events and expectations of the day. On the morrow, a visitor who arrived at Providence from Boston told us the story; and I had thenceforth an excellent opportunity of hearing all the remarks that could be made by persons of all ways of thinking and feeling, on this affair.

It excited much less attention than it deserved; less than would be believed possible by those at a distance who think more seriously of persecution for opinion, and less tenderly of slavery than a great many of the citizens of Boston. To many in the city of Boston the story I have told would be news and to yet more in the country, who know that some trouble was caused by abolition meetings in the city, but who are not aware that their own will, embodied in the laws, was overborne to gratify the mercenary interests of a few, and the political fears of a few more.

The first person with whom I conversed about this riot was the president of a university. We were perfectly agreed as to the causes and character of the outrage. This gentleman went over to Boston for a day or two; and when he returned, I saw him again. He said he was happy to tell me that we have been needlessly making ourselves uneasy about the affair: that there had been no mob, the persons assembled having been all gentlemen.

An eminent lawyer at Boston was one of the next to speak upon it. "O, there was no mob," said he. "I was there myself, and saw they were all gentlemen. They were all in fine broad-cloth."

"Not the less a mob for that," said I.

"Why, they protected Garrison. He received no harm. They protected Garrison."

"From whom, or what?"

"O, they would not really hurt him. They only wanted to show that they would not have such a person live among them."

"Why should not he live among them? Is he guilty under any law?"

"He is an insufferable person to them."

"So may you be to-morrow. If you can catch Garrison breaking the laws, punish him under the laws. If you cannot, he has as much right to live where he pleases as you."

Two law pupils of this gentleman presently entered. One approved of all that had been done, and praised the spirit of the gentlemen of Boston. I asked whether they had not broken the law. Yes. I asked him if he knew what the law was. Yes; but it could not be always kept. If a man was caught in a house setting it on fire, the owner might shoot him; and Garrison was such an incendiary. I asked him for proof. He had nothing but hearsay to give. The case, as I told him, came to this. A. says Garrison is an

incendiary. B. says he is not. A. proceeds on his own opinion to break the law, lest Garrison should do so.

The other pupil told me of the sorrow of heart with
which he saw the law, the life of the republic, set at
naught by those who should best understand its nature
and value. He saw that the time was come for the true men
of the republic to oppose a bold front to the insolence of
the rich and the powerful, who were bearing down the
liberties of the people for a matter of opinion. The young
men, he saw, must brace themselves up against the tyranny of the monied mob, and defend the law; or the liberties of the country were gone. I afterwards found many
such among the young men of the wealthier classes. If
they keep their convictions, they and their city are safe.

No prosecutions followed. I asked a lawyer, an abolitionist, why. He said there would be difficulty in getting a
verdict; and, if it was obtained, the punishment would be
merely a fine, which would be paid on the spot, and the
triumph would remain with the aggressors. This seemed
to me no good reason.

I asked an eminent judge the same question; and
whether there was not a public prosecutor who might
prosecute for breach of the peace, if the abolitionists
would not, for the assault on Garrison. He said it might
be done; but he had given his advice against it. Why? The
feeling was so strong against the abolitionists,—the rioters
were so respectable in the city,—it was better to let the
whole affair pass over without notice.

Of others, some knew nothing of it, because it was about
such a low set of people; some could not take any interest
in what they were tired of hearing about; some had not
heard anything of the matter; some thought the abolitionists were served quite right; some were sure the gentlemen
of Boston would not do anything improper; and some
owned that there was such bad taste and meddlesome-
ness in the abolitionists, that people of taste kept out of
the way of hearing anything about them.

Notwithstanding all this, the body of the people are
sound. Many of the young lawyers are resolved to keep
on the watch, to maintain the rights of the abolitionists in

the legislature, and in the streets of the city. Many hundreds of the working men agreed to leave their work on the first rumour of riot, get sworn in as special constables, and keep the peace against the gentry; acting vigorously against the mob ringleaders, if such should be the magistrates of Boston themselves. I visited many of the villages in Massachusetts; and there everything seemed right. The country people are abolitionists, by nature and education, and they see the iniquity of mob-law. A sagacious gentleman told me that it did him good to hear, in New York, of this mob, because it proved the rest of Massachusetts to be in a sound state. It is always 'Boston *versus* Massachusetts;' and when the city, or the aristocracy there, who think themselves the city, are very vehemently wrong, it is a plain proof that the country people are eminently right. This may, for the humour of the thing, be strongly put; but there is much truth in it.

The philosophy of the case is very easy to understand; and supremely important to be understood.

The law, in a republic, is the embodiment of the will of the people. As long as the republic is in a natural and healthy state, containing no anomaly, and exhibiting no gross vices, the function of the law works easily, and is understood and reverenced. Its punishments bear only upon individuals, who have the opposition of society to contend with for violating its will, and who are helpless against the righteous visitations of the law.

If there be any anomaly among the institutions of a republic, the function of the law is certain to be disturbed, sooner or later: and that disturbance is usually the symptom by the exhibition of which the anomaly is first detected, and then cured. It was so with free-masonry. It will be so with slavery; and with every institution inconsistent with the fundamental principles of democracy. The process is easily traceable. The worldly interests of the minority,—of perhaps a single class,—are bound up with the anomaly:—of the minority, because, if the majority had been interested in any anti-republican institution, the republic would not have existed. The minority may go on for a length of time in apparent harmony with the expressed will of the many,—the law. But the time comes when their anomaly clashes with the law. For instance, the merchants of the north trade in products which are, as they believe, created out of a denial that all men are born free and equal, and that the just powers of rulers are derived from the consent of the governed; while the contrary principles are the root which produces the law. Which is to be given up, when both cannot be held? If the pecuniary interest of merchants is incompatible with freedom of speech in fellow-citizens, which is to suffer?—The will of the majority, the lawmaker, is to decide. But it takes some time to awaken the will of the majority; and till it awakes, the interest of the faction is active, and overbears the law. The retribution is certain; the result is safe. But the evils meanwhile are so tremendous, that no exertion should be spared to open the eyes of the majority to the insults offered to its will.

One compound fallacy is allowed daily to pass unexposed and unstigmatized. "You make no allowance," said a friend who was strangely bewildered by it,—"you make no allowance for the great number of excellent people who view the anomaly and the law as you do, but who keep quiet, because they sincerely believe that by speaking and acting they should endanger the Union." This explains the conduct of a crowd of "excellent people," neither merchants, nor the friends of slave-holders, nor approving slavery, or mobbing, or persecution for opinion; but who revile or satirize the abolitionists, and, for the rest, hold their tongues. But is it possible that such do not see that if slavery be wrong, and if it be indeed bound up with the Union, the Union must fall? Every day which passes over the unredressed wrongs of any class which a republic holds in her bosom; every day which brings persecution on those who act out the principles which all profess; every day which adds a sanction to brute force, and impairs the sacredness of law; every day which prolongs impunity to the oppressor and discouragement to the oppressed, is a more evil day than that which should usher in the work of renovation.

But the dictum is not true. This bitter satire upon the

constitution, and upon all who have complacently lived under it, is not true. The Union is not incompatible with freedom of speech. The Union does not forbid men to act according to their convictions. The Union has never depended for its existence on hypocrisy, insult, and injury; and it never will.

Let citizens but take heed individually to respect the law, and see that others do,—that no neighbour transgresses it, that no statesman despises it unrebuked, that no child grows up ignorant or careless of it; and the Union is as secure as the ground they tread upon. If this be not done, everything is in peril, for the season; not only the Union, but property, home, life and integrity.

SECTIONAL PREJUDICE

It is the practice at Washington to pay the Members of Congress, not only a per diem allowance, but their travelling expenses; at so much per twenty miles. Two Members of Congress from Missouri made charges widely different in amount. Complaints were made that the Members were not confined to a mail route, and that the country had to pay for any digressions the honourable gentlemen might be in the humour to make. Upon this, a Member observed that, so far from wishing to confine the congressional travellers to a mail route, he would, if possible, prescribe the condition that they should travel, both in coming and going, through every State of the Union. Any money thus expended, would be, he considered, a cheap price to pay for the conquest of prejudices and dispersion of unfriendly feelings, which would be the consequence of the rambles he proposed.

The southern members love to boast of the increase of colleges, so that every State will soon be educating its own youth. The northern men miss the sweet sounds of acknowledgment which used to meet their ears, as often as past days were referred to—the grateful mention of the New England retreats where the years of preparation for active life were spent. The southern men are mortified at the supposition that everything intellectual must come out of New England. When they boast that Virginia has produced almost all their Presidents, they are met by the boast that New England has furnished almost all the school-masters, professors, and clergy of the country. While the north is still fostering a reverence for the Union, the south loses no opportunity of enlarging lovingly on the virtue of passionate attachment to one's native state.

There is much nature and much reason in all this. It is true that there is advantage in the youth of the whole country being brought together within college walls, at the age when warm friendships are formed. They can hardly quarrel very desperately in Congress, after having striven, and loved, and learned together, in their bright early days. The cadets at West Point spoke warmly to me of this. They told me that when a youth is coming from afar, the youths who have arrived from an opposite point of the compass prepare to look cold upon him and quiz him, and receive him frigidly enough; but the second Sunday seldom comes round before they wonder at him and themselves, and acknowledge that he might almost have been born in their own State. On the other hand, it is true that it would be an absurdity and a hardship to the dwellers in the south and west to have no means of educating their youth at home; but to be obliged to send them a thousand miles in pursuit of necessary learning. It is also true that medical colleges should abound; that peculiar diseases, incident to climate and locality, may be studied on the spot. In this, as in many other cases, some good must be sacrificed for the attainment of a greater good.

The question is, need sectional prejudices increase under the new arrangements? Are there no means of counteracting this great evil, except the ancient methods? Is West Point the last spot whereon common interests may rally, and whence state jealousies may be excluded?

I should be sorry if the answer were unfavourable; for this Sectional Prejudice, carried beyond the point of due political vigilance, is folly,—childish folly. Events prove it to be so.

Yet "hatred" is not too strong a term for this sectional prejudice. Many a time in America have I been conscious of that pang and shudder which are felt only in the presence of hatred. I question whether the enmity between the British and the Americans, at the most exasperating crisis of the war, could ever have been more intense than some that I have seen flashing in the eyes, and heard from the lips, of Americans against fellow-citizens in distant sections of their country. I have scarcely known whether to laugh or to mourn when I have been told that the New England people are all pedlars or canting priests; that the people of the south are all heathens; and those of the west all barbarians.

The most mortifying instance that I witnessed of this sectional prejudice was at Cincinnati. It was the most mortifying, on two accounts; because it did not give way before intercourse; and because its consequences are likely to be very serious to the city and, if it spreads, to the whole west.

Less than fifty years ago, it contained fewer than a hundred whites; and buffalo lodged in a cane brake where the city now stands; while the State at present contains upwards of a million of inhabitants, the city between thirty and forty thousand; and Cincinnati has four daily, and five or six weekly, newspapers, besides a variety of other periodicals.

The most remarkable circumstance, and the most favourable, with regard to the peopling of Cincinnati is, that its population contains contributions of almost every element that goes to constitute society; and each in its utmost vigour. There are here few of the arbitrary associations which exist among the members of other societies. Young men come with their wives, in all directions, from afar; with no parents, cousins, sects, or parties about them. Here is an assemblage from almost every nation under heaven,—a contribution from the resources of almost every country; and all unburdened, and ready for natural association and vigorous action. Like takes to like, and friendships are formed from congeniality, and not from accident or worldly design. But here it is that sectional prejudice interferes, to set up arbitrary associations where, of all places, they should be shunned. There are many New Englanders among the clergy, lawyers, and merchants; and this portion of society will not freely mix with the westerners. When I was one day expressing my admiration, and saying that it was a place for people of ambition, worldly or philanthropic, to live in, one of its noblest citizens said, "Yes, we have a new creation going on here; won't you come and dabble in the mud?" If the merchants of Genoa were princes, the citizens of Cincinnati, as of every first city of a new region, are princes and prophets at once. They can foresee the future, if they please; and shape it, if they will: and petty personal regards are unworthy of such a destiny. It is melancholy to see how the crusading chiefs quarrelled for precedence on the soil of the Holy Land: it would be more so to see the leaders of this new enterprise desecrating their higher mission by a like contention.

CITIZENSHIP OF PEOPLE OF COLOUR

BEFORE I entered New England, while I was ascending the Mississippi, I was told by a Boston gentleman that the people of colour in the New England States were perfectly well-treated; that the children were educated in schools provided for them; and that their fathers freely exercised the franchise. This gentleman certainly believed he was telling me the truth. That he, a busy citizen of Boston, should know no better, is now as striking an exemplification of the state of the case to me as a correct representation of the facts would have been. There are two causes for his mistake. He was not aware that the schools for the coloured children in New England are, unless they escape by their insignificance, shut up, or pulled down, or the school-house wheeled away upon rollers over the frontier of a pious State, which will not endure that its coloured citizens should be educated. He was not aware of a gentleman of colour, and his family, being locked out of their own hired pew in a church, because their white brethren will not worship by their side. But I will not proceed with an enumeration of injuries, too familiar to Americans to excite any feeling but that of weariness; and too disgusting to all others to be endured. The other cause of this gentleman's mistake was, that he did not, from long custom, feel some things to be injuries, which he would call anything but good treatment, if he had to bear them himself. Would he think it good treatment to be forbidden to eat with fellow-citizens; to be assigned to a particular gallery in his church; to be excluded from college, from municipal office, from professions, from scientific and literary associations? If he felt himself excluded from every department of society, but its humiliations and its drudgery, would he declare himself to be "perfectly well-treated in Boston?" Not a word more of statement is needed.

The coloured race are citizens. They stand, as such, in the law, and in the acknowledgment of every one who knows the law. They are citizens, yet their houses and schools are pulled down, and they can obtain no remedy at law. They are thrust out of offices, and excluded from the most honourable employments, and stripped of all the best benefits of society by fellow-citizens who, once a year, solemnly lay their hands on their hearts, and declare that all men are born free and equal, and that rulers derive their just powers from the consent of the governed.

This system of injury is not wearing out. Lafayette, on his last visit to the United States, expressed his astonishment at the increase of the prejudice against colour. He remembered, he said, how the black soldiers used to mess with the whites in the revolutionary war. It should ever be remembered that America is the country of the best friends the coloured race has ever had. The more truth there is in the assertions of the oppressors of the blacks, the more heroism there is in their friends. The greater the excuse for the pharisees of the community, the more divine is the equity of the redeemers of the coloured race. If it be granted that the coloured race are naturally inferior, naturally depraved, disgusting, cursed,—it must be granted that it is a heavenly charity which descends among them to give such solace as it can to their incomprehensible existence. As long as the excuses of the one party go to enhance the merit of the other, the society is not to be despaired of, even with this poisonous anomaly at its heart.

Happily, however, the coloured race is not cursed by God, as it is by some factions of his children. The less clear-sighted of them are pardonable for so believing. Circumstances, for which no living man is answerable, have generated an erroneous conviction in the feeble mind of man, which sees not beyond the actual and immediate. No remedy could ever have been applied, unless stronger minds than ordinary had been brought into the case. But it so happens, wherever there is an anomaly, giant minds rise up to overthrow it: minds gigantic, not in understanding, but in faith. While the mass of common men and women are despising, and disliking, and fearing, and keeping down the coloured race, blinking the fact that they are citizens, the few of Nature's aristocracy are putting forth a strong hand to lift up this degraded race out of oppression, and their country from the reproach of it. If they were but one or two, trembling and toiling in solitary energy, the world afar would be confident of their success. But they number hundreds and thousands; and if ever they feel a passing doubt of their progress, it is only because they are pressed upon by the meaner multitude. Over the sea, no one doubts of their victory. It is as certain as that the risen sun will reach the meridian. Already have people of colour crossed the thresholds of many whites, as guests, not as drudges or beggars. Already are they admitted to worship, and to exercise charity, among the whites.

The world has heard and seen enough of the reproach incurred by America, on account of her coloured population. It is now time to look for the fairer side. Already is the world beyond the sea beginning to think of America, less as the country of the double-faced pretender to the name of Liberty, than as the home of the single-hearted, clear-eyed Presence which, under the name of Abolitionism, is majestically passing through the land which is soon to be her throne.

POLITICAL NON-EXISTENCE OF WOMEN

ONE of the fundamental principles announced in the Declaration of Independence is, that governments derive their just powers from the consent of the governed. How can the political condition of women be reconciled with this?

Governments in the United States have power to tax women who hold property; to divorce them from their husbands; to fine, imprison, and execute them for certain offences. Whence do these governments derive their powers? They are not "just," as they are not derived from the consent of the women thus governed.

Governments in the United States have power to enslave certain women; and also to punish other women for inhuman treatment of such slaves. Neither of these powers are "just;" not being derived from the consent of the governed.

Governments decree to women in some States half their husbands' property; in others one-third. In some, a woman, on her marriage, is made to yield all her property to her husband; in others, to retain a portion, or the whole, in her own hands. Whence do governments derive the unjust power of thus disposing of property without the consent of the governed?

The democractic principle condemns all this as wrong; and requires the equal political representation of all rational beings. Children, idiots, and criminals, during the season of sequestration, are the only fair exceptions.

The case is so plain that I might close it here; but it is interesting to inquire how so obvious a decision has been so evaded as to leave to women no political rights whatever. The question has been asked, from time to time, in more countries than one, how obedience to the laws can be required of women, when no woman has, either actually or virtually, given any assent to any law. No plausible answer has, as far as I can discover, been offered; for the good reason, that no plausible answer can be devised. The most principled democratic writers on government have

on this subject sunk into fallacies, as disgraceful as any
advocate of despotism has adduced. In fact, they have
thus sunk from being, for the moment, advocates of despotism. Jefferson in America, and James Mill at home, subside, for the occasion, to the level of the author of the
Emperor of Russia's Catechism for the young Poles.

Jefferson says,* "Were our State a pure democracy, in
which all the inhabitants should meet together to transact all their business, there would yet be excluded from
their deliberations,

"1. Infants, until arrived at years of discretion;

"2. Women, who, to prevent depravation of morals, and
ambiguity of issue, could not mix promiscuously in the
public meetings of men;

"3. Slaves, from whom the unfortunate state of things
with us takes away the rights of will and of property."

If the slave disqualification, here assigned, were shifted
up under the head of Women, their case would be nearer
the truth than as it now stands. Woman's lack of will and
of property, is more like the true cause of her exclusion
from the representation, than that which is actually set
down against her. As if there could be no means of conducting public affairs but by promiscuous meetings! As if
there would be more danger in promiscuous meetings for
political business than in such meetings for worship, for
oratory, for music, for dramatic entertainments,—for any
of the thousand transactions of civilized life! The plea is
not worth another word.

Mill says, with regard to representation, in his Essay on
Government, "One thing is pretty clear; that all those individuals, whose interests are involved in those of other
individuals, may be struck off without inconvenience. . . .
In this light, women may be regarded, the interest of almost all of whom is involved, either in that of their fathers
or in that of their husbands."

The true democratic principle is, that no person's interests can be, or can be ascertained to be, identical with

* Correspondence vol. iv. p. 295.

those of any other person. This allows the exclusion of none but incapables.

The interests of women who have fathers and husbands can never be identical with theirs, while there is a necessity for laws to protect women against their husbands and fathers. This statement is not worth another word.

Some who desire that there should be an equality of property between men and women, oppose representation, on the ground that political duties would be incompatible with the other duties which women have to discharge. The reply to this is, that women are the best judges here. God has given time and power for the discharge of all duties; and, if he had not, it would be for women to decide which they would take, and which they would leave. But their guardians follow the ancient fashion of deciding what is best for their wards. The Emperor of Russia discovers when a coat of arms and title do not agree with a subject prince. The King of France early perceives that the air of Paris does not agree with a free-thinking foreigner. The English Tories feel the hardship that it would be to impose the franchise on every artizan, busy as he is in getting his bread. The Georgian planter perceives the hardship that freedom would be to his slaves. And the best friends of half the human race peremptorily decide for them as to their rights, their duties, their feelings, their powers. In all these cases, the persons thus cared for feel that the abstract decision rests with themselves; that, though they may be compelled to submit, they need not acquiesce.

I cannot enter upon the commonest order of pleas of all;—those which relate to the virtual influence of woman; her swaying the judgment and will of man through the heart; and so forth. One might as well try to dissect the morning mist. I knew a gentleman in America who told me how much rather he had be a woman than the man he is;—a professional man, a father, a citizen. He would give up all this for a woman's influence. I thought he was mated too soon. He should have married a lady, also of my acquaintance, who would not at all object to being a slave, if ever the blacks should have the upper hand; "it is so right that the one race should be subservient to the other!"

Or rather,—I thought it a pity that the one could not be a woman, and the other a slave; so that an injured individual of each class might be exalted into their places, to fulfil and enjoy the duties and privileges which they despise, and, in despising, disgrace.

That woman has power to represent her own interests, no one can deny till she has been tried. The modes need not be discussed here: they must vary with circumstances. The fearful and absurd images which are perpetually called up to perplex the question,—images of women on woolsacks in England, and under canopies in America, have nothing to do with the matter. The principle being once established, the methods will follow, easily, naturally, and under a remarkable transmutation of the ludicrous into the sublime. The kings of Europe would have laughed mightily, two centuries ago, at the idea of a commoner, without robes, crown, or sceptre, stepping into the throne of a strong nation. Yet who dared to laugh when Washington's super-royal voice greeted the New World from the presidential chair, and the old world stood still to catch the echo?

The principle of the equal rights of both halves of the human race is all we have to do with here. It is the true democratic principle which can never be seriously controverted, and only for a short time evaded. Governments can derive their just powers only from the consent of the governed.

V. Economy

"That thou givest them they gather. Thou openest thine hand; they are filled wih good."

104th Psalm

THE traveller from the Old World to the New is apt to lose himself in reflection when he should be observing. Speculations come in crowds in the wilderness. He finds himself philosophizing with every step he takes, as luxuriously as by his study fireside, or in his rare solitary walk at home.

In England, everything comes complete and finished under notice. Each man may be aware of some one process of formation, which it is his business to conduct; but all else is presented to him in its entireness. The statesman knows what it is to compose an act of parliament; to proceed from the first perception of the want of it, through the gathering together of facts and opinions, the selection from these, the elaborating, adjusting, moulding, specifying, excluding, consolidating, till it becomes an entire something, which he throws down for parliament to find fault with. When it is passed, the rest of society looks upon it as a whole, as a child does upon a table or a doll, without being aware of any process of formation. The shoemaker, thus, takes his loaf of bread, and the clock that ticks behind his door, as if they came down from the clouds as they are, in return for so much of his wages; and he analyzes nothing but shoes. The baker and watchmaker receive their shoes in the same way, and analyze nothing but bread and clocks. Too many gentlemen and ladies analyze nothing at all. If better taught, and introduced at an early age into the world of analysis, nothing, in the whole course of education, is probably so striking to their minds. They begin a fresh existence from the day when they first obtain a glimpse into this new region of discovery.

Such an era is the traveller's entrance upon the wilder regions of America. His old experience is all reversed. He sees nothing of art in its entireness; but little of nature in her instrumentality. Nature is there the empress, not the handmaid. Art is her inexperienced page, and no longer the Prospero to whom she is the Ariel.

It is an absorbing thing to watch the process of world-making:—both the formation of the natural and the conventional world. I witnessed both in America; and when I look back upon it now, it seems as if I had been in another planet.

The position or prospects of men in a new country may best be made intelligible by accounts of what the traveller saw and heard while among them. Pictures serve the purpose better than reports. I will, therefore, give pictures of some of the many varieties of dwellers that I saw, amidst their different localities, circumstances, and modes of living. No one of them is aware how vivid an idea he impresses on the mind of humanity; nor how distinct a place he fills in her records. No one of them, probably, is aware how much happier he is than Alexander, in having before him more worlds to conquer.

My narratives, or pictures, must be but a few selected from among a multitude. My chapter would extend to a greater length than any old novel, if I were to give all I possess.

The United States are not only vast in extent: they are inestimably rich in material wealth. There are fisheries and granite quarries along the northern coasts; and shipping from the whole commercial world within their ports. There are tanneries within reach of their oak woods, and manufactures in the north from the cotton growth of the south.

There is unlimited wealth of corn, sugar-cane and beet, hemp, flax, tobacco, and rice. There are regions of pasture land. There are varieties of grape for wine, and mulberries for silk. There is salt. There are mineral springs. There is marble, gold, lead, iron, and coal. There is a chain of mountains, dividing the great fertile western valley from the busy eastern region which lies between the mountains and the Atlantic. These mountains yield the springs by which the great rivers are to be fed for ever, to fertilize the great valley, and be the vehicle of its commerce with the world. Out of the reach of these rivers, in the vast breadth of the north, lie the great lakes, to be likewise the servants of commerce, and to afford in their fisheries the means of life and luxury to thousands. These inland seas temper the climate, summer and winter, and insure health to the heart of the vast continent. Never was a country more gifted by nature.

It is blessed also in the variety of its inhabitants. However it may gratify the pride of a nation to be descended from one stock, it is ultimately better that it should have been compounded from many nations. The blending of qualities, physical and intellectual, the absorption of national prejudices, the increase of mental resources, will be found in the end highly conducive to the elevation of the national character. America will find herself largely blessed in this way, however much she may now complain of the immigration of strangers.

There can scarcely be a finer set of elements for the composition of a nation than the United States now contain. It will take centuries to fuse them; and by that time, pride of ancestry,—vanity of physical derivation,—will be at an end. The ancestry of moral qualities will be the only pedigree preserved; and of these every civilized nation under heaven possesses an ample, and probably an equal, share. Let the United States then cherish their industrious Germans and Dutch; their hardy Irish; their intelligent Scotch; their kindly Africans, as well as the intellectual Yankee, the insouciant Southerner, and the complacent Westerner. All are good in their way; and augment the moral value of their country, as diversities of soil, climate, and productions, do its material wealth.

Among the most interesting personages in the United States, are the Solitaries;—solitary families, not individuals. Europeans, who think it much to lodge in a country cottage for six weeks in the summer, can form little idea of the life of a solitary family in the wilds. I did not see the most sequestered, as I never happened to lose my way in the forests or on the prairies: but I witnessed some modes of life which realized all I had conceived of the romantic, or of the dismal.

One rainy October day, I saw a settler at work in the forest, on which he appeared to have just entered. His clearing looked, in comparison with the forest behind him, of about the size of a pincushion. He was standing, up to the knees in water, among the stubborn stumps, and charred stems of dead trees. He was notching logs with his axe, beside his small log-hut and stye. There was swamp behind, and swamp on each side;—a pool of mud around each dead tree, which had been wont to drink the moisture. There was a semblance of a tumble-down fence: no orchard yet; no grave-yard; no poultry; none of the graces of fixed habitation had grown up. On looking back to catch a last view of the scene, I saw two little boys, about three and four years old, leading a horse home from the forest; one driving the animal behind with an armful of bush, and the other reaching up on tiptoe to keep his hold of the halter; and both looking as if they would be drowned in the swamp. If the mother was watching from the hut, she must have thought this strange dismal play for her little ones. The hard-working father must be toiling for his children; for the success of his after life can hardly atone to him for such a destitution of comfort as I saw him in the midst of. Many such scenes are passed on every road in the western parts of the States. They become cheering when the plough is seen, or a few sheep are straggling on the hill side, seeming lost in space.

One day, at Niagara, I had spent hours at the Falls, till, longing for the stillness of the forest, I wandered deep into its wild paths, meeting nothing but the belled heifer, grazing, and the slim, clean swine which live on the mast and roots they can find for themselves. I saw some motion in a thicket, a little way from the path, and went to see what it was. I found a little boy and girl, working away, by turns, with an axe, at the branches of a huge hickory, which had been lately felled. "Father" had felled the hickory the day before, and had sent the children to make faggots from the branches. They were heated and out of breath. I had heard of the toughness of hickory, and longed to know what the labour of wood-cutting really was. Here was an irresistible opportunity for an experiment. I made the children sit down on the fallen tree, and find out the use of my ear-trumpet, while I helped to make their faggot. When I had hewn through one stout branch, I was quite sufficiently warmed, and glad to sit down to hear the children's story. Their father had been a weaver and a preacher in England. He had brought out his wife and six children. During the week, he worked at his land, finding some employment or another for all of his children who could walk alone; and going some distance on Sundays to preach. This last particular told volumes. The weaver has not lost heart over his hard field-labour. His spirit must be strong and lively, to enable him to spend his seventh day thus, after plying the axe for six. The children did not seem to know whether they liked Manchester or the forest best; but they looked stout and rosy.

No solitude can be more romantic than that at the mouth of the Mammoth Cave in Kentucky; so called, not because any mammoth-bones have been found there, but because it is the largest explored cave in the world. I was told, not only by the guides, but by a gentleman who is learned in caves, that it can be travelled through, in different directions, to the extent of sixty miles. We could not think of achieving the entire underground journey; but we resolved to see all we could; and, for that purpose, preferred devoting the half of two days to the object, to one entire day, the weariness of which would probably curtail our rambles. After a most interesting and exciting journey of nearly two nights and a day from Nashville, Tennessee, our party, consisting of four, arrived at Bell's hotel, twelve miles from the cave, at half-past seven, on a bright May morning. We slept till one o'clock, and then set off in a stage and four for the cave. My expectations had been so excited, that every object on the road seemed to paint itself on my very spirit; and I now feel as if I saw the bright hemp fields, the oak copses, the gorgeous wild flowers, and clear streams, running over their limestone beds, that adorned our short journey.

The house at the cave stands on the greenest sward that earth and dews can produce; and it grows up to the very walls of the dwelling. The well, with its sweep,—a long pole, with a rope and bucket at one end, laid across the top of a high post,—this primitive well, on the same plot of turf, and the carriage in which two travellers—young men—had just arrived, were the only occupiers of the grass, besides the house. We lost no time in proceeding to the cave.

The entrance of the cave serves as an ice-house to the family of the guide. They keep their meat there, and go to refresh themselves when relaxed by the heat. The temperature is delightful, after the first two or three minutes; and we were glad to leave our cloaks by the way side. The ladies tied handkerchiefs over their heads, and tucked up their gowns for the scramble over the loose limestone; looking thereby very picturesque, and not totally unlike the witches in Macbeth. The gloom, the echo of the footsteps, the hollow sound of voices, the startling effect of lights seen unexpectedly in a recess, in a crevice, or high overhead,—these impressions may be recalled in those who have wandered in caves, but can never be communicated to those who have not. It is in vain to describe a cave. Call it a chaos of darkness and rocks, with wandering and inexplicable sounds and motions, and all is done. Everything appears alive: the slowly growing stalactites, the water ever dropping into the plashing pool, the whispering airs,— all seem conscious. The coolness, vastness, suggestions of architecture, and dim disclosures, occasion different feelings from any that are known under the lights of the sky. The air in the neighbourhood of the waterfall was delicious to breathe; and the pool was so clear that I could not, for some time, see the water, in a pretty full light. That Rembrandt light on the drip of water, on the piled rocks, and on our figures,—light swallowed up before it could reach the unseen canopy under which we stood, can never be forgotten. Milton's lake of fire might have brought the roof into view:—nothing less.

The young guides, brothers, were fine dashing youths, as Kentucky youths are. They told us some horrible tales, and one very marvellous story about darkness and bewilderment in the labyrinth of the cave. They told us (before they knew that any of us were English) that "all the lords and lights of England had been to see the cave, except the king." While they were about it, they might as well have included his majesty. Perhaps they have, by this time; good stories being of very rapid growth. They reported that ladies hold on in the cave better than gentlemen. One of the party supposed this was because they were lighter; but the guide believed it was owing to their having more curiosity.

The gush of sun-light pouring in at the mouth of the cave, green and soft, as we emerged from the darkness, was exquisitely beautiful. So was the foliage of the trees, after the rigid forms which had been printing themselves upon our eye-sight for so many hours. As we sat at the entrance, to accustom ourselves to the warm outward air, I saw, growing high in the steep woods, the richest of kalmias, in full bloom. One of the gentlemen ran to bring me some; and when it came, it was truly a feast to the eye. How apt are we to look upon all things as made for us! How many seasons has this kalmia bloomed?

We were truly sorry to bid farewell to our motherly hostess, and her "smart" sons. Theirs is a singular mode of life; and it left nearly as vivid an impression on our minds as their mighty neighbour, the cave. If any of us should ever happen to be banished, and to have a home to seek, I fancy we should look out for a plot of green sward, among flowering kalmias, near the mouth of an enormous cave, with humming birds flitting about it by day, and fire-flies and summer lightning by night.

In strong contrast in my mind with such a scene as this, stands a gay encampment in the wilderness, at which I soon after arrived. The watering places among the Virginia mountains are as new and striking a spectacle as the United States can afford. The journeyings of those who visit them are a perpetual succession of contrasts. I may as well give the whole journey from Cincinnati to the eastern base of the Alleghenies.

We left Cincinnati at noon on the 25th of June: as sultry a summer's day as ever occurs on the Ohio. The glare was reflected from the water with a blinding and scorching heat; and feather fans were whisking all day in the ladies' cabin of our steam-boat. Hot as it was, I could not remain in the shady cabin. The shores of the Ohio are so beautiful, that I could not bear to lose a single glimpse between the hills. It is holiday-travelling to have such a succession of pictures as I saw there made to pass noiselessly before one's eyes. There were the children running among the gigantic trees on the bank, to see the boat pass; the girl with her milk-pail, half way up the hill; the horseman on the ridge, or the wagoner with his ox-team pausing on the slope. Then there was the flitting blue jay under the cool shadow of the banks; the butterflies crossing the river in zig-zag flight; the terrapins (small turtles) floundering in the water, with their pert little heads above the surface; and the glancing fire-flies every night.

The company on board were of the lowest class we ever happened to meet with in our travels. They were obliging enough; as everybody is throughout the country, as far as my experience goes; but otherwise they were no fair specimens of American manners. One woman excited my curiosity from the beginning; but I entertained a much more agreeable feeling towards her when we parted, after several days' travelling in company. Her first deed was to ask where we were going; and her next, to take my book out of my lap, and examine it. Much of the rest of her time was occupied in dressing her hair, which was, notwithstanding, almost as rough as a negro's. She wore in her head a silver comb, another set with brilliants, and a third, an enormous tortoiseshell, so stuck in, on one side, as to remind the observer, irresistibly, of a unicorn. She pulled down her hair in company, and put it up again, many times in a day, whenever, as it seemed to me, she could not think of anything else to be doing. Her young companion, meantime, sat rubbing her teeth with dragon-root. The other cabin company seemed much of the same class. I was dressing in my state room between four and five the next morning, when an old lady, who was presently going ashore, burst in, and snatched the one tumbler glass from my hand. She was probably as much amazed at my having carried it out of sight as I was at her mode of recovering it.

On passing Catletsburgh we bade adieu to glorious Kentucky. At that point, our eyes rested on three sovereign States at one glance, Ohio, Kentucky, and Virginia. We landed at Guyandot, and proceeded by stage the next morning to Charleston, on the Kanawha river. The ascent of the mountains above New River is trying to weak nerves. The horses have to stop, here and there, to rest; and it appears that if they were to back three steps, it would be death. In a few minutes the stage stopped. "If any of the passengers wish to go to the Hawk's Nest. . . . . ." shouted the driver. He gave us ten minutes, and pointed with his whip to a beaten path in the wood to the right. It seems to me now that I was unaccountably cool and careless about it. I was absorbed by what I had seen, or I might have known, from the direction we were taking, that we were coming out above the river again. We had not many yards to go. We issued suddenly from the covert of the wood, upon a small platform of rock;—a Devil's Pulpit it would be called, if its present name were not so much better;—a platform of rock, springing from the mountain side, without any visible support, and looking sheer down upon an angle of the roaring river, between eleven and twelve hundred feet below. Nothing whatever intervenes. Spread out beneath, shooting up around, are blue mountain peaks, extending in boundless expanse. No one, I believe, could look down over the edge of this airy shelf, but for the stunted pines which are fast rooted in it. With each arm clasping a pine-stem, I looked over, and saw more, I cannot but think, than the world has in reserve to show me.

It is said that this place was discovered by Chief Justice Marshall, when, as a young man, he was surveying among the mountains. But how many Indians knew it before? How did it strike the mysterious race who gave place to the Indians? Perhaps one of these may have stood there to see the summer storm careering below; to feel that his foothold was too lofty to be shaken by the thunderpeals that burst beneath; to trace the quiverings of the lightnings afar, while the heaven was clear above his own head. Perhaps this was the stand chosen by the last Indian, from which to cast his lingering glance upon the glorious regions from which the white intruders were driving his race. If so, here he must have pined and died, or hence he must have cast himself down. I cannot conceive that from this spot any man could turn away, to go into exile. But it cannot be that Marshall was more than the earliest of Saxon race who discovered this place. Nature's thrones are not left to be first mounted by men who can be made Chief Justices. We know not what races of wild monarchs may have had them first.

We travelled the rest of the day through an Alpine region, still full of beauty. The road is so new that the stopping places seemed to have no names. Our first re-entrance upon the world was at Lewisburg, at noon, on the 29th. It appears to be a neat village. The militia were parading: very respectable men, I do not doubt, but not much like soldiers. In a quarter of an hour we were off for the White Sulphur Springs, nine miles (of dusty road) from Lewisburg, and arrived there at half-past two, just as the company were dispersing about the walks, after dinner.

Nothing could be more striking than the contrast between our stage-coach society and that which was thronging the green area into which we were driven. We were heated, wearied, shabby, and all of one dust colour, from head to foot, and, I doubt not, looking very sheepish under the general stare. Every body else was gay and spruce, and at full leisure to criticise us. Gentlemen in the piazza in glossy coats and polished pumps; ladies in pink, blue, and white, standing on green grass, shading their delicate faces and gay head-dresses under parasols; never was there a more astonishing contrast than all this presented with what we had been seeing of late. The friends who were expecting us, however, were not ashamed of us, and came bounding over the green to welcome us, and carry us within reach of refreshment.

It was doubtful whether "a cabin" could be spared to us. We were fortunate in being so favoured as to be put in possession of one in the course of the afternoon. Several carriages full of visitors arrived within a few days, each with its load of trunks, its tin pail dangling behind (wherewith to water the horses in the wilderness) and its crowd of expecting and anxious faces at the windows, and were turned back to seek a resting-place elsewhere. That we were accommodated at all, I believe to this day to be owing to some secret self-denying ordinance on the part of our friends.

On one side of the green, are the large rooms, in which the company at the Springs dine, play cards, and dance. Also, the bar-room, and stage, post, and superintendent's offices. The cabins are disposed round the other sides, and dropped down, in convenient situations behind. These cabins consist of one, two, or more rooms, each containing a bed, a table, a looking-glass, and two or three chairs. All company is received in a room with a bed in it: there is no help for it. The better cabins have a piazza in front; and all have a back door opening upon the hill side; so that the attendants, and their domestic business, are kept out of sight.

The sulphur fountain is in the middle of the southern end of the green; and near it is the sulphur bathing-house. The fountain rises in the midst of a small temple, which is surmounted by a statue of Hygeia, presented to the establishment by a grateful visitor from New Orleans.

The water, pure and transparent, and far more agreeable to the eye than to the taste, forms a pool in its octagon-shaped cistern; and hither the visitors lounge, three times a day, to drink their two or three half-pint tumblers of nauseousness.

These springs had been visited only about fifteen years.

No philosophising on cases appears to have been instituted:
no recording, classifying, inferring, and stating. The patients come from distances of a thousand miles in every
direction, with a great variety of complaints; they grow
better or do not; they go away, and nobody is the wiser
for their experience. It would be difficult to trace them,
and to make a record of anything more than their experience while on the spot. The application of these waters will
probably continue for a long time to be purely empirical.
All that is really known to the patients themselves is, that
they are first sleepy, then ravenous; that they must then
leave the White Sulphur Spring, and go to the Warm
Springs, to be bathed; then to the Sweet Springs, to be
braced; and then home, to send all their ailing friends into
Virginia next year.

Upwards of two hundred visitors were accommodated
when I was in the White Sulphur Valley; and cabins
were being built in all directions. The valley, a deep basin
among the mountains, presents such beauties to the eye,
as perhaps few watering-places in the world can boast.
There has been no time yet to lay them open, for the
benefit of the invalids; but there are plans for the formation of walks and drives through the woods, and along the
mountain sides. At present, all is wild, beyond the pre-
cincts of the establishment; and, for the pleasure of the
healthy, for those who can mount, and ramble, and scramble, it seems a pity that it should not remain so.

The establishment is under the management of the
proprietor, who has been offered 500,000 dollars for it, that
it may be conducted by a company of share-holders, who
would introduce the necessary improvements. When I was
there, the proprietor was still holding off from this bargain,
the company not being willing to continue to him the
superintendence of the concern. I hope that arrangements,
satisfactory to all parties, may have been made by this
time. The average gross receipts of a season were reported
to be 50,000 dollars. It was added that these might easily
be doubled, if all were done that might be.

After breakfast, we sauntered about the green and
visited various new acquaintances in their piazzas. Then

we went home for our bonnets, and rambled through the woods, till we were sent back by the rain, and took shelter beside the fountain. The effect was strange of seeing there a family of emigrants, parents and nine children, who were walking from North Carolina into Illinois. There must have been twins among these children, so many of them looked just alike. The contrast between this group of way-worn travellers, stopping out of curiosity to taste the waters, and the gay company among whom they very properly held up their independent heads, was striking to a stranger.

We dined at two; and afterwards found that a fire would be comfortable, though it was the last day of June. As many friends as our room would hold came home with us, and sat on the bed, table, and the few chairs we could muster, while one made the wood fire, and another bought ice-creams, which a country lad brought to the door. These ice-creams seemed to be thin custard, with a sprinkling of snow in it; but the boy declared that they were ice-creams when he left home. When we had finished our dessert, washed and returned the glasses, and joked and talked till the new-comers of our party grew ashamed of their drowsiness, we crossed the green to diversify the afternoon amusements of certain of our friends. Some were romping with their dogs; some reading books brought by themselves; (for there is no library yet;) some playing at chess or backgammon; all deploring the rain.

After tea, we stormed the great scales, and our whole party were individually weighed. It must be an interesting occupation to the valetudinarians of the place to watch their own and each other's weight, from day to day, or from week to week. For my part, I found my weight just what it always has been, the few times in my life that I have remembered to ascertain it. Such unenviable persons can never make a pursuit of the scales, as others can whose gravity is more discriminating.—From the scales, we adjourned to the ball-room, where I met friends and acquaintances from Mobile and New Orleans; saw new-comers from the Carolinas and Georgia; was introduced to personages of note from Boston; recognized some whom I had known at Philadelphia; and sat between two gentlemen who had fought a duel. There was music, dancing, and refreshments; laughing and flirting here; grave conversation there;—all the common characteristics of a ball, with the added circumstances that almost every State in the Union was here represented; and that we were gathered together in the heart of the mountains.

One more visit remained to be paid this day. We had promised to look in upon some friends who were not at the ball, in order to try the charms and virtues of egg-nogg, which had been lauded to us by an eminent statesman, who has had opportunity, during his diplomatic missions, to learn what there is best in this world. The egg-nogg having been duly enjoyed, we at length went home, to write letters as long as we could hold up our heads, after so extremely busy a day:—a day which may be considered a fair specimen of life at the White Sulphur Springs.

Nothing can be quieter or more refreshing, after a winter's visiting at Boston or New York, than such an abode in a country village as I made trial of last May. The weeks slipped away only too fast. Dr. and Mrs. F., their little boy [Charley], six years old, and myself, were fortunate enough to prevail with a farmer's widow at Stockbridge, Massachusetts, to take us into her house. The house was conspicuous from almost every part of the sweet valley into which it looked; the valley of the Housatonic. It was at the top of a steep hill; a sort of air palace.

We all dined together at two. One of the daughters absented herself at breakfast, that she might arrange our rooms; but both were present at dinner, dressed, and ready for their afternoon's occupation of working and reading. One was fond of flowers, and had learned a great deal about them. She was skilful in drying them, and could direct us to the places in the woods and meadows where they grew. Some members of the family, more literary than the rest, were gone westward; but there was a taste for books among them all. I often saw a volume on the table of the widow's parlour, with her spectacles in it. She told me, one day, of her satisfaction in her children, that they were given to good pursuits, and all received church members. All young people in these villages are more or less instructed. Schooling is considered a necessary of life. I happened to be looking over an old almanack one day, when I found, among the directions relating to the preparations for winter on a farm, the following: "Secure your cellars from frost. Fasten loose clap-boards and shingles. Secure a good school-master." It seemed doubtful, at the first glance, whether some new farming utensil had not been thus whimsically named; as the brass plate which hooks upon the fender, or upper bar of the grate, is called "the footman;" but the context clearly showed that a man with learning in his head was the article required to be provided before the winter.

It was as a favour that the widow Jones took us in. She does not let lodgings. She opened her house to us, and made us a part of her family. Two of her daughters were at home, and a married son lived at hand. We had a parlour, with three windows, commanding different views of the valley: two good-sized chambers, conveniently furnished, and a large closet between; our board with the family, and every convenience that could be provided: and all for two dollars per week each, and half price for the child. She was advised to ask more, but she refused, as she did not wish to be "grasping." It was a merry afternoon when we followed the wagon up the hill to our new abode, and unpacked, and settled ourselves for our long-expected month of May. Never was unpacking a pleasanter task.

It was some trouble to me, in America, that I could not get opportunity to walk so much as I think necessary to health. It is not the custom there: partly owing to the climate, the extreme heat of summer, and cold of winter; and partly to the absence of convenient and pretty walks in and about the cities; a want which, I trust, will be supplied in time. In Stockbridge much pedestrian exercise may be and is accomplished; and I took the opportunity of indulging in it, much to the surprise of some persons, who were not aware how English ladies can walk. One very warm afternoon, we were going on a visit to Lenox, five miles off. My friends went in a wagon; I preferred walking.

The widow's son watched me along the road, and then remarked, "You will see no more of her till you get to Lenox.
I would not walk off at that rate, if they gave me Lenox
when I got there."

In the evenings, we made a descent upon the village,
or the village came up to us. In the latter case, our
hostess was always ready with a simple and graceful welcome, and her best endeavours to provide seats for our
many friends. If we staid below till after nine, the family
had gone to rest on our return. We had only to lift the
latch, light our candles, and make our way to the milk-
pans, if we were thirsty. For twenty-five years, the widow
has lived on the top of her hill, with only a latch to her
door. She sleeps undefended, for she has no enemies;
and in her village there are no thieves.

The contrast is striking between the country life of New
England and that of the west. I staid for some weeks in the
house of a wealthy land-owner in Kentucky. Our days were
passed in great luxury; and some of the hottest of them
very idly. The house was in the midst of grounds, gay with
verdure and flowers, in the opening month of June; and
our favourite seats were the steps of the hall, and chairs
under the trees. From thence we could watch the play of
the children on the grass-plat, and some of the drolleries
of the little negroes. The red bird and the blue bird flew
close by; and the black and white woodpecker with crim-
son head, tapped at all the tree-trunks, as if we were no
interruption. We relished the table fare, after that with
which we had been obliged to content ourselves on board
the steam-boats. The tender meat, fresh vegetables, good
claret and champagne, with the daily piles of strawberries
and towers of ice-cream, were welcome luxuries. There
were thirty-three horses in the stables, and we roved about
the neighbouring country accordingly.

One morning I took a lesson in rifle-shooting; the gentlemen having brought out their weapons for a few hours'
sport among the squirrels. A rifle does not bounce like a
musket, and affords, therefore, an easy beginning. I took
aim at twenty-five paces, and hitting within an inch,
thought it best to leave off with credit. A child of eighteen

months stood in the middle of the gravel-walk, very composedly, while the rifles were popping off; and his elder brothers were busy examining the shots. Children seem born to their future pursuits, in new countries. Negro children seem all born riders and drivers. It was an amusement to see little children that in England could not hold themselves on a large horse, playing pranks with a whole equipage that they were leading to water.

In the evening we repaired to the cool grass-plat, to amuse ourselves with the pretty sport of trying which should find out the first star. It was then ascertained that two gentlemen present were well qualified to entertain us with stories of horrible western murders,—more fearful than any other murders. So we sat till late at night, amidst summer lightning and the glancing of fire-flies, listening to the most harrowing and chilling set of tales of human misdeeds and their retributions, that it ever was my fortune to listen to. The Christmas firesides of England yield no impressions of horror like the plain facts of a life in the wilderness, told under the trees, in a sultry night, while the pale lightning is exploding on the horizon.

Such is a fair specimen of our life in the West. Contrasts rise up before my mind's eye, as the scenes of my journeying present themselves; contrasts in the face of the country, as striking as in the modes of living.

When I was at Salem, in Massachusetts, the friends whose hospitality I was enjoying proposed an excursion to Cape Ann, (the northern point of Massachusetts' bay,) and round the peninsula which constitutes the township of Gloucester. This excursion impressed me strongly, from the peculiar character of the scenery: but I know not whether it is an impression which can be conveyed by description. Whether it be or not, I would recommend all strangers to go and visit this peninsula; and, if convenient, in fine autumn weather, when the atmosphere lends its best aid to the characteristic charms of the landscape.

The population of the peninsula is homogeneous. There is probably no individual beyond Gloucester whose parentage may not be referred to a particular set of people, at a particular date in English history. It has great wealth of granite and fish. It is composed of granite; and almost its only visitors are fish.

It is a singular region. If a little orchard plot is seen, here and there, it seems rescued by some chance from being grown over with granite. It was pleasant to see such a hollow, with its apple tree, the ladder reared against it, the basket beneath, and the children picking up the fallen fruit. The houses look as if they were squeezed in among the rocks. The granite rises straight behind a house, encroaches on each side, and overhangs the roof, leaving space only for a sprinkling of grass about the door, for a red shrub or two to wave from a crevice, and a drip of water to flow down among gay weeds. Room for these dwellings is obtained by blasting the rocks. Formerly, people were frightened at fragments falling through the roof after a blasting: but now, it has become too common an occurrence to alarm any body. One precaution is enforced: no one is allowed to keep more than twenty-eight pounds of powder in one town or village; and the powder-houses may be seen, insulated on rocks, and looking something like watch-boxes, at some distance from every settlement. The school-houses are also remarkable buildings. The school-house may always be known at a glance: a single square room, generally painted white or pale green, and reared on a grassy eminence, with a number of small heads to be seen through the windows, or little people gathered about the door. There are twenty-one school-houses in this township of Gloucester, the population of which is nine thousand.

We saw what we could of Gloucester before sunset. There are some very good houses, newly-built; and the place has the air of prosperity that gladdens the eye wherever it turns, in New England. We ran down to the shore. It is overlooked by a windmill, from whose grassy platform we beheld the scene in the singular light which here succeeds an autumn sunset. The sky and sea were, without exaggeration, of a deep scarlet: Ten Pound Island sat black upon the waters, with its yellow beacon just lighted. Fishing vessels lay still, every rope being reflected in the red mirror; and a boat, in which a boy was sculling across the harbour, was the only moving object.

After tea, a clergyman and his wife called; and then a long succession of the hospitable inhabitants of Gloucester came to bid us welcome: from which it appeared that small articles of intelligence circulate as rapidly here as in other country-places. In another respect, Gloucester resembled all the villages and small towns I passed through: in the pretty attention of presenting flowers. In some of the larger cities, bouquets of rich and rare flowers were sent to me, however severe might have been the frost, or however dreary the season. In the smallest villages, I had offerings, quite as welcome, in bunches of flowers from the woods and meadows. Many of these last were new to me, and as gladly received as the luscious hyacinths which greeted me every morning at Charleston. At Lenox, in Massachusetts, where I spent one night, my table was covered with meadow-flowers, and with fine specimens of Jack-in-the-pulpit, and the moccassin-flower, or lady's slipper: and at Gloucester, when I returned from my early visit to the beach, where I had been to see the fishermen go out, I found a gorgeous bouquet of autumn flowers; dahlias more various and rich than could have been supposed to grow in such a region.

On our return to Salem, we diverged a little from our road, near Manchester, to see a farm, whose situation would make an envious person miserable. The house lies under the shelter of a wooded hill, and enjoys a glorious view of Massachusetts Bay. The property lies between two bays, and has a fine fishing-station off the point. The fields look fertile, and a wide range of pasturage skirts the bay. A woman and children were busy in the orchard, with a cart and barrels, taking in a fine crop of apples; and we could only hope that they were sensible of their privilege in living in such a place. These are the regions, teeming with the virtues of the Pilgrims, and as yet uninfected by the mercenary and political cowardice of the cities, where the most gladdening aspects of human life are to be seen.

The newly-settled districts of the southern States are as unlike as possible to all this. They are extreme opposite cases. If human life presents its fairest aspects in the retired townships of New England,—some of its very worst, perhaps, are seen in the raw settlements of Alabama and Mississippi.

When we drew near to Columbus, Georgia, we were struck with amazement at the stories that were told, and the anecdotes that were dropped, in the stage, about recent attempts on human life in the neighbourhood; and at the number of incidents of the same kind which were the news of the day along the road. Our driver from Macon had been shot at, in attempting to carry off a young lady. A gentleman, boarding in the hotel at Columbus, was shot in the back, in the street, and laid by for months. No inquiry was made, or nothing came of it. The then present governor of the State of Mississippi had recently stood over two combatants, pistol in hand, to see fair play. This *was* stated as a remarkable fact. The landlord of the house where we stopped to breakfast on the day we were to reach Columbus, April 9th, 1835, was, besides keeping a house of entertainment, a captain of militia, and a member of the legislature of Georgia. He was talking over with his guests a late case of homicide in a feud between the Myers and Macklimore families. He declared that he would have laws like those of the Medes and Persians against homicide; and, in the same breath, said that if he were a Myers, he would shoot Mr. Macklimore and all his sons.

We arrived at Columbus before sunset, and determined to stay a day to see how the place had got on since Captain Hall saw it cut out of the woods, ten years before. During the evening, I could do nothing but watch the Indians from my window. The place swarmed with them; a few Choctaws, and the rest Creeks. A sad havoc has taken place among them since; and this neighbourhood has been made the scene of a short but fierce war. But all looked fair and friendly when we were there. Groups of Indians were crouching about the entries of the stores, or looking in at the windows. The squaws went by, walking one behind another, with their hair, growing low on the forehead, loose, or tied at the back of the head, forming a fine contrast with the young lady who had presided at our breakfast-table at five that morning, with her long hair braided and adorned with brilliant combs, while her fingers shone in pearl and gold rings. These squaws carried large Indian baskets on their backs, and shuffled along, bare-footed, while their lords paced before them, well mounted; or, if walking, gay with blue and red clothing and embroidered leggings, with tufts of hair at the knees, while pouches and white fringes dangled about them. They looked like grave merry-andrews; or, more still, like solemn fanatical harvest men going out for largess. By eight o'clock they had all disappeared; but the streets were full of them again the next morning.

Our hostess was civil, and made no difficulty about giving us a late breakfast by ourselves, in consideration of our fatigues. Before one o'clock we dined, in company with seventy-five persons, at one long table. The provisions were good, but ill-cooked; and the knives so blunt that it was a mystery to me how the rest of the company obtained so quick a succession of mouthfuls as they did.

The Chattahoochee, on whose banks Columbus stands, is unlike any river I saw in the United States, unless it be some parts of the Susquehanna. Its rapids, overhung by beech and pine woods, keep up a perpetual melody, grateful alike to the ear of the white and the red man. It is broad and full, whirling over and around the rocks with which it is studded, and under the frail wooden foot-bridge which spans a portion of its width, between the shore and a pile of rocks in the middle of the channel. On this foot-bridge I stood, and saw a fish caught in a net laid among the eddies. A dark fisherman stood on each little promontory; and a group was assembled about some canoes in a creek on the opposite Alabama shore, where the steepness of the hills seemed scarcely to allow a foothold between the rushing water and the ascent. The river is spanned by a long covered bridge, which we crossed the same night on our way into Alabama.

There are three principal streets in Columbus, with many smaller, branching out into the forest. Some pretty bits of greensward are left, here and there, with a church, or a detached house upon each—village-like. There are some good houses, five hotels, and a population of above 2,000,—as nearly as I could make out among the different accounts of the accession of inhabitants since the census. The stores looked creditably stocked; and a great many gentlemanly men were to be seen in the streets. It bears the appearance of being a thriving, spacious, handsome village, well worth stopping to see.

We left it, at seven in the evening, by the long bridge, at the other end of which we stopped for the driver to hold a parley, about a parcel, with a woman, who spoke almost altogether in oaths. A gentleman in the stage remarked, that we must have got quite to the end of the world. The roads were as bad as roads could be; and we rolled from side to side so incessantly, as to obviate all chance of sleeping. The passengers were very patient during the hours of darkness; but, after daylight, they seemed to think they had been long enough employed in shifting their weight to keep the coach on its four wheels. "I say, driver," cried one, "you won't upset us, now daylight is come?" "Driver," shouted another, "keep this side up." "Gentlemen," replied the driver, "I shall mind nothing you say till the ladies begin to complain." A reply equally politic and gallant.

At half-past five, we stopped to breakfast at a log dwelling, composed of two rooms, with an open passage between. We asked for water and towel. There was neither basin nor towel; but a shallow tin dish of water was served up in the open passage where all our fellow-travellers were standing. We asked leave to carry our dish into the right-hand room. The family were not all dressed. Into the left-hand room. A lady lodged there!

We saw to-day, the common sight of companies of slaves travelling westwards; and the very uncommon one of a party returning into South Carolina. When we overtook such a company proceeding westwards, and asked where they were going, the answer commonly given by the slaves was, "Into Yellibama."—Sometimes these poor creatures were encamped, under the care of the slave-trader, on the banks of a clear stream, to spend a day in washing their clothes. Sometimes they were loitering along the road; the old folks and infants mounted on the top of a wagon-load of luggage; the able-bodied, on foot, perhaps silent, perhaps laughing; the prettier of the girls, perhaps with a flower in the hair, and a lover's arm around her shoulder. There were wide differences in the air and gait of these people. It is usual to call the most depressed of them brutish in appearance. In some sense they are so; but I never saw in any brute an expression of countenance so low, so lost, as in the most degraded class of negroes. There is some life and intelligence in the countenance of every animal; even in that of "the silly sheep," nothing so dead as the vacant, unheeding look of the depressed slave is to be seen. To-day, there was a spectacle by the road-side which showed that this has nothing to do with negro nature; though no such proof is needed by those who have seen negroes in favourable circumstances, and know how pleasant an aspect those grotesque features may wear. To-day we passed, in the Creek Territory, an establishment of Indians who held slaves. Negroes are anxious to be sold to Indians, who give them moderate work, and accommodations as good as their own. Those seen to-day among the Indians, were sleek, intelligent, and cheerful-looking, like the most favoured house-slaves, or free servants of colour, where the prejudice is least strong.

We left the Creek Territory just as the full moon rose, and hoped to reach Montgomery by two hours before midnight.

On our arrival at past eleven o'clock, we found we were expected; but no one would have guessed it. In my chamber, there was neither water, nor sheets, nor anything that afforded a prospect of my getting to rest, wet as my clothes were. We were hungry, and tired, and cold; and there was no one to help us but a slave, who set about her work as slaves do. We ate some biscuits that we had with us, and gave orders, and made requests with so much success as to have the room in tolerable order by an hour after midnight. When I awoke in the morning, the first thing I saw was, that two mice were running after one another round my trunk, and that the floor of the room seemed to contain the dust of a twelvemonth. The breakfast was to atone for all. The hostess and another lady, three children, and an array of slaves, placed themselves so as to see us eat our breakfast; but it seemed to me that the contents of the table were more wonderful to look at than ourselves. Besides the tea and coffee, there were corn-bread, buns, buckwheat cakes, broiled chicken, bacon, eggs, rice, hominy, fish, fresh and pickled, and beef-steak. The hostess strove to make us feel at home, and recommended her plentiful meal by her hearty welcome to it. She was anxious to explain that her house was soon to be in better order. Her husband was going to Mobile to buy furniture; and, just now, all was in confusion, from her head slave having swallowed a fish bone, and being unable to look after the affairs of the house. When our friends came to carry us to their plantation, she sent in refreshments, and made herself one of the party, in all heartiness.

It was Sunday, and we went to the Methodist church, hoping to hear the regular pastor, who is a highly-esteemed preacher. But a stranger was in the pulpit, who gave us an extraordinary piece of doctrine, propounded with all possible vehemence. His text was the passage about the tower of Siloam; and his doctrine was that great sinners would somehow die a violent death. Perhaps this might be thought a useful proposition in a town where life is held so cheap as in Montgomery; but we could not exactly understand how it was derived from the text. The place was intensely light and hot, there being no blinds to the windows, on each side of the pulpit: and the quietness of the children was not to be boasted of.

On the way to our friends' plantation, we passed a party of negroes, enjoying their Sunday drive. They never appear better than on such occasions, as they all ride and drive well, and are very gallant to their ladies. We passed a small prairie, the first we had seen; and very serene and pretty it looked, after the forest. It was green and undulating, with a fringe of trees.

Our friends, now residing seven miles from Montgomery, were from South Carolina; and the lady, at least, does not relish living in Alabama. It was delightful to me to be a guest in such an abode as theirs. They were about to build a good house: meantime, they were in one which I liked exceedingly: a log-house, with the usual open passage in the middle. Roses and honeysuckles, to which humming-birds resort, grew before the door. Abundance of books, and handsome furniture and plate, were within the house, while daylight was to be seen through its walls. In my well furnished chamber, I could see the stars through the chinks between the logs. During the summer, I should be sorry to change this primitive kind of abode for a better.

It is not difficult to procure the necessaries and comforts of life. Most articles of food are provided on the plantation. Wine and groceries are obtained from Mobile or New Orleans; and clothing and furniture from the north. Tea is twenty shillings English per lb.; brown sugar, three-pence-halfpenny; white sugar, sixpence-halfpenny. A gentleman's family, where there are children to be educated, cannot live for less than from seven hundred pounds to one thousand pounds per annum. The sons take land and buy slaves very early; and the daughters marry almost in childhood; so that education is less thought of, and sooner ended, than in almost any part of the world. The pioneers of civilisation, as the settlers in these new districts may be regarded, care for other things more than for education; or they would not come. They are, from whatever motive, money-getters; and few but money-getting qualifications are to be looked for in them. It was partly amusing, and partly sad, to observe the young people of these regions; some, fit for a better mode of life, discontented; some youths pedantic, some maidens romantic, to a degree which makes the stranger almost doubt the reality of the scenes and personages before his eyes. The few better educated who come to get money, see the absurdity, and feel the wearisomeness of this kind of literary cultivation; but the being in such society is the tax they must pay for making haste to be rich.

I heard in Montgomery of a wealthy old planter in the neighbourhood, who has amassed millions of dollars, while his children can scarcely write their names. Becoming aware of their deficiencies, as the place began to be peopled from the eastward, he sent a son of sixteen to school, and a younger one to college; but they proved "such gawks," that they were unable to learn, or even to remain in the society of others who were learning; and their old father has bought land in Missouri, whither he was about to take his children, to remove them from the contempt of their neighbours. They are doomed to the lowest office of social beings; to be the mechanical, unintelligent pioneers of man in the wilderness. Surely such a warning as this should strike awe into the whole region, lest they should also perish to all the best purposes of life, by getting to consider money, not as a means, but an end.

I suppose there must be such pioneers; but the result is a society which it is a punishment to its best members to live in. There is pedantry in those who read; prejudice in those who do not; coxcombry among the young gentlemen; bad manners among the young ladies; and an absence of all reference to the higher, the real objects of life. When to all this is added that tremendous curse, the possession of irresponsible power, (over slaves,) it is easy to see how character must become, in such regions, what it was described to me on the spot, "composed of the chivalric elements, badly combined:" and the wise will feel that, though a man *may* save his soul anywhere, it is better to live on bread and water where existence is most idealized, than to grow suddenly rich in the gorgeous regions where mind is corrupted or starved amidst the luxuriance of nature. The hard-working settler of the north-west, who hews his way into independence with his own hands, is, or may be, exempt from the curse of this mental corruption or starvation; but it falls inevitably and heavily upon those who fatten upon the bounty of Nature, in the society of money-getters like themselves, and through the labours of degraded fellow-men, whom they hold in their injurious power.

On many estates that we saw, the ladies make it their business to cut out all the clothes for the negroes. Many a fair pair of hands have I seen dyed with blue, and bearing the marks of the large scissors. The slave women cannot be taught, it is said, to cut out even their scanty and unshapely garments economically. Nothing can be more hideous than their working costume. There would be nothing to lose on the score of beauty, and probably much gained, if they could be permitted to clothe themselves. But it is universally said that they cannot learn. A few ladies keep a woman for this purpose, very naturally disliking the coarse employment.

We visited the negro quarter; a part of the estate which filled me with disgust, wherever I went. It is something between a haunt of monkeys and a dwelling-place of human beings. The natural good taste, so remarkable in free negroes, is here extinguished. Their small, dingy, untidy houses, their cribs, the children crouching round the fire, the animal deportment of the grown-up, the brutish chagrins and enjoyments of the old, were all loathsome. There was some relief in seeing the children playing in the sun, and sometimes fowls clucking and strutting round the houses; but otherwise, a walk through a lunatic asylum is far less painful than a visit to the slave quarter of an estate. The children are left, during working hours, in the charge of a woman; and they are bright, and brisk, and merry enough, for the season, however slow and stupid they may be destined to become.

I spent some days at a plantation a few miles from Montgomery, and heard there of an old lady who treats her slaves in a way very unusual, but quite safe, as far as appears. She gives them knowledge, which is against the law; but the law leaves her in peace and quiet. She also commits to them the entire management of the estate, requiring only that they should make her comfortable, and letting them take the rest. There is an obligation by law to keep an overseer; to obviate insurrection. How she manages about this, I omitted to inquire: but all goes on well; the cultivation of the estate is creditable, and all parties are contented. This is only a temporary ease and contentment. The old lady must die; and her slaves will either be sold to a new owner, whose temper will be an accident; or, if freed, must leave the State: but the story is satisfactory in as far as it gives evidence of the trust-worthiness of the negroes.

It was now the middle of April. In the kitchen garden the peas were ripening, and the strawberries turning red, though the spring of 1835 was very backward. We had salads, young asparagus, and radishes.

The following may be considered a pretty fair account of the provision for a planter's table, at this season; and, except with regard to vegetables, I believe it does not vary much throughout the year. Breakfast at seven; hot wheat bread, generally sour; corn-bread, biscuits, waffles, hominy, dozens of eggs, broiled ham, beef-steak or broiled fowl, tea and coffee. Lunch at eleven; cake and wine, or liqueur. Dinner at two; now and then soup (not good,) always roast turkey and ham; a boiled fowl here, a tongue there; a small piece of nondescript meat, which generally turns out to be pork disguised; hominy, rice, hot corn-bread, sweet potatoes; potatoes mashed with spice, very hot; salad and radishes, and an extraordinary variety of pickles. Of these, you are asked to eat everything with everything else. If you have turkey and ham on your plate, you are requested to add tongue, pork, hominy, and pickles. Then succeed pies of apple, squash, and pumpkin; custard, and a variety of preserves as extraordinary as the preceding pickles: pine-apple, peach, limes, ginger, guava jelly, cocoa-nut, and every sort of plums. These are almost all from the West-Indies. Dispersed about the table are shell almonds, raisins, hickory, and other nuts; and, to crown the whole, large blocks of ice-cream. Champagne is abundant, and cider frequent. Ale and porter may now and then be seen; but claret is the most common drink. During dinner a slave stands at a corner of the table, keeping off the flies by waving a large bunch of peacock's feathers fastened into a handle,—an ampler fan than those of our grandmothers.

Supper takes place at six, or seven. Sometimes the family sits round the table; but more commonly the tray is handed round, with plates which must be held in the lap. Then follow tea and coffee, waffles, biscuits, sliced ham or hung-beef, and sweet cake. Last of all, is the offer of cake and wine at nine or ten.

The profits of cotton-growing, when I was in Alabama,

were thirty-five per cent. One planter whom I knew had bought fifteen thousand dollars' worth of land within two years, which he could then have sold for sixty-five thousand dollars. He expected to make, that season, fifty or sixty thousand dollars of his growing crop. It is certainly the place to become rich in; but the state of society is fearful. One of my hosts, a man of great good-nature, as he shows in the treatment of his slaves, and in his family relations, had been stabbed in the back in the reading-room of the town, two years before, and no prosecution was instituted. Another of my hosts carried loaded pistols for a fortnight, just before I arrived, knowing that he was lain in wait for by persons against whose illegal practices he had given information to a magistrate, whose carriage was therefore broken in pieces, and thrown into the river. A lawyer with whom we were in company one afternoon, was sent for to take the deposition of a dying man who had been sitting with his family in the shade, when he received three balls in the back from three men who took aim at him from behind trees. The tales of jail-breaking and rescue were numberless; and a lady of Montgomery told me that she had lived there four years, during which time no day, she believed, had passed without some one's life having been attempted, either by duelling or assassination. It will be understood that I describe this region as presenting an extreme case of the material advantages and moral evils of a new settlement, under the institution of slavery. The most prominent relief is the hospitality,—that virtue of young society. It is so remarkable, and to the stranger so grateful, that there is danger of its blinding him to the real state of affairs. In the drawing-room, the piazza, the barouche, all is so gay and friendly, there is such a prevailing hilarity and kindness, that it seems positively ungrateful and unjust to pronounce, even in one's own heart, that all this way of life is full of wrong and peril. Yet it is impossible to sit down to reflect, with every order of human beings filling an equal space before one's mental eye, without being struck to the soul with the conviction that the state of society, and no less of individual families, is false and hollow, whether their members are aware of

it or not; that they forget that they must be just before
they can be generous. The severity of this truth is much
softened to sympathetic persons on the spot; but it returns
with awful force when they look back upon it from afar.

In the slave quarter of a plantation hereabouts I saw a
poor wretch who had run away three times, and been re-
captured. The last time he was found in the woods, with
both legs frost-bitten above the knees, so as to render am-
putation necessary. I passed by when he was sitting on
the door-step of his hut, and longed to see him breathe his
last. But he is a young man, likely to drag out his helpless
and hopeless existence for many a dreary year. I dread to
tell the rest; but such things must be told sometimes, to
show to what a pass of fiendish cruelty the human spirit
may be brought by merely witnessing the exercise of irresponsible power over the defenceless. I give the very
words of the speaker, premising that she is not American
by birth or education, nor yet English.

The master and mistress of this poor slave, with their
children, had always treated him and his fellow-slaves very
kindly. He made no complaint of them. It was not from
their cruelty that he attempted to escape. His running
away was therefore a mystery to the person to whom I
have alluded. She recapitulated all the clothes that had
been given to him; and all the indulgences, and forgive-
nesses for his ingratitude in running away from such a
master, with which he had been blessed. She told me that
she had advised his master and mistress to refuse him
clothes, when he had torn his old ones with trying to make
his way through the woods; but his master had been too
kind, and had again covered his nakedness. She turned
round upon me, and asked what could make the ungrateful wretch run away a third time from such a master?

"He wanted to be free."

"Free! from such a master!"

"From any master."

"The villain! I went to him when he had had his legs
cut off, and I said to him, it serves you right . . . . ."

"What! when you knew he could not run away any
more?"

"Yes, that I did; I said to him, you wretch! but for your master's sake I am glad it has happened to you. You deserve it, that you do. If I were your master I would let you die; I'd give you no help nor nursing. It serves you right; it is just what you deserve. It's fit that it should happen to you. . . . !"

"You did not—you dared not so insult the miserable creature!" I cried.

"Oh, who knows," replied she, "but that the Lord may bless a word of grace in season!"

Some readers may conceive this to be a freak of idiotcy. It was not so. This person is shrewd and sensible in matters where rights and duties are not in question. Of these she is, as it appears, profoundly ignorant; in a state of superinduced darkness; but her character is that of a clever, and, with some, a profoundly religious woman. Happily, she has no slaves of her own: at least, no black ones.

This little history of a portion of my southern journey may give an idea of what life is in the wilder districts of the south. I will offer but one more sketch, and that will exemplify life in the wilder districts of the north. The picture of my travels in and around Michigan will convey the real state of things there, at present.

Our travelling party consisted of Mr. and Mrs. L., the before-mentioned Charley, his father and mother, and myself. We were prepared to see everything to advantage; for there was strong friendship among us all; and a very unusual agreement of opinion on subjects which education, temperament, or the circumstances of the time, made most interesting to us.

We landed at Detroit, from Lake Erie, at seven o'clock in the morning of the 13th of June, 1836. We reached the American just in time for breakfast. At that long table, I had the pleasure of seeing the healthiest set of faces that I had beheld since I left England. The breakfast was excellent, and we were served with much consideration; but the place was so full, and the accommodations of Detroit are so insufficient for the influx of people who are betaking themselves thither, that strangers must patiently put up with much delay and inconvenience till new houses of entertainment are opened.

The society of Detroit is very choice; and, as it has continued so since the old colonial days, through the territorial days, there is every reason to think that it will become, under its new dignities, a more and more desirable place of residence. Some of its inferior society is still very youthful; a gentleman, for instance, saying in the reading-room, in the hearing of one of our party, that, though it did not sound well at a distance, Lynching* was the only way to treat Abolitionists: but the most enlightened society is, I believe, equal to any which is to be found in the United States.

We had two great pleasures this day; a drive along the quiet Lake St. Clair, and a charming evening party at General Mason's. After a pilgrimage through the State of New York, a few exciting days at Niagara, and a disagreeable voyage along Lake Erie, we were prepared to enjoy to the utmost the novelty of a good evening party; and we were as merry as children at a ball. It was wholly unexpected to find ourselves in accomplished society on the far side of Lake Erie; and there was something stimulating in the contrast between the high civilisation of the evening, and the primitive scenes that we were to plunge into the next day. Though we had to pack up and write, and be off very early in the morning, we were unable to persuade ourselves to go home till late; and then we talked over Detroit as if we were wholly at leisure.

15th. An obliging girl at the American provided us with

* It is possible that this term may not yet be familiar to some of my English readers. It means summary punishment. The modes now in use among those who take the law into their own hands in the United States, are tarring and feathering, scourging with a cow-hide, banishing, and hanging. The term owes its derivation to a farmer of the name of Lynch, living on the Mississippi, who, in the absence of court and lawyers, constituted himself a judge, and ordered summary punishment to be inflicted on an offender. He little foresaw the national disgrace which would arise from the extension of the practice to which he gave his name.

coffee and biscuits at half-past five, by which time our "exclusive extra" was at the door.

As soon as we had entered the woods, the roads became as bad as, I suppose, roads ever are. Something snapped, and the driver cried out that we were "broke to bits." The team-bolt had given way. Our gentlemen, and those of the mail-stage, which happened to be at hand, helped to mend the coach.

We went into a settler's house, where we were welcomed to rest and refresh ourselves. Three years before, the owner bought his eighty acres of land for a dollar an acre. He could now sell it for twenty dollars an acre. He shot, last year, a hundred deer, and sold them for three dollars a-piece. He and his family need have no fears of poverty. We dined well, nine miles before reaching Ypsilanti. The log-houses,—always comfortable when well made, being easily kept clean, cool in summer, and warm in winter,— have here an air of beauty about them. The hue always harmonizes well with the soil and vegetation. Those in Michigan have the bark left on, and the corners sawn off close; and are thus both picturesque and neat.

At Ypsilanti, I picked up an Ann Arbor newspaper. It was badly printed; but its contents were pretty good; and it could happen nowhere out of America, that so raw a settlement as that at Ann Arbor, where there is difficulty in procuring decent accommodations, should have a newspaper.

16th. We were off by half-past six; and, not having rested quite enough, and having the prospect of fourteen miles before breakfast, we, with one accord, finished our sleep in the stage. We reached Tecumseh by half-past nine, and perceived that its characteristic was chair-making. Every other house seemed to be a chair manufactory. One bore the inscription, "Cousin George's Store:" the meaning of which I do not pretend to furnish. Perhaps the idea is, that purchasers may feel free and easy, as if dealing with cousin George. Everybody has a cousin George. Elsewhere, we saw a little hotel inscribed, "Our House;" a prettier sign than "Traveller's Rest," or any other such tempting invitation that I am acquainted with. At

Tecumseh, I saw the first strawberries of the season. All that I tasted in Michigan, of prairie growth, were superior to those of the west, grown in gardens.

We did not reach Sturgis's Prairie till night. We had heard so poor an account of the stage-house, that we proceeded to another, whose owner has the reputation of treating his guests magnificently, or not at all. He treated us on *juste milieu* principles. He did what he could for us; and that could not be called magnificent. The house was crowded with emigrants. When, after three hours waiting, we had supper, two full-grown persons were asleep on some blankets in the corner of the room, and as many as fifteen or sixteen children on chairs and on the floor. Our hearts ached for one mother. Her little girl, two years old, had either sprained or broken her arm, and the mother did not know what to do with it. The child shrieked when the arm was touched, and wailed mournfully at other times. We found in the morning, however, that she had had some sleep. I have often wondered since how she bore the motion of the wagon on the worst parts of the road. It was oppressively hot. I had a little closet, whose door would not shut, and which was too small to give me room to take off the soft feather-bed. The window would not keep open without being propped by the tin water-jug; and though this was done, I could not sleep for the heat. This reminds me of the considerate kindness of an hotel-keeper in an earlier stage of our journey. When he found that I wished to have my window open, there being no fastening, he told me he would bring his own tooth-brush for a prop, —which he accordingly did.

I never could understand how wagons were made in the back-country; they seemed to be elastic, from the shocks and twisting they would bear without giving way. To form an accurate idea of what they have to bear, a traveller should sit on a seat without springs, placed between the hind wheels, and thus proceed on a corduroy road. The effect is less fatiguing and more amusing, of riding in a wagon whose seats are on springs, while the vehicle itself is not. In that case, the feet are dancing an involuntary jig, all the way; while the rest of the body is in a state of entire repose.

The drive was so exciting and pleasant, the rain having ceased, that I was taken by surprise by our arrival at Michigan City. The driver announced our approach by a series of flourishes on one note of his common horn, which made the most ludicrous music I ever listened to. How many minutes he went on, I dare not say; but we were so convulsed with laughter that we could not alight with becoming gravity, amidst the groups in the piazza of the hotel. The man must be first cousin to Paganini.

Such a city as this was surely never before seen. It is three years since it was begun; and it is said to have one thousand five hundred inhabitants. It is cut out of the forest, and curiously interspersed with little swamps, which we no doubt saw in their worst condition after the heavy rains. New, good houses, some only half finished, stood in the midst of the thick wood. A large area was half cleared. The finished stores were scattered about; and the streets were littered with stumps. The situation is beautiful. The undulations of the ground, within and about it, and its being closed in by lake or forest on every side, render it unique. An appropriation has been made by Government for a harbour; and two piers are to be built out beyond the sand, as far as the clay soil of the lake. Mr. L. and I were anxious to see the mighty fresh water sea. We made inquiry in the piazza; and a sandy hill, close by, covered with the pea vine, was pointed out to us. We ran up it, and there beheld what we had come so far to see. There it was, deep, green, and swelling on the horizon, and whitening into a broad and heavy surf as it rolled in towards the shore. Hence, too, we could make out the geography of the city. The whole scene stands insulated in my memory, as absolutely singular; and, at this distance of time, scarcely credible. I was so well aware on the spot that it would be so, that I made careful and copious notes of what I saw: but memoranda have nothing to do with such emotions as were caused by the sight of that enormous body of tumultuous waters, rolling in apparently upon the helpless forest,—everywhere else so majestic.

On our road to Chicago, the next day,—a road winding in and out among the sand-hills, we were called to alight, and run up a bank to see a wreck. It was the wreck of the Delaware;—the steamer in which it had been a question whether we should not proceed from Niles to Chicago.

In the wood which borders the prairie on which Chicago stands, we saw an encampment of United States' troops. Since the rising of the Creeks in Georgia, some months before, there had been apprehensions of an Indian war along the whole frontier. It was believed that a correspondence had taken place among all the tribes, from the Cumanches, who were engaged to fight for the Mexicans in Texas, up to the northern tribes among whom we were going.

Chicago looks raw and bare, standing on the high prairie above the lake-shore. The houses appeared all insignificant, and run up in various directions, without any principle at all. A friend of mine who resides there had told me that we should find the inns intolerable, at the period of the great land sales, which bring a concourse of speculators to the place. It was even so. The very sight of them was intolerable; and there was not room for our party among them all. I do not know what we should have done, (unless to betake ourselves to the vessels in the harbour,) if our coming had not been foreknown, and most kindly provided for. We were divided between three families, who had the art of removing all our scruples about intruding on perfect strangers. None of us will lose the lively and pleasant associations with the place, which were caused by the hospitalities of its inhabitants.

I never saw a busier place than Chicago was at the time of our arrival. The streets were crowded with land speculators, hurrying from one sale to another. A negro, dressed up in scarlet, bearing a scarlet flag, and riding a white horse with housings of scarlet, announced the times of sale. At every street-corner where he stopped, the crowd flocked round him; and it seemed as if some prevalent mania infected the whole people. The rage for speculation might fairly be so regarded. As the gentlemen of our party walked the streets, store-keepers hailed them from their doors, with offers of farms, and all manner of land-lots, advising them to speculate before the price of land rose higher. A young lawyer, of my acquaintance there, had realised five hundred dollars per day, the five preceding days, by merely making out titles to land. Another friend had realised, in two years, ten times as much money as he had before fixed upon as a competence for life.

Others, besides lawyers and speculators by trade, make a fortune in such extraordinary times. A poor man at Chicago had a pre-emption right to some land, for which he paid in the morning one hundred and fifty dollars. In the afternoon, he sold it to a friend of mine for five thousand dollars. A poor Frenchman, married to a squaw, had a suit pending, when I was there, which he was likely to gain, for the right of purchasing some land by the lake for one hundred dollars, which would immediately become worth one million dollars.

There was much gaiety going on at Chicago, as well as business. On the evening of our arrival a fancy fair took place. As I was too much fatigued to go, the ladies sent me a bouquet of prairie flowers. There is some allowable pride in the place about its society. It is a remarkable thing to meet such an assemblage of educated, refined, and wealthy persons as may be found there, living in small, inconvenient houses on the edge of a wild prairie. There is a mixture, of course. I heard of a family of half-breeds setting up a carriage, and wearing fine jewellery. When the present intoxication of prosperity passes away, some of the inhabitants will go back to the eastward; there will be an accession of settlers from the mechanic classes; good houses will have been built for the richer families, and the singularity of the place will subside. It will be like all the other new and thriving lake and river ports of America. Meantime, I am glad to have seen it in its strange early days.

I have now given sketches of some of the most remarkable parts of the country, hoping that a pretty distinct idea might thus be afforded of their primary resources, and of

the modes of life of their inhabitants. I have said nothing
of the towns, in this connexion; town-life in America having
nothing very peculiar about it, viewed in the way of general survey. The several departments of industry will now
be particularly considered.

VI.   Agriculture

"Plus un peuple nombreux se rapproche, moins le gouverne-
ment peut usurper sur le Souverain. L'avantage d'un gouverne-
ment tyrannique est donc en ceci, d'agir à grandes distances.
A l'aide des points d'appui qu'il se donne, sa force augmente
au loin, comme celle des léviers. Celle du peuple, au contraire,
n'agit que concentrée: elle s'évapore et se perd en s'étendant,
comme l'effet de la poudre éparse à terre, et qui ne prend feu
que grain à grain. Les pays les moins peuplés sont ainsi les-plus
propres à la tyrannie. Les bêtes féroces ne règnent que dans
les déserts."

Rousseau

THE pride and delight of Americans is in their quantity of
land. I do not remember meeting with one to whom it had
occurred that they had too much. Among the many complaints of the minority, this was never one. I saw a gentleman strike his fist on the table in an agony at the country
being so "confoundedly prosperous:" I heard lamentations
over the spirit of speculation; the migration of young men
to the back country; the fluctuating state of society from
the incessant movement westwards; the immigration of
labourers from Europe; and the ignorance of the sparse
population. All these grievances I heard perpetually complained of; but in the same breath I was told in triumph
of the rapid sales of land; of the glorious additions which
had been made by the acquisition of Louisiana and

Florida, and of the probable gain of Texas. Land was
spoken of as the unfailing resource against over manufacture; the great wealth of the nation; the grand security
of every man in it.

On this head, the two political parties seem to be more
agreed than on any other. The Federalists are the great
patrons of commerce; but they are as proud of the national
lands as the broadest of the Democrats. The Democrats,
however, may be regarded as the patrons of agriculture,
out of the slave States. There seems to be a natural relation between the independence of property and occupation
enjoyed by the agriculturist, and his watchfulness over
State Rights and the political importance of individuals.
The simplicity of country life, too, appears more congenial
with the workings of democratic institutions, than the complex arrangements of commerce and manufactures.

The possession of land is the aim of all action, generally
speaking, and the cure for all social evils, among men in
the United States. If a man is disappointed in politics or
love, he goes and buys land. If he disgraces himself, he
betakes himself to a lot in the west. If the demand for any
article of manufacture slackens, the operatives drop into
the unsettled lands. If a citizen's neighbours rise above him
in the towns, he betakes himself where he can be monarch
of all he surveys. An artisan works, that he may die on
land of his own. He is frugal, that he may enable his son
to be a landowner. Farmers' daughters go into factories
that they may clear off the mortgage from their fathers'
farms; that they may be independent landowners again.
All this is natural enough in a country colonised from an
old one, where land is so restricted in quantity as to be
apparently the same thing as wealth. It is natural enough
in a young republic, where independence is of the highest
political value. It is natural enough in a country where
political economy has never been taught by its only effectual propounder—social adversity. And, finally, it falls
out well for the old world, in prospect of the time when
the new world must be its granary.

The Democratic party are fond of saying that the United
States are intended to be an agricultural country. It seems

to me that they are intended to be everything. The Niagara basin, the Mississippi valley, and the South, will be able to furnish the trading world with agricultural products for ever,—for aught we can see. But it is clear that there are other parts of the country which must have recourse to manufactures and commerce.

The first settlers in New England got land, and thought themselves rich. Their descendants have gone on to do the same; and they now find themselves poor. With the exception of some Southerners, ruined by slavery, who cannot live within their incomes, I met with no class in the United States so anxious about the means of living as the farmers of New England.

The Massachusetts farmers were the first to decline; but now the comparative adversity of agriculture has extended even into Vermont. A few years ago, lenders of money into Vermont received thirty per cent. interest from farmers: now they are glad to get six per cent.; and this does not arise from the farmers having saved capital of their own. They have but little property besides their land. Their daughters, and even their sons, resort to domestic service in Boston for a living. Boston used to be supplied from Vermont with fowls, butter, and eggs: but the supply has nearly ceased. This is partly owing to an increased attention to the growth of wool for the manufacturers; but partly also to the decrease of capital and enterprise among the farmers.

In Massachusetts the farmers have so little property besides their land, that they are obliged to mortgage when they want to settle a son or daughter, or make up for a deficient crop. The great Insurance Company at Boston is the formidable creditor to many. This Company will not wait a day for the interest. If it is not ready, loss or ruin ensues. Many circumstances are now unfavourable to the old-fashioned Massachusetts farmer. Domestic manufactures, which used to employ the daughters, are no longer worth while, in the presence of the factories. The young men, who should be the daughters' husbands, go off to the west. The idea of domestic service is not liked. There is an expensive family at home, without sufficient employment;

and they may be considered poor. These are evils which
may be shaken off any day. I speak of them, not as demanding much compassion, but as indicating a change in
the state of affairs; and especially that New England is de-
signed to be a manufacturing and commercial region. It
is already common to see agriculture joined with other
employments. The farmers of the coast are, naturally, fishermen also. They bring home fish, manure their land with
the offal; sow their seed, and go out again to fish while it
is growing. Shoemaking is now joined with farming. In the
long winter evenings, all the farmers' families around Lynn
are busy shoemaking; and in the spring, they turn out into
the fields again. The largest proportion of factory girls too
is furnished by country families.

There is, of course, a knowledge of the difficulty on the
spot; but not always a clear view of coming events, which
include a remedy. The commonest way of venting any
painful sensibility on the subject, is declamation against
luxury; or rather, against the desire for it in those who are
supposed unable to afford it. This will do no good. If the
Pilgrim Fathers themselves had had luxury before their
eyes, they would have desired to have it; and they would
have been right. Luxury is, in itself, a great good. Luxury
is *delicious fare*,—of any and every kind: and He who bestowed it meant all men to have it. The evil of luxury is in
its restriction; in its being made a cause of separation between men, and a means of encroachment by some on the
rights of others. Frugality is a virtue only when it is required by justice and charity. Luxury is vicious only when
it is obtained by injustice, and carried on into intemperance. It is a bad thing that a Massachusetts farmer should
mortgage his farm, in order that his wife and daughters
may dress like the ladies of Boston; but the evil is not in
the dress; it is rather in his clinging to a mode of life
which does not enable him to pay his debts. The women
desire dress, not only because it is becoming, but because
they revolt from sinking, even outwardly, into a lower
station of life than they once held. What they have to do
is to make up their minds to be consistent. They must
either go down with their farm, for love of it, and the ways

which belong to it: or they must make a better living in some other manner. They cannot have the old farm and its ways, and luxury too. Nobody has a right to decide for them which they ought to choose; and declaiming against luxury will therefore do no good. It is, however, pretty clear which they will choose, while luxury and manufactures are growing before their eyes; and, in that case, declaiming against luxury can do little but harm: it will only destroy sympathy between the declaimers and those who may find the cap fit.

One benevolent lady strongly desires and advises that manufactures should be put down; and the increased population all sent away somewhere, that New England may be as primitive and sparsely peopled as in days when it was, as she supposes, more virtuous than now. Whenever she can make out what virtue is, so as to prove that New England was ever more virtuous than now, her plans may find hearers; but not till then. I mention these things merely to show how confirmed is the tendency of New England to manufactures, in preference to agriculture.

It is scarcely possible to foresee, with distinctness, the destination of the southern States, east of the Alleghenies, when the curse of slavery shall be removed. Up to that period, continual deterioration is unavoidable. Efforts are being made to compensate for the decline of agriculture by pushing the interests of commerce. This is well; for the opening of every new rail-road, of every new pier, is another blow given to slavery. The agriculture of Virginia continues to decline; and her revenue is chiefly derived from the rearing of slaves as stock for the southern market. In the north and west parts of this State, where there is more farming than planting, it has long been found that slavery is ruinous; and when I passed through, in the summer of 1835, I saw scarcely any but whites, for some hundreds of miles along the road, except where a slave trader was carrying down to the south the remains that he had bought up. Unless some new resource is introduced, Virginia will be almost impoverished when the traffic in slaves comes to an end; which, I have a strong persuasion, will be the case before very long. The Virginians them-

selves are, it seems, aware of their case. I saw a factory at
Richmond, worked by black labour, which was found, to
the surprise of those who tried the experiment, to be of
very good quality.

No mismanagement short of employing slaves will account for the deterioration of the agricultural wealth of
these States. When the traveller observes the quality of
some of the land now under cultivation, he wonders how
other estates could have been rendered so unprofitable as
they are. The rich Congaree bottoms, in South Carolina,
look inexhaustible; but some estates, once as fine, now lie
barren and deserted. I went over a plantation, near Columbia, South Carolina, where there were four thousand
acres within one fence, each acre worth fifteen hundred
dollars. This land has been cropped yearly with cotton
since 1794, and is now becoming less productive; but it is
still very fine. The cotton seed is occasionally returned to
the soil; and this is the only means of renovation used. Four
hundred negroes work this estate. We saw the field
trenched, ready for sowing. The sowing is done by hand,
thick, and afterwards thinned. I saw the cotton elsewhere,
growing like twigs. I saw also some in pod. There are three
or four pickings of pods in a season; of which the first
gathering is the best. Each estate has its cotton press. In
the gin, the seed is separated from the cotton; and the
latter is pressed and packed for sale.

Adversity is the best teacher of economy here, as elsewhere. In the first flush of prosperity, when a proprietor
sits down on a rich virgin soil, and the price of cotton is
rising, he buys bacon and corn for his negroes, and other
provisions for his family, and devotes every rod of his land
to cotton-growing. I knew of one in Alabama, who, like his
neighbours, paid for his land and the maintenance of his
slaves with the first crop, and had a large sum over, wherewith to buy more slaves and more land. He paid eight
thousand dollars for his land, and all the expenses of the
establishment, and had, at the end of the season, eleven
thousand dollars in the bank. It was thought, by a wise
friend of this gentleman's, that it was a great injury, instead of benefit to his fortune, that his labourers were not

free. To use this wise man's expression, "it takes two white men to make a black man work;" and he was confident that it was not necessary, on any pretence whatever, to have a single slave in Alabama. Where all the other elements of prosperity exist, as they do in that rich new State, any quality and amount of labour might be obtained, and the permanent prosperity of the country might be secured.

I saw at Charleston the first great overt act of improvement that I am aware of in South Carolina. One step has been taken upwards; and when I saw it, I could only wish that the slaves in the neighbourhood could see, as clearly as a stranger could, the good it portended to them. It is nothing more than that an enterprising gentleman has set up a rice-mill, and that he avails himself to the utmost of its capabilities; but this is made much of in that land of small improvement; as it ought to be. The chaff is used to enrich the soil; and the proprietor has made lot after lot of bad land very profitable for sale with it, and is thus growing rapidly rich. The sweet flour, which lies between the husk and the grain, is used for fattening cattle. The broken rice is sold cheap; and the rest finds a good market. There are nine persons employed in the mill, some white and some black; and many more are busy in preparing the lots of land, and in building on them. Clusters of houses have risen up around the mill.

Alabama, Mississippi, and Louisiana, present the extreme case of the fertility of the soil, the prosperity of proprietors, and the woes of slaves. I found the Virginians spoke with sorrow and contempt of the treatment of slaves in North and South Carolina: South Carolina and Georgia, of the treatment of slaves in the richer States to the west: and, in these last, I found the case too bad to admit of aggravation. It was in these last that the most heart-rending disclosures were made to me by the ladies, heads of families, of the state of society, and of their own intolerable sufferings in it. As I went further north again, I found an improvement. There was less wealth in the hands of individuals, a better economy, more intelligent slaves, and more discussion how to get rid of slavery. Tennessee is, in some sort, naturally divided on the question. The eastern part of the State is hilly, and fit for farming; for which slave labour does not answer. The western part is used for cotton-planting; and the planters will not yet hear of free labour. The magnificent State of Kentucky has no other drawback to its prosperity than slavery; and its inhabitants are so far convinced of this that they will, no doubt, soon free themselves from it. They cannot look across the river, and witness the prosperity of Illinois, Indiana, and Ohio, without being aware that, with their own unequalled natural advantages, they could not be so backward as they are, from any other cause.

The prospects of agriculture in the States northwest of the Ohio are brilliant. The stranger who looks upon the fertile prairies of Illinois and Indiana, and the rich alluvions of Ohio, feels the iniquity of the English corn laws as strongly as in the alleys of Sheffield and Manchester. The world ought never to hear of a want of food,—no one of the inhabitants of its civilised portions ought ever to be without the means of obtaining his fill, while the mighty western valley smiles in its fertility. If the aristocracy of England, for whom those laws were made, and by whom they are sustained, could be transported to travel, in open wagons, the boundless prairies, and the shores of the great rivers which would bring down the produce, they would groan to see from what their petty, selfish interests had shut out the thousands of half-starved labourers at home.

The prettiest amateur farm I saw was that of the late Dr. Hosack, at Hyde Park, on the Hudson. Dr. Hosack had spared no pains to improve his stock, and his methods of farming, as well as the beauty of his pleasure-grounds. His merits in the former departments the agricultural societies in England are much better qualified to appreciate than I; and they seem to have valued his exertions; to judge by the medals and other honourable testimonials from them which he showed to me. As for his pleasure-grounds, little was left for the hand of art to do. The natural terrace above the river, green, sweeping, and undulating, is surpassingly beautiful. Dr. Hosack's good taste led him to leave it alone, and to spend his pains on the gardens and conservatory behind. Of all the beautiful country-seats on the Hudson, none can, I think, equal Hyde Park; though many bear a more imposing appearance from the river.

The most remarkable order of land-owners that I saw in the United States was that of the Shakers and the Rappites; both holding all their property in common, and both enforcing celibacy. The interest which would be felt by the whole of society in watching the results of a community of property is utterly destroyed by the presence of the other distinction; or rather of the ignorance and superstition of which it is the sign.

The moral and economical principles of these societies ought to be most carefully distinguished by the observer. This being done, I believe it will be found that whatever they have peculiarly good among them is owing to the soundness of their economical principles; whatever they have that excites compassion, is owing to the badness of their moral arrangements.

I visited two Shaker communities in Massachusetts. The first was at Hancock, consisting of three hundred persons, in the neighbourhood of another at Lebanon, consisting of seven hundred persons. There are fifteen Shaker establishments or "families" in the United States, and their total number is between five and six thousand. There is no question of their entire success, as far as wealth is concerned. A very moderate amount of labour has secured to them in perfection all the comforts of life that they know how to enjoy, and as much wealth besides as would command the intellectual luxuries of which they do not dream. The earth does not show more flourishing fields, gardens, and orchards, than theirs. The houses are spacious, and in all respects unexceptionable. The finish of every external thing testifies to their wealth, both of material and leisure. The floor of their place of worship, (the scene of their peculiar exercises,) the roofs of their houses, their stair-carpets, the feet of their chairs, the springs of their gates, and their spitting-boxes,—for even these neat people have spitting-boxes—show a nicety which is rare in America. Their table fare is of the very best quality. If happiness lay in bread and butter, and such things, these people have attained the *summum bonum*. Their store shows what they can produce for sale. A great variety of simples, of which they sell large quantities to London; linen-drapery, knitted wares, sieves, baskets, boxes, and confectionary; palm and feather fans, pin-cushions, and other such trifles; all these may be had in some variety, and of the best quality. If such external provision, with a great amount of accumulated wealth besides, is the result of co-operation and community of property among an ignorant, conceited, inert society like this, what might not the same principles of association achieve among a more intelligent set of people, stimulated by education, and exhilarated by the enjoyment of all the blessings which Providence has placed within the reach of man?

The wealth of the Shakers is not to be attributed to their celibacy. They are receiving a perpetual accession to their numbers from among the "world's people," and these accessions are usually of the most unprofitable kind. Widows with large families of young children, are perpetually joining the community, with the view of obtaining a plentiful subsistence with very moderate labour. The increase of their numbers does not lead to the purchase of more land. They supply their enlarged wants by the high cultivation of the land they have long possessed; and the superfluity of capital is so great that it is difficult to conceive what will be done with it by a people so nearly dead to intellectual enjoyments. If there had been no celibacy among them, they would probably have been far more wealthy than they are; the expenses of living in community being so much less, and the produce of co-operative labour being so much greater than in a state of division into families. The truth of these last positions can be denied by none who have witnessed the working of a co-operative system. The problem is to find the principle by which all shall be induced to labour their share. Any such principle being found, the wealth of the community follows of course.

Whether any principle to this effect can be brought to bear upon any large class of society in the old world, is at present the most important dispute, perhaps, that is agitating society. It will never now rest till it has been made matter of experiment. If a very low principle has served the purpose, for a time at least, in the new world, there seems much ground for expectation that a far higher one may be found to work as well in the more complicated case of English society. There is, at least, every encouragement to try. While there are large classes of people here whose condition can hardly be made worse; while the present system (if such it may be called) imposes care on the rich, excessive anxiety on the middle classes, and desperation on the poor: while the powerful are thus, as it were, fated to oppress; the strivers after power to circumvent and counteract; and the powerless to injure, it seems only reasonable that some section, at least, of this warring population should make trial of the peaceful principles which are working successfully elsewhere. The co-operative methods of the Shakers and Rappites might be tried without any adoption of their spiritual pride and cruel superstition. These are so far from telling against the system, that they prompt the observer to remark how much has been done in spite of such obstacles.

The followers of Mr. Rapp are settled at Economy, on the Ohio, eighteen miles below Pittsburgh. Their number was five hundred when I was there; and they owned three thousand acres of land. Much of their attention seems to be given to manufactures. They rear silkworms, and were the earliest silk-weavers in the United States. At my first visit they were weaving only a flimsy kind of silk handkerchief; last summer I brought away a piece of substantial, handsome black satin. They have sheep-walks, and a large woollen manufactory. Their factory was burnt down in 1834; the fire occasioning a loss of sixty thousand dollars; a mere trifle to this wealthy community. Their vineyards, corn-fields, orchards, and gardens gladden the eye. There is an abundance so much beyond their need that it is surprising that they work; except for want of something else to do. The Dutch love of flowers was visible in the plants that were to be seen in the windows, and the rich carnations and other sweets that bloomed in the garden and green-house. The whole place has a superior air to that of either of the Shaker "families" that I saw. The women were better dressed; more lively, less pallid; but, I fear, not much wiser. Mr. Rapp exercises an unbounded influence over his people. They are prevented learning any language but German, and are not allowed to converse with strangers. The superintendent keeps a close watch over them in this respect. Probationers must serve a year before they can be admitted: and the managers own that they dread the entrance of young people, who might be "unsettled;" that is, not sufficiently subservient.

Mr. Rapp is now very old. His son is dead. It remains to be seen what will become of his community, with its immense accumulation of wealth, when it has lost its dictator. It does not appear that they can go on in their present state without a dictator They smile superciliously upon Mr. Owen's plan, as admitting "a wrong principle,"—marriage. The best hope for them is that they will change their minds on this point, admitting the educational improvements which will arise out of the change, and remaining in community with regard to property.

Though the members of these remarkable communities are far from being the only agriculturists in whom the functions of proprietor and labourer are joined, the junction is in them so peculiar as to make them a separate class, holding a place between the landowners of whom I have before spoken, and the labourers of whom I shall have to treat.

DISPOSAL OF LAND

THE political economists of England have long wondered why the Americans have not done what older nations would be glad to do, if the opportunity had not gone by;—reserved government lands, which, as it is the tendency of rent to rise, might obviate any future increase of taxation. There are more good reasons than one why this cannot be done in America.

The expenses of the general government are so small that the present difficulty is to reduce the taxation so as to leave no more than a safe surplus revenue in the treasury;

and there is no prospect of any increase of taxation; as the taxpayers are likely to grow much faster than the expenses of the government.

The people of the United States choose to be proprietors of land, not tenants. No one can yet foresee the time when the relation of landlord and tenant (except in regard to house property) will be extensively established in America. More than a billion of acres remain to be disposed of first.

The weightiest reason of all is that, in the United States, the people of to-day are the government of to-day; the people of fifty years hence will be the government of fifty years hence; and it would not suit the people of to-day to sequestrate their property for the benefit of their successors, any better than it would suit the people of fifty years hence to be legislated for by those of to-day. A democratic government must always be left free to be operated upon by the will of the majority of the time being. All that the government of the day can do is to ascertain what now appears to be the best principle by which to regulate the disposal of land, and then to let the demand and supply take their natural course.

Some circumstances seem at present to favour the process of enlightenment; others are adverse to it. Those which are favourable are, the high prosperity of manufactures and commerce, the essential requisite of which is the concentration of labourers: the increasing immigration of labourers from Europe, and the happy experience which they force upon the back settler of the advantage of an increased proportion of labour to land; and the approaching crisis of the slavery question; when every one will see the necessity of measures which will keep the slaves where they are.

The circumstances unfavourable to an understanding of the true state of the case about the disposal of land are, the deep-rooted persuasion that land itself is the most valuable wealth, in all places, and under all circumstances: and the complication of interests connected with the late acquisition of Louisiana and Florida, and the present usurpation of Texas.

Louisiana was obtained from the French, not on account

of the fertile new land which it comprehended, but because it was essential to the very existence of the United States that the mouth of the Mississippi should not be in the possession of another people. The Americans obtained the mouth of the Mississippi; and with it, unfortunately, large tracts of the richest virgin soil, on which slavery started into new life, and on which "the perspiration of the eastern States" (as I have heard the settlers of the west called) rested, and grew barbarous while they grew rich. A fact has lately transpired in the northern States which was already well known in the south,—that the purchase of Florida was effected for the sake of the slave-holders. It is now known that the President was overwhelmed with letters from slave-owners, complaining that Florida was the refuge of their runaways; and demanding that this retreat should be put within their power. Florida was purchased. Many and great evils have already arisen out of its acquisition. To cover these, and blind the people to the particular and iniquitous interests engaged in the affair, the sordid faction benefited raises a perpetual boast in the ears of the people about their gain of new territory, and the glory and profit of having added so many square miles to their already vast possessions.

It would be a happy thing for them if they should know all soon enough to direct their national reprobation upon the Texan adventurers, and wash their hands of the iniquity of that business. This would soon be done, if they could look upon the whole affair from a distance, and see how the fair fame of their country is compromised by the avarice and craft of a faction. The probity of their people, their magnanimity in money matters, have always been conspicuous, from the time of the cession of their lands by the States to the General Government, till now: and, now they seem in danger of forfeiting their high character through the art of the few, and the ignorance of the many. The few are obtaining their end by flattering the passion of the many for new territory, as well as by engaging their best feelings on behalf of those who are supposed to be fighting for their rights against oppressors.

It is much to be feared that, even if Texas were acknowl-

edged to-morrow to be a Mexican State, an injury would
be found to have been done to the American people, which
it will take a long time and much experience to repair. No
pains have been spared to confirm the delusion, that the
possession of more and more land is the only thing to be
desired, alike by the selfish and the patriotic; by those
who would hastily build up their own fortunes, and by
those who desire the aggrandisement of their country. No
one mourned with me more earnestly over this popular
delusion than a member of Congress, who has since been
one of the most vehement advocates of the Texan cause,
and has thereby done his best to foster the delusion. He
told me that the metaphysics of society in the south afford
a curious study to the observer; and that they are humbling to a resident. He told me that, so far from the honour
and happiness of any region being supposed to lie in the
pursuit of the higher objects of life, any man would be
pronounced "imbecile" who, having enough for his moderate wants, should prefer the enjoyment of his patrimony,
his family relations, and intercourse with the society in
which he was brought up, to wandering away in pursuit
of more land. He complained that he was heart-sick when
he heard of American books: that there was no character
of permanence in anything;—all was fluctuation, except the
passion for land, which, under the name of enterprise, or
patriotism, or something else that was creditable, would
last till his countrymen had pushed their out-posts to the
Pacific. He insisted that the only consolation arose from
what was to be hoped when pioneering must, perforce,
come to a stop. He told me of one and another of his intelligent and pleasant young neighbours, who were quitting
their homes and civilised life, and carrying their brides "as
bondwomen" into the wilderness, because fine land was
cheap there.

The people of the United States have, however, kept
their eyes open to one great danger, arising from this love
of land. They have always had in view the disadvantage
of rich men purchasing tracts larger than they could cultivate. They saw that it was contrary to the public interest
that individuals should be allowed to interpose a desert

between other settlers whose welfare depends much on their having means of free communication, and a peopled neighbourhood; and that it is inconsistent with republican modes that overgrown fortunes should arise by means of an early grasping of large quantities of a cheap kind of property, which must inevitably become of the highest value in course of time. The reduction in the price of land would probably have been greater, but for the temptation which the cheapening would hold out to capitalists.

RURAL LABOUR

ENGLISH farmers settling in the United States used to be a joke to their native neighbours. The Englishman began with laughing, or being shocked, at the slovenly methods of cultivation employed by the American settlers: he was next seen to look grave on his own account; and ended by following the American plan.

The American ploughs round the stumps of the trees he has felled, and is not very careful to measure the area he ploughs, and the seed he sows. The Englishman clears half the quantity of land,—clears it very thoroughly; ploughs deep, sows thick, raises twice the quantity of grain on half the area of land, and points proudly to his crop. But the American has, meantime, fenced, cleared, and sown more land, improved his house and stock, and kept his money in his pocket. The Englishman has paid for the labour bestowed on his beautiful fields more than his fine crop repays him. When he has done thus for a few seasons, till his money is gone, he learns that he has got to a place where it answers to spend land to save labour; the reverse of his experience in England.

It would puzzle a philosopher to compute how long some prejudices will subsist in defiance of, not only evidence, but personal experience. These same Americans, who laugh (reasonably enough) at the prejudiced English farmer, seem themselves incapable of being convinced on a point quite as plain as that between him and themselves. The very ground of their triumph over him is their knowledge of the much smaller value of land, and greater value of labour, in America than in England: and yet, there is no one subject on which so many complaints are to be heard from every class of American society as the immigration of foreigners. It is wonderful, to a stranger, to see how they fret and toil, and scheme and invent, to supply the deficiency of help, and all the time quarrel with the one means by which labour is brought to their door. The immigration of foreigners was the one complaint by which I was met in every corner of the free States; and I really believe I did not converse with a dozen persons who saw the ultimate good through the present apparent evil.

It is not much to be wondered at that gentlemen and ladies, living in Boston and New York, and seeing, for the first time in their lives, half-naked and squalid persons in the street, should ask where they come from, and fear lest they should infect others with their squalor, and wish they would keep away. It is not much to be wondered at that the managers of charitable institutions in the maritime cities should be weary of the claims advanced by indigent foreigners: but it is surprising that these gentlemen and ladies should not learn by experience that all this ends well, and that matters are taking their natural course. It would certainly be better that the emigrants should be well clothed, educated, respectable people; (except that, in that case, they would probably never arrive;) but the blame of their bad condition rests elsewhere, while their arrival is, generally speaking, almost a pure benefit. Some are intemperate and profligate; and such are, no doubt, a great injury to the cities where they harbour; but the greater number show themselves decent and hardworking enough, when put into employment. Every American acknowledges that few or no canals or rail-roads would be in existence now, in the United States, but for the Irish labour by which they have been completed: and the best cultivation that is to be seen in the land is owing to the Dutch and Germans it contains. What would housekeepers do for domestic service without foreigners? If the American ports had been barred against immigration, and the sixty thousand foreigners per annum, with all their progeny, had been excluded, where would now have been the public works of the United States, the agriculture, the shipping? The most emphatic complainers of the immigration of foreigners are those who imagine that the morals of society suffer thereby. My own conviction is that the morals of society are, on the whole, thereby much improved. My own opinion is that most of the evils charged upon the immigrants are chargeable upon the mismanagement of them in the ports. The atrocious corruption of the New York elections, where an Irishman, just landed, and employed upon the drains, perjures himself, and votes nine times over, is chargeable, not upon immigration, nor yet upon universal suffrage, but upon faults in the machinery of registration.

The bad moral consequences of a dispersion of agricultural labour, and the good moral effects of an adequate combination, are so serious as to render it the duty of good citizens to inform themselves fully of the bearings of this question before they attempt to influence other minds upon it. Those who have seen what are the morals and manners of families who live alone in the wilds, with no human opinion around them, no neighbours with whom to exchange good offices, no stimulus to mental activity, no social amusements, no church, *no life*, nothing but the pursuit of the outward means of living,—any one who has witnessed this will be ready to agree what a blessing it would be to such a family to shake down a shower of even poor Irish labourers around them. To such a family no tidings ought to be more welcome than of the arrival of ship-load after ship-load of immigrants at the ports, some few of whom may wander hitherwards, and by entering into a combination of labour to obtain means of living, open a way to the attainment of the ends. Sixty thousand immigrants a-year! What are these spread over so many thousand square miles? If the country could be looked down upon from a balloon, some large clusters of these would be seen detained in the cities, because they could not be spared into the country; other clusters would be seen about the canals and rail-roads; and a very slight

[handwritten margin note: People against immigrants think that the morals of their society suffer because of them; however, they are rather improved.]

sprinkling in the back country, where their stations would be marked by the prosperity growing up around them.

The expedients used in the country settlements to secure a combination of labour when it is absolutely necessary, show how eminently deficient it is. Every one has heard of the "frolic" or "bee," by means of which the clearing of lots, the raising of houses, the harvesting of crops is achieved. Roads are made, and kept by contributions of labour and teams, by settlers. For the rest, what can be done by family labour alone is so done, with great waste of time, material, and toil. The wonderful effects of a "frolic," in every way, should serve, in contrast with the toil and difficulty usually expended in producing small results, to incline the hearts of settlers towards immigrants, and to plan how an increase of them may be obtained.

Minds are, I hope, beginning to turn in this direction. In New England, where there is the most combination of labour, and the poorest land, it is amusing to see the beginning of discoveries on this head. I find, in the United States' Almanack for 1835, an article on agricultural improvements, (presupposing a supply of labour as the primary requisite,) which bears all the marks of freshness and originality, of having been a discovery of the writer's.

"If such improvements as are possible, or even easy," (where there is labour at hand,) "were made in the husbandry of this country, many and great advantages would be found to arise. As twice the number of people might be supported on the same quantity of land, all our farming towns would become twice as populous as they are likely to be in the present state of husbandry. There would be, in general, but half the distance to travel to visit one's friends and acquaintances. Friends might oftener see and converse with each other. Half the labour would be saved in carrying the corn to mill, and the produce to market; half the journeying saved in attending our courts; and half the expense in supporting government, and in making and repairing roads; half the distance saved in going to the smith, weaver, clothier, &c.; half the distance saved in going to public worship, and most other meetings; for where steeples are four miles apart, they would be only two or three. Much time, expense and labour would, on these accounts, be saved; and civilisation, with all the social virtues, would, perhaps, be proportionally promoted and increased."

Before this can be done, there must be hands to do it. Steeples must remain four or fourteen miles apart, till there are beings enough in the intervening space to draw them together. I saw, on the Mississippi, a woman in a canoe, paddling up against the stream; probably, as I was told, to visit a neighbour twenty or thirty miles off. The only comfort was that the current would bring her back four times as quickly as she went up. What a blessing would a party of emigrant neighbours be to a woman who would row herself twenty miles against the stream of the Mississippi for companionship!

I was told, in every eastern city, that it was a common practice with parish officers in England to ship off their paupers to the United States. I took some pains to investigate the grounds of this charge, and am convinced that it is a mistake; that the accusation has arisen out of some insulated case. I was happy to be able to show my American friends how the supposed surplus population of the English agricultural counties has shrunk, and in most cases disappeared, under the operation of the new Poor Law, so that, even if the charge had ever been true, it could not long remain so. By the time that we shall be enabled to say the same of the parishes of Ireland, the Americans will, doubtless, have discovered that they would be glad of all the labourers we had ever been able to spare; if only we could send them in the form of respectable men and women, instead of squalid paupers, looking as if they were going from shore to shore, to rouse the world to an outcry against the sins and sorrows of our economy.

It will scarcely be credited by those who are not already informed on the subject, that a proposition has been made to send out of the country an equal number of persons to the amount brought into it; ship loads of labourers going to and fro, like buckets in a well: that this proposition has been introduced into Congress, and has been made the basis of appropriations in some State legislatures: that itinerant lecturers are employed to advocate the scheme: that it is preached from the pulpit, and subscribed for in the churches, and that in its behalf are enlisted members of the administration, a great number of the leading politicians, clergy, merchants, and planters, and a large proportion of the other citizens of the United States. It matters little how many or how great are the men engaged in behalf of a bad scheme, which is so unnatural that it cannot but fail:—it matters little, as far as the scheme itself is concerned; but it is of incalculable consequence as creating an obstruction. For itself, the miserable abortion—the Colonisation scheme—might be passed over; for its active results will be nothing; but it is necessary to refer to it in its passive character of an obstruction. It is necessary to refer thus to it, not only as a matter of fact, but because, absurd and impracticable as the scheme clearly is, when viewed in relation to the whole state of affairs in America, it is not so easy on the spot to discern its true character. So many perplexing considerations are mixed up with it by its advocates; so many of those advocates are men of earnest philanthropy, and well versed in the details of the scheme, while blind to its general bearing, that it is difficult to have general principles always in readiness to meet opposing facts; to help adopting the partial views of well-meaning and thoroughly persuaded persons; and to know where to doubt, and what to disbelieve. I went to America extremely doubtful about the character of this institution. I heard at Baltimore and Washington all that could be said in its favour, by persons conversant with slavery, which I had not then seen. Mr. Madison, the President of the Colonisation Society, gave me his favourable views of it. Mr. Clay, the Vice-President, gave me his. So did almost every clergyman and other member of society whom I met for some months. Much time, observation, and reflection were necessary to form a judgment for myself, after so much prepossession, even in so clear a case as I now see this to be. Others on the spot must have the same allowance as was necessary for me: and, if any pecuniary interest be involved in the question, much more. But, I am firmly persuaded that any clear-headed man, shutting himself up in his closet for a day's study of the question, or taking a voyage, so as to be able to look back upon the entire country he has left,—being careful to take in the whole of its economical aspect, (to say nothing, at present, of the moral,) can come to no other conclusion than that the scheme of transporting the coloured population of the United States to the coast of Africa is absolutely absurd; and, if it were not so, would be absolutely pernicious. But, in matters of economy, the pernicious and the absurd are usually identical.

What is now the state of the case? Slavery, of a very mild kind, has been abolished in the northern parts of the Union, where agricultural labour can be carried on by whites, and where such employments bear a very reduced proportion to manufacturing and commercial occupations. Its introduction into the north-western portions of the country has been prohibited by those who had had experience of its evils. Slavery, generally of a very aggravated character, now subsists in thirteen States out of twenty-six, and those thirteen are the States which grow the tobacco, rice, cotton and sugar; it being generally alleged that rice and sugar cannot be raised by white labour, while some maintain that they may. I found few who doubted that tobacco and cotton may be grown by white labour, with the assistance from brute labour and machinery which would follow upon the disuse of human capital. The amount of the slave population is now above two millions and a half. It increases rapidly in the States which have been impoverished by slavery; and is killed off, but not with equal rapidity, on the virgin soils to which alone it is, in any degree, appropriate. It has become unquestionably inappropriate in Maryland, Delaware, Virginia, and Kentucky. To these I should be disposed to add Missouri, and North Carolina, and part of Tennessee and South Carolina. The States which have more slave labour than their deteriorated lands require, sell it to those which have a deficiency of labour to their rich lands. Virginia, now in a very depressed condition, derives her chief revenue from the rearing of slaves, as stock, to be sent to Alabama, Mississippi, and Louisiana. The march of circumstance has become too obvious to escape the attention of the most short-sighted. No one can fail to perceive that slavery, like an army of locusts, is compelled to shift its place, by the desolation it has made. Its progress is southwards; and now, having reached the sea there, southwestwards. If there were but an impassable barrier there, its doom would be certain, and not very remote. This doom was apparently sealed a while ago, by the abolition of slavery in Mexico, and the fair chance there seemed of Missouri and Arkansas being subjected to a restriction of the same purport with that imposed on the new States, north-west of the Ohio. This doom has been, for the present, cancelled by the admission of slavery into Missouri and Arkansas, and by the seizure of Texas by American citizens. The open question, however, only regards its final limits. Its speedy abolition in many of the States may be, and is, regarded as certain.

The institution of slavery was a political anomaly at the time of the Revolution. It has now become an economical one also. Nothing can prevent the generality of persons from seeing this, however blind a few, a very few persons on the spot may be to the truth.*

It is proposed by the Colonisation Society that free persons of colour shall be sent to establish and conduct a civilised community on the shores of Africa. The variety of prospects held out by this proposition to persons of different views is remarkable. To the imaginative, there is the picture of the restoration of the coloured race to their paternal soil: to the religious, the prospect of evangelising Africa. Those who would serve God and Mammon are de-

* It may surprise some that I speak of those who are blind to slavery being an anomaly in economy as 'few.' Among the many hundreds of persons in the slave States, with whom I conversed on the subject of slavery, I met with only one, a lady, who defended the institution altogether: and with perhaps four or five who defended it as necessary to a purpose which must be fulfilled, and could not be fulfilled otherwise. All the rest who vindicated its present existence did so on the ground of the impossibility of doing it away. A very large number avowed that it was indefensible in every point of view.

lighted at being able to work their slaves during their own lives, and then leave them to the Colonisation Society with a bequest of money, (when money must needs be left behind,) to carry them over to Africa. Those who would be doing, in a small way, immediately, let certain of their slaves work for wages which are to carry them over to Africa. Those who have slaves too clever or discontented to be safe neighbours, can ship them off to Africa. Those who are afraid of the rising intelligence of their free coloured neighbours, or suffer strongly under the prejudice of colour, can exercise such social tyranny as shall drive such troublesome persons to Africa. The clergy, public lecturers, members of legislatures, religious societies, and charitable individuals, both in the north and south, are believed to be, and believe themselves to be, labouring on behalf of slaves, when they preach, lecture, obtain appropriations, and subscribe, on behalf of the Colonisation Society. Minds and hearts are laid to rest,—opiated into a false sleep.

Here are all manner of people associated for one object, which has the primary advantage of being ostensibly benevolent. It has had Mr. Madison for its chief officer: Mr. Clay for its second. It has had the aid, for twenty years, of almost all the presses and pulpits of the United States, and of most of their politicians, members of government, and leading professional men and merchants, and almost all the planters of twelve states, and all the missionary interest. Besides the subscriptions arising from so many sources, there have been large appropriations made by various legislatures. What is the result?—Nothing. *Ex nihilo nihil fit.* Out of a chaos of elements no orderly creation can arise but by the operation of a sound principle: and sound principle here, there is none.

In twenty years, the Colonisation Society has removed to Africa between two and three thousand persons;* while the annual increase of the slave population is, by the lowest computation, sixty thousand; and the number of free blacks is upwards of three hundred and sixty-two thousand.

* With the condition of the African colony, we have here nothing to do. We are now considering the Colonisation Society in its professed relation to American slavery.

The chief officers of the Colonisation Society look forward to being able, in a few years, to carry off the present annual increase, and a few more; by which time the annual increase will amount to many times more than the Society will have carried out from the beginning.

While labourers are flocking into other parts of the country, at the rate of sixty thousand per annum, and are found to be far too few for the wants of society, the Colonisation scheme proposes to carry out more than this number; and fails of all its ostensible objects till it does so. A glance at the causes of slavery, and at the present economy of the United States, shows such a scheme to be a bald fiction.

It alienates the attention and will of the people, (for the purposes of the few,) from the principle of the abolition of slavery, which would achieve any honest objects of the Colonisation Society, and many more. Leaving, for the present, the moral consideration of the case, abolition would not only leave the land as full of labourers as it is now, but incalculably augment the supply of labour by substituting willing and active service, and improved methods of husbandry, for the forced, inferior labour, and wasteful arrangements which are always admitted to be co-existent with slavery.

Whenever I am particularly strongly convinced of anything, in opposition to the opinion of any or many others, I entertain a suspicion that there is more evidence on the other side than I see. I felt so, even on this subject of slavery, which has been clear to English eyes for so long. I went into the slave States with this suspicion in my mind; and I preserved it there as long as possible. I believe that I have heard every argument that can possibly be adduced in vindication or palliation of slavery, under any circumstances now existing; and I declare that, of all displays of intellectual perversion and weakness that I have witnessed, I have met with none so humbling and so melancholy as the advocacy of this institution. I declare that I know the whole of its theory;—a declaration that I dare not make with regard to, I think, any other subject whatever: the result is that I believe there is nothing rational to be said in vindication or palliation of the protraction of slavery in

the United States.—Having made this avowal, it will not be
expected that I should fill my pages with a wide superficies
of argument which will no more bear a touch than pond-
ice, on the last day of thaw. As I disposed in my mind
the opposite arguments of slave-holders, I found that they
ate one another up, like the two cats that Sheridan told
of; but without leaving so much as an inch of tail.

It is obvious that all laws which encourage the departure
of the blacks must be repealed, when their slavery is
abolished. The one thing necessary, in the economical view
of the case, is that efficient measures should be taken to
prevent an unwise dispersion of these labourers: measures,
I mean, which should in no way interfere with their personal liberty, but which should secure to them generally
greater advantages on the spot than they could obtain by
roaming. Any such tendency will be much aided by the
strong local attachments for which negroes are remarkable. It is not only that slaves dread all change, from the
intellectual and moral dejection to which they are reduced;
fearing even the removal from one plantation to another,
under the same master, from the constant vague apprehension of something dreadful. It is not only this, (which,
however, it would take them some time to outgrow,) but
that all their race show a kind of feline attachment to
places to which they are accustomed, which will be of excellent service to kind masters when the day of emancipation comes. For the rest, efficient arrangements can and
will doubtless be made to prevent their wandering further
than from one master to another. The abolition of slavery
must be complete and immediate: that is to say, as a man
either is or is not the property of another, as there can be
no degrees of ownership of a human being, there must be
an immediate and complete surrender of all claim to negro
men, women, and children as property: but there may
and will doubtless be arrangements made to protect, guide,
and teach these degraded beings, till they have learned
what liberty is, and how to use it. Liberty to change their
masters must, under certain reasonable limitations, be allowed; the education of their children must be enforced.
The amount of wages will be determined by natural laws,

and cannot be foreseen, further than that they must necessarily be very ample for a long time to come. It will probably be found desirable to fix the price of the government lands, with a view to the coloured people, at that amount which will best obviate squatting, and secure the respectable settlement of some who may find their way to the west.

Suggestions of this kind excite laughter among the masters of slaves, who are in the habit of thinking that they know best what negroes are, and what they are capable of. I have reasons for estimating their knowledge differently, and for believing that none know so little of the true character and capabilities of negroes as their owners. They might know more, but for the pernicious and unnatural secrecy about some of the most important facts connected with slave-holding, which is induced partly by pride, partly by fear, partly by pecuniary interest. If they would do themselves and their slaves the justice of inquiring with precision what is the state of Hayti; what has taken place in the West Indies; what the emancipation really was there; what its effects actually are, they would obtain a clearer view of their own prospects. So they would, if they would communicate freely about certain facts nearer home: not only conversing as individuals, but removing the restrictions upon the press by which they lose far more than they gain, both in security and fortune,—to say nothing of intelligence. Of the many families in which I enjoyed intercourse, there was, I believe, none where I was not told of some one slave of unusual value, for talent or goodness, either in the present or a former generation. A collection of these alone, as they stand in my journal, would form no mean testimony to the intellectual and moral capabilities of negroes: and if to these were added the tales which I could tell, if I also were not bound under the laws of mystery of which I have been complaining, many hearts would beat with the desire to restore to their human rights those whose fellow-sufferers have given ample proof of their worthiness to enjoy them. The consideration which binds me to silence upon a rich collection of facts, full of moral beauty and promise, is regard to the safety of many whose heroic obedience to the laws of

God has brought them into jeopardy under the laws of slave-holders, and the allies of slave-holders. Nor would I, by any careless revelations, throw the slightest obstacle in the way of the escape of any one of the slaves who may be about to shirk their masters, by methods with which I happen to be acquainted.

It can, however, do nothing but good to proclaim the truth that slaves do run away in much greater numbers than is supposed by any but those who lose them, and those who help them. By which I mean many others besides the abolitionists *par excellence*. Perhaps I might confine the knowledge to these last; for I believe no means exist by which the yearly amount of loss of this kind may be verified and published in the south. Everybody who has been in America is familiar with the little newspaper picture of a black man, hieing with his stick and bundle, which is prefixed to the advertisements of runaways. Every traveller has probably been struck with the number of these which meets his eye; but unless he has more private means of information, he will remain unaware of the streams of fugitives continually passing out of the States. There is much reserve about this in the south, from pride; and among those elsewhere who could tell, from far other considerations. The time will come when the whole story, in its wonder and beauty, may be told by some who, like myself, have seen more of the matter, from all sides, than it is easy for a native to do. Suffice it, that the loss by runaways, and the generally useless attempts to recover them, is a heavy item in the accounts of the cotton and sugar-growers of the south; and one which is sure to become heavier till there shall be no more bondage to escape from. It is obvious that the slaves who run away are among the best: an escape being usually the achievement of a project early formed; concealed, pertinaciously adhered to, and endeared by much toil and sacrifice undergone for its sake, for a long course of years. A weak mind is incapable of such a series of acts, with a unity of purpose. They are the choicest slaves who run away. Of the cases known to me, the greater number of the men, and some of the women, have acted throughout upon an idea;

(called by their owners "a fancy,"—a very different thing;) while some few of the men have started off upon some sudden infliction of cruelty; and many women on account of intolerable outrage, of the grossest kind. Several masters told me of leave given to their slaves to go away, and of the slaves refusing to avail themselves of it. If this was meant to tell in favour of slavery, it failed of its effect. The argument was too shallow to impose upon a child. Of course, they were the least valuable slaves to whom this permission was given: and their declining to depart proved nothing so much as the utter degradation of human beings who could prefer receiving food and shelter from the hand of an owner to the possession of themselves.

Amidst the mass of materials which accumulated on my hands during the process of learning from all parties their views on this question, I hardly know where to turn, and what to select, that will most briefly and strongly show that the times have outgrown slavery. This is the point at which every fact and argument issue, whatever may be the intention of those who adduce it. The most striking, perhaps, is the treatment of the Abolitionists: a subject to be adverted to hereafter. The insane fury which vents itself upon the few who act upon the principles which the many profess, is a sign of the times not to be mistaken. It is always the precursor of beneficial change. Society in America seems to be already passing out of this stage into one even more advanced. The cause of abolition is spreading so rapidly through the heart of the nation; the sound part of the body politic is embracing it so actively, that no disinterested observer can fail to be persuaded that even the question of time is brought within narrow limits.

After giving one or two testimonies to the necessity of a speedy change of system, I will confine myself to relating a few signs of the times which I encountered in my travels through the south.

In 1782, Virginia repealed the law against manumission; and in nine years, there were ten thousand slaves freed in that State. Alarmed for the institution, her legislature re-enacted the law. What has been the consequence?—Let us take the testimony of the two leading newspapers of the capital of Virginia, given at a time when the Virginian legislature was debating the subject of slavery; and when there was, for once, an exposure of the truth from those best qualified to reveal it. In 1832, the following remarks appeared in the "Richmond Enquirer."

"It is probable, from what we hear, that the committee on the coloured population will report some plan for getting rid of the free people of colour. But is this all that can be done? Are we for ever to suffer the greatest evil which can scourge our land not only to remain, but to increase in its dimensions? 'We may shut our eyes and avert our faces, if we please,' (writes an eloquent South Carolinian, on his return from the north a few weeks ago,) 'but there it is, the dark and growing evil, at our doors: and meet the question we must at no distant day. God only knows what it is the part of wise men to do on that momentous and appalling subject. Of *this* I am very sure, that the difference —nothing short of frightful—between all that exists on one side of the Potomac, and all on the other, is owing to *that cause alone*. The disease is deep seated; it is at the heart's core; it is consuming, and has all along been consuming, our vitals; and I could laugh, if I *could* laugh on such a subject, at the ignorance and folly of the politician who ascribes that to an act of the government, which is the inevitable effect of the eternal laws of nature. What is to be done? O my God, I don't know; but something must be done.'

"Yes, something must be done; and it is the part of no honest man to deny it; of no free press to affect to conceal it. When this dark population is growing upon us; when every new census is but gathering its appalling numbers upon us; when within a period equal to that in which this federal constitution has been in existence, those numbers will increase to more than two millions within Virginia; when our sister States are closing their doors upon our blacks for sale; *and when our whites are moving westwardly in greater numbers than we like to hear of;* when this, the fairest land on all this continent, for soil and climate and situation combined, might become a sort of garden spot if it were worked by the hands of white men alone, *can we, ought we* to sit quietly down, fold our arms, and say to each other, 'well, well, this thing will not come to the worst in our day? We will leave it to our children and our grand-children and great-grand-children to take care of themselves, and to brave the storm.' Is this to act like wise men? Heaven knows we are no fanatics. We detest the madness which actuated the *Amis des Noirs.* But something ought to be done. Means, sure but gradual, systematic but discreet, ought to be adopted for reducing the mass of evil which is pressing upon the south, and will still more press upon her the longer it is put off. We ought not to shut our eyes, nor avert our faces. And though we speak almost without a hope that the committee or the legislature will do anything, at the present session, to meet this question, yet we say now, in the utmost sincerity of our hearts, that our wisest men cannot give too much of their attention to this subject, nor can they give it too soon."

The other paper, the "Richmond Whig," had the same time, the following:

"We affirm that the great mass of Virginia herself triumphs that the slavery question has been agitated, and reckons it glorious that the spirit of her sons did not shrink from grappling with the monster. We affirm that, in the heaviest slave districts of the State, thousands have hailed the discussion with delight, and contemplate the distant, but ardently desired result, as the supreme good which Providence could vouchsafe to their country."

This is doubtless true. One of the signs of the times which struck me was the clandestine encouragement received by the abolitionists of the north from certain timid slave-holders of the south, who send money for the support of abolition publications, and an earnest blessing. They write, "For God's sake go on! We cannot take your publications; we dare not countenance you; but we wish you God speed! You are our only hope." There is nothing to be said for the moral courage of those who feel and write thus, and dare not express their opinions in the elections. Much excuse may be made for them by those who know the horrors which await the expression of anti-slavery sentiments in many parts of the south. But, on the other hand, the abolitionists are not to be blamed for considering all slave-holders under the same point of view, as long as no improved state of opinion is manifested in the representation; the natural mirror of the minds of the represented.

Chief Justice Marshall, a Virginian, a slave-holder, and a member of the Colonisation Society, (though regarding this society as being merely a palliative, and slavery incurable but by convulsion,) observed to a friend of mine, in the winter of 1834, that he was surprised at the British for supposing that they could abolish slavery in their colonies by act of parliament. His friend believed it would be done. The Chief Justice could not think that such economical institutions could be done away by legislative enactment. His friend pleaded the fact that the members of the British House of Commons were pledged, in great numbers, to their constituents on the question. When it was done, the Chief Justice remarked on his having been mistaken; and that he rejoiced in it. He now saw hope for his beloved Virginia, which he had seen sinking lower and lower among the States. The cause, he said, was that work is disreputable in a country where a degraded class is held to enforced labour.* He had seen all the young, the flower of the State, who were not rich enough to remain at home in idleness, betaking themselves to other regions, where they might work without disgrace. Now there was hope; for he considered that in this act of the British, the decree had gone forth against American slavery, and its doom was sealed.

There was but one sign of the times which was amusing to me; and that was the tumult of opinions and prophecies offered to me on the subject of the duration of slavery, and the mode in which it would be at last got rid of; for I never heard of any one but Governor M'Duffie who supposed that it can last for ever. He declared last year, in his

* Governor M'Duffie's message to the legislature of South Carolina contains the proposition that freedom can be preserved only in societies where either work is disreputable, or there is an hereditary aristocracy, or a military despotism. He prefers the first, as being the most republican.

message to the legislature of South Carolina, that he considers slavery as the corner-stone of their republican liberties: and that, if he were dying, his latest prayer should be that his children's children should live nowhere but amidst the institutions of slavery. This message might have been taken as a freak of eccentricity merely, if it had stood alone. But a committee of the legislature, with Governor Hamilton in the chair, thought proper to endorse every sentiment in it. This converts it into an indication of the perversion of mind commonly prevalent in a class when its distinctive pecuniary interest is in imminent peril. I was told, a few months prior to the appearance of this singular production, that though Governor M'Duffie was a great ornament to the State of South Carolina, his opinions on the subject of slavery were *ultra,* and that he was left pretty nearly alone in them. Within a year, those who told me so went, *in public,* all lengths with Governor M'Duffie.

I believe I might very safely and honourably give the names of those who prophesied to me in the way I have mentioned; for they rather court publicity for their opinions, as it is natural and right that they should, as long as they are sure of them. But it may suffice to mention that they are all eminent men, whose attention has been strongly fixed, for a length of years, upon the institution in question.

A. believes that slavery is a necessary and desirable stage in civilisation: not on the score of the difficulty of cultivating new lands without it, but on the ground of the cultivation of the negro mind and manners. He believes the Haytians to have deteriorated since they became free. He believes the white population destined to absorb the black, though holding that the two races will not unite after the third mixture. His expectation is that the black and mulatto races will have disappeared in a hundred and fifty years. He has no doubt that cotton and tobacco may be well and easily grown by whites.

B. is confident that the condition of slaves is materially improved, yet believes that they will die out, and that there will be no earlier catastrophe. He looks to colonisation, however, as a means of lessening the number. This same

gentleman told me of a recent visit he had paid to a connexion of his own, who had a large "force," consisting
chiefly of young men and women: not one child had been
born on the estate for three years. This looks very like
dying out; but does it go to confirm the materially improved condition of the slaves?

C. allows slavery to be a great evil; and, if it were now
non-existent, would not ordain it, if he could. But he thinks
the slaves far happier than they would have been at home
in Africa, and considers that the system works perfectly.
He pronounces the slaves "the most contented, happy, industrious peasantry in the world." He believes this virtue
and content would disappear if they were taught anything whatever; and that if they were free, they would be,
naturally and inevitably, the most vicious and wretched
population ever seen. His expectation is that they will increase to such a degree as to make free labour, "*which always supersedes slave labour,*" necessary in its stead; that
the coloured race will wander off to new regions, and be
ultimately "absorbed" by the white. He contemplates no
other than this natural change, which he thinks cannot take
place in less than a century and a half. A year later, this
gentleman told a friend of mine that slavery cannot last
above twenty years. They must be stringent reasons which
have induced so great a change of opinion in twelve
months.

D. thinks slavery an enormous evil, but doubts whether
something as bad would not arise in its stead. He is a
colonisationist, and desires that the general government
should purchase the slaves, by annual appropriations, and
ship them off to Africa, so as to clear the country of the
coloured people in forty or fifty years. If this is not done,
a servile war, the most horrible that the world has seen, is
inevitable. Yet he believes that the institution, though infinitely bad for the masters, is better for the slaves than
those of any country in Europe for its working classes. He
is convinced that the tillage of all the crops could be
better carried on by whites, with the assistance of cattle
and implements, than by negroes.

E. writes, (October 1835,) "Certain it is that if men of property and intelligence in the north have that legitimate influence which that class has here, nothing will come of this abolition excitement. All we have to say to them is, 'Hands off!' Our *political* rights* are clear, and shall not be invaded. *We know too much about slavery to be slaves ourselves.* But I repeat, nothing will come of the present, or rather recent excitement, for already it is in a great degree passed. And the time is coming when a struggle between pauperism and property, or, if you choose, between labour and capital in the north, stimulated by the spirit of Jacksonism, will occupy the people of that quarter to the exclusion of our affairs. If any external influence is ever to affect the institution of slavery in the south, it will not be the vulgar and ignorant fanaticism of the northern States, intent upon a cheap charity which is to be done at our expense; but that influence will be found in English literature, and the gradual operation of public opinion. Slavery, so to speak, may be evaporated;—it cannot be drawn off. If it were, the whole land would be poisoned and desolated."

The best reply to this letter will be found in the memora-

* The dispute between the abolitionists and their adversaries is always made to turn on the point of distinction between freedom of discussion and political interference. With the views now entertained by the south, she can never be satisfied on this head. She requires nothing short of a dead silence upon the subject of human rights. This demand is made by her state governors of the state governors of the north. It will, of course, never be granted. The course of the abolitionists seems to themselves clear enough; and they act accordingly. They labour *politically* only with regard to the District of Columbia, over which Congress holds exclusive jurisdiction. Their other endeavour is to promote the discussion of the moral question throughout the free States. They use no direct means to this end in the slave States;—in the first place, because they have no power to do so; and in the next, because the requisite movement there is sure to follow upon that in the north. It is wholly untrue that they insinuate their publications into the south. Their only political transgression (and who will call it a moral one?) is, helping fugitive slaves. The line between free discussion and political interference has never yet been drawn to the satisfaction of both parties, and never will be.

ble speech of Mr. Preston, one of the South Carolina senators, delivered in Congress, last spring.

Mr. Preston's speech describes the spread of abolition
opinions as being rapid and inevitable. He proves the
rapidity by citing the number of recently-formed abolition
societies in the north; and the inevitableness, by exhibiting
the course which such convictions had run in England and
France. He represents the case as desperate. He advises,—
not yielding, but the absolute exclusion of opinion on the
subject,—exclusion from Congress, and exclusion from the
slave States. This is well. The matter may be considered to
be given up, unless this is merely the opinion of an individual. The proposal is about as hopeful as it would be to
draw a cordon round the Capitol to keep out the four
winds; or to build a wall up to the pole-star to exclude
the sunshine.

One more sample of opinions. A gentleman who edits a
highly-esteemed southern newspaper, expresses himself
thus. "There is a wild fanaticism at work to effect the overthrow of the system, although in its fall would go down
the fortunes of the south, and to a great extent those of
the north and east;—in a word, the whole fabric of our
Union, in one awful ruin. What then ought to be done?
What measures ought to be taken to secure the safety of
our property and our lives? We answer, let us be vigilant
and watchful to the last degree over all the movements of
our enemies both at *home* and abroad. Let us declare
through the public journals of our country, that the question of slavery is not, and shall not be open to discussion;
—that the system is deep-rooted amongst us, and must remain for ever;—that the very moment any private individual attempts to lecture us upon its evils and immorality,
and the necessity of putting measures into operation to secure us from them, in the same moment his tongue shall
be cut out and cast upon the dung-hill. We are freemen,
sprung from a noble stock of freemen, able to boast as
noble a line of ancestry as ever graced this earth;—we have
burning in our bosoms the spirit of freemen—live in an age
of enlightened freedom, and in a country blessed with its
privileges—under a government that has pledged itself to

protect us in the enjoyment of our peculiar domestic institutions in peace, and undisturbed. We hope for a long continuance of these high privileges, and have now to love, cherish, and defend, property, liberty, wives and children, the right to manage our own matters in our own way, and, what is equally dear with all the rest, the inestimable right of dying upon our own soil, around our own firesides, in struggling to put down all those who may attempt to infringe, attack, or violate any of these sacred and inestimable privileges."

If these opinions of well-prepared persons, dispersed through the slave States, and entrusted with the public advocacy of their interests, do not betoken that slavery is tottering to its fall, there are no such things as signs of the times.

The prohibition of books containing anything against slavery, has proceeded to a great length. Last year, Mrs. Barbauld's works were sent back into the north by the southern booksellers, because the "Evenings at Home" contain a "Dialogue between Master and Slave." Miss Sedgwick's last novel, "The Linwoods," was treated in the same way, on account of a single sentence about slavery. The "Tales of the Woods and Fields," and other English books, have shared the same fate. I had a letter from a southern lady, containing some regrets upon the necessity of such an exclusion of literature, but urging that it was a matter of *principle* to guard from attacks "an institution ordained by the favour of God for the happiness of man:" and assuring me that the literary resources of South Carolina were rapidly improving.—So they had need; for almost all the books already in existence will have to be prohibited, if nothing condemnatory of slavery is to be circulated. This attempt to nullify literature was followed up by a threat to refuse permission to the mails to pass through South Carolina: an arrangement which would afflict its inhabitants more than it could injure any one else.

The object of all this is to keep the children in the dark about how the institution is regarded abroad. This was evident to me at every step: and I received an express caution not to communicate my disapprobation of slavery to the children of one family, who could not, their parents declare, even feel the force of my objections. One of them was "employed, the whole afternoon, in dressing out little Nancy for an evening party; and she sees the slaves much freer than herself." Of course, the blindness of this policy will be its speedy destruction. It is found that the effect of public opinion on the subject upon young men who visit the northern States, is tremendous, when they become aware of it: as every student in the colleges of the north can bear witness.

The students of Lane Seminary, near Cincinnati, of which Dr. Beecher is the president, became interested in the subject, three or four years ago, and formed themselves into an Abolition Society, debating the question, and taking in newspapers. This was prohibited by the tutors, but persevered in by the young men, who conceived that this was a matter with which the professors had no right to meddle. Banishment was decreed; and all submitted to expulsion but fourteen. Of course, each of the dispersed young men became the nucleus of an Abolition Society, and gained influence by persecution. It was necessary for them to provide means to finish their education. One of them, Amos Dresser, itinerated, (as is usual in the sparsely-peopled west,) travelling in a gig, and selling Scott's Bible, to raise money for his educational purposes. He reached Nashville, in Tennessee; and there fell under suspicion of abolition treason; his baggage being searched, and a whole abolition newspaper, and a part of another being found among the packing-stuff of his stock of bibles. There was also an unsubstantiated rumour of his having been seen conversing with slaves. He was brought to trial by the Committee of Vigilance; seven elders of the presbyterian church at Nashville being among his judges. After much debate as to whether he should be hanged, or flogged with more or fewer lashes, he was condemned to receive twenty lashes, with a cow-hide, in the market-place of Nashville. He was immediately conducted there, made to kneel down on the flint pavement, and punished according to his sentence; the mayor of Nashville presiding, and the public executioner being the agent. He was warned to leave the city within twenty-four hours: but was told, by some charitable person who had the bravery to take him in, wash his stripes, and furnish him with a disguise, that it would not be safe to remain so long. He stole away immediately, in his dreadful condition, on foot; and when his story was authenticated, had heard nothing of his horse, gig, and bibles, which he values at three hundred dollars. Let no one, on this, tremble for republican freedom. Outrages upon it, like the above, are but extremely transient signs of the times. They no more betoken the permanent condition of the republic, than the shivering of one hour of ague exhibits the usual state of the human body.

The other young men found educational and other assistance immediately; and a set of noble institutions has grown out of their persecution. There were professors ready to help them; and a gentleman gave them a farm in Ohio, on which to begin a manual labour college, called the Oberlin Institute. It is on a most liberal plan young women who wish to become qualified for "Christian teaching" being admitted; and there being no prejudice of colour. They have a sprinkling both of Indians and of negroes. They do all the farm and house work, and as much study besides as is good for them. Some of the young women are already fair Hebrew and Greek scholars. In a little while, the estate was so crowded, and the new applications were so overpowering, that they were glad to accept the gift of another farm. When I left the country, within three years from their commencement, they had either four or five flourishing institutions in Ohio and Michigan, while the Lane Seminary drags on feebly with its array of tutors, and dearth of pupils.

Notwithstanding the many symptoms of an unmanly and anti-republican fear which met my observation in these regions, it was long before I could comprehend the extent of it; especially as I heard daily that the true enthusiastic love of freedom could exist in a republic, only in the presence of a servile class. I am persuaded that the southerners verily believe this; that they actually imagine their northern brethren living in an exceedingly humdrum

way, for fear of losing their equality. It is true that there
is far too much subservience to opinion in the northern
States: particularly in New England. There is there a self-
imposed bondage which must be outgrown. But this is no
more like the fear which prevails in the south than the
apprehensiveness of a court-physician is like the terrors of
Tiberius Cæsar.

Wherever I went, in the south, in whatever town or
other settlement I made any stay, some startling circumstance connected with slavery occurred, which I was assured was unprecedented. No such thing had ever occurred
before, or was likely to happen again. The repetition of
this assurance became, at last, quite ludicrous.

The fear of which I have spoken as prevalent, does not
extend to the discussion of the question of slavery with
strangers. My opinions of slavery were known, through the
press, before I went abroad: the hospitality which was
freely extended to me was offered under a full knowledge
of my detestation of the system. This was a great advantage, in as much as it divested me entirely of the character of a spy, and promoted the freest discussion, wherever
I went. There was a warm sympathy between myself and
very many, whose sufferings under the system caused me
continual and deep sorrow, though no surprise. Neither
was I surprised at their differing from me as widely as they
do about the necessity of immediate action, either by re-
sistance or flight, while often agreeing, nearly to the full,
in my estimate of the evils of the present state of things.
They have been brought up in the system. To them, the
moral deformity of the whole is much obscured by its
nearness; while the small advantages, and slight pretti-
nesses which it is very easy to attach to it, are prominent,
and always in view. These circumstances prevented my
being surprised at the candour with which they not only
discussed the question, but showed me all that was to be
seen of the economical management of plantations; the
worst as well as the best. Whatever I learned of the system, by express showing, it must be remembered, was
from the hands of the slave-holders themselves. Whatever
I learned, that lies deepest down in my heart, of the moral

evils, the unspeakable vices and woes of slavery, was from the lips of those who are suffering under them on the spot.

There was an outcry, very vehement, and very general among the friends of slavery, in both north and south, against the cruelty of abolitionists in becoming the occasion of the laws against slaves being made more severe. In my opinion, this affords no argument against abolition, even if the condition of the slaves of to-day were aggravated by the stir of opinion. The negroes of the next generation are not to be doomed to slavery for fear of somewhat more being inflicted on their parents: and, severe as the laws already are, the consequence of straining them tighter still would be that they would burst. But the fact is, that so far from the condition of the slave being made worse by the efforts of his distant friends, it has been substantially improved. I could speak confidently of this as a necessary consequence of the value set upon opinion by the masters; but I know it also from what I myself saw; and from the lips of many slave-holders. The slaves of South Carolina, Georgia, Alabama, and Louisiana, have less liberty of communication with each other; they are deprived of the few means of instruction that they had; they are shut in earlier in the evening, and precluded from supping and dancing for half the night, as they used to do; but they are substantially better treated; they are less worked by hard masters; less flogged; better fed and clothed. The eyes of the world are now upon the American slave and his master: the kind master goes on as he did before: the hard master dares not be so unkind as formerly. He hates his slave more than ever, for slavery is more troublesome than ever; but he is kept in order, by the opinion of the world abroad and the neighbours around; and he dares not vent his hatred on his human property, as he once could.

The word 'hatred' is not too strong for the feeling of a large proportion of slave-holders towards particular slaves; or, as they would call them, (the word 'slave' never being heard in the south,) their 'force,' their 'hands,' their 'negroes,' their 'people.' I was frequently told of the 'endearing relation' subsisting between master and slaves; but,

at the best, it appeared to me the same 'endearing relation'
which subsists between a man and his horse, between a
lady and her dog. As long as the slave remains ignorant,
docile, and contented, he is taken good care of, humoured,
and spoken of with a contemptuous, compassionate kindness. But, from the moment he exhibits the attributes of a
rational being,—from the moment his intellect seems likely
to come into the most distant competition with that of
whites, the most deadly hatred springs up;—not in the
black, but in his oppressors. It is a very old truth that we
hate those whom we have injured. Never was it more clear
than in this case. I had, from time to time in my life, witnessed something of human malice; I had seen some of
the worst aspects of domestic service in England; of village
scandal; of political rivalship; and other circumstances pro-
vocative of the worst passions; but pure, unmitigated hatred, the expression of which in eye and voice makes one's
blood run cold, I never witnessed till I became acquainted
with the blacks of America, their friends and oppressors:
the blacks and their friends the objects; their oppressors
the far more unhappy subjects. It so happens that the most
remarkable instances of this that I met with were clergymen and ladies. The cold livid hatred which deformed,
like a mask, the faces of a few, while deliberately slander-
ing, now the coloured race, and now the abolitionists, could
never be forgotten by me, as a fearful revelation, if the
whole country were to be absolutely christianized to-morrow. Mr. Madison told me, that if he could work a miracle,
he knew what it should be. He would make all the blacks
white; and then he could do away with slavery in twenty-
four hours. So true it is that all the torturing associations of
injury have become so connected with colour, that an institution which hurts everybody and benefits none, which
all rational people who understand it dislike, despise, and
suffer under, can with difficulty be abolished, because of
the hatred which is borne to an irremovable badge.

This hatred is a sign of the times; and so are the alleged
causes of it; both are from their nature so manifestly temporary. The principal cause alleged is the impossibility of
giving people of colour any idea of duty, from their want

of natural affection. I was told in the same breath of their attachment to their masters, and devotion to them in sickness; and of their utter want of all affection to their parents and children, husbands and wives. For "people of colour," read "slaves," and the account is often correct. It is true that slaves will often leave their infants to perish, rather than take any trouble about them; that they will utterly neglect a sick parent or husband; while they will nurse a white mistress with much ostentation. The reason is obvious. Such beings are degraded so far below humanity that they will take trouble, for the sake of praise or more solid reward, after they have become dead to all but grossly selfish inducements. Circumstances will fully account for a great number of cases of this sort: but to set against these, there are perhaps yet more instances of domestic devotion, not to be surpassed in the annals of humanity. Of these I know more than I can here set down; partly from their number, and partly from the fear of exposing to injury the individuals alluded to.

At a very disorderly hotel in South Carolina, we were waited upon by a beautiful mulatto woman and her child, a pretty girl of about eight. The woman entreated that we would buy her child. On her being questioned, it appeared that it was "a bad place" in which she was: that she had got her two older children sold away, to a better place; and now, her only wish was for this child to be saved. On being asked whether she really desired to be parted from her only remaining child, so as never to see her again, she replied that "it would be hard to part," but for the child's sake she did wish that we would buy her.

Their whole notion of religion is of power and show, as regards God; of subjection to a new sort of reward and punishment, as regards themselves; and invisible reward and punishment have no effect on them. A negro, conducting worship, was heard to pray thus; and broad as the expressions are, they are better than an abject, unintelligent adoption of the devotional language of whites. "Come down, O Lord, come down,—on your great white horse, a kickin' and snortin'." An ordinary negro's highest idea of majesty is of riding a prancing white horse. As for their own concern in religion, I know of a "force" where a preacher had just made a strong impression. The slaves had given up dancing, and sang nothing but psalms: they exhibited the most ludicrous spiritual pride, and discharged their business more lazily than ever, taunting their mistress with, "You no holy. We be holy. You no in state o' salvation." Such was the effect upon the majority.

Such is the effect of religion upon those who have no rights, and therefore no duties. Great efforts are being now made by the clergy of four denominations* to obtain converts in the south. The fact, pointed out to me by Mr. Madison, that the "chivalrous" south is growing strict, while the puritanic north is growing genial, is a very remarkable sign of the times, as it regards slavery. All sanctions of the institution being now wanted, religious sanctions are invoked among others. The scene has been acted before, often enough to make the catastrophe clearly discernible. There are no true religious sanctions of slavery. Though I found that the divines of the four denominations were teaching a compromising Christianity, to propitiate the masters, and gross superstitions to beguile the slaves, —vying with each other in the latter respect, that they might outstrip one another in the number of their converts, —I rejoiced in their work. Anything is better for the slaves than apathetic subjection; and, under all this falsification, enough Christian truth has already come in to blow slavery to atoms.

The testimony of slave-holders was most explicit as to no moral improvement having taken place, in consequence of the introduction of religion. There was less singing and dancing; but as much lying, drinking, and stealing as ever: less docility, and a vanity even transcending the common vanity of slaves,—to whom the opinion of others is all which they have to gain or lose. The houses are as dirty as ever, (and I never saw a clean room or bed but once, within the boundaries of the slave States;) the family are still contented with their "clean linen, as long as it does not smell badly." A new set of images has been presented to the

* Presbyterians, Episcopalians, Methodists and Baptists.

slaves; but there still remains but one idea, by and for which any of them live; the idea of freedom.

The rapid increase of the suffrage in the north, compared with the south, affords an indication of some speedy change of circumstances. Three fifths of the slave population is represented; but this basis of representation is so narrow in contrast with that of the populous States where every man has the suffrage, that the south must decrease and the north increase, in a way which cannot long be borne by the former. The south has no remedy but in abolishing the institution by which her prosperity is injured, and her population comparatively confined. It will be long before white labour becomes so reputable there as elsewhere; and the present white residents cannot endure the idea of the suffrage being freely given, within any assignable time, to those who are now their slaves, or to their dusky descendants. It is in contemplation of this difficulty that the loudest threats are heard of secession from the Union; a movement which, as I have before said, would be immediately prevented, or signally punished. The abolition of slavery is the only resource.

How stands the case, finally?—A large proportion of the labour of the United States is held on principles wholly irreconcilable with the principles of the constitution: whatever may be true about its origin, it is now inefficient, wasteful, destructive, to a degree which must soon cause a change of plan: some who see the necessity of such a change, are in favour of reversing the original policy;—slavery having once been begun in order to till the land, they are now for usurping a new territory in order to employ their slaves: others are for banishing the labour which is the one thing most needful to their country, in every way. While all this confusion and mismanagement exist, here is the labour, actually on the land, ready to be employed to better purpose; and in the treasury are the funds by which the transmutation of slave into free labour might be effected,—at once in the District of Columbia; and by subsequent arrangements in the slave States. Many matters of detail would have to be settled: the distribution would be difficult; but it is not impossible. Virginia, whose revenue is derived from the rearing of slaves for the south, whose property is the beings themselves, and not their labour, must, in justice, receive a larger compensation than such States as Alabama and Louisiana, where the labour is the wealth, and which would be therefore immediately enriched by the improvement in the quality of the labour which would follow upon emancipation. Such arrangements may be difficult to make; but "when there's a will there's a way;" and when it is generally perceived that the abolition of slavery must take place, the great principle will not long be allowed to lie in fetters of detail. The Americans have done more difficult things than this; though assuredly none greater. The restoration of two millions and a half of people to their human rights will be as great a deed as the history of the world will probably ever have to exhibit. In none of its pages are there names more lustrous than those of the clear-eyed and fiery-hearted few who began and are achieving the virtuous revolution.

VII. Morals of Economy

"And yet of your strength there is and can be no clear feeling, save by what you have prospered in, by what you have done. Between vague, wavering capability, and fixed, indubitable performance, what a difference! A certain inarticulate self-consciousness dwells dimly in us; which only our works can render articulate, and decisively discernible. Our works are the mirror wherein the spirit first sees its natural lineaments. Hence, too, the folly of that impossible precept 'know thyself,' till it be translated into this partially possible one, 'know what thou canst work at.'"

Sartor Resartus, p. 166. *Boston Edition*

THE glory of the world passeth away. One kind of worldly glory passes away, and another comes. Like a series of clouds sailing by the moon, and growing dim and dimmer as they go down the sky, are the transitory glories which are only brightened for an age by man's smile: dark vapours, which carry no light within themselves. How many such have floated across the expanse of history, and melted away! It was once a glory to have a power of life and death over a patriarchal family: and how mean does this now appear, in comparison with the power of life and death which every man has over his own intellect.

It was once a glory to be idle, and a shame to work,— at least with any member or organ but one,—the brain. Those who have been able to get through life with the least possible work have been treated as the happiest: those who have had the largest share imposed upon them have been passively pitied as the most miserable. If the half-starved artisan, if the negro slave, could, when lying down at length to rest, see and exhibit the full vision of their own lives, they would complain far less of too much work than of too little freedom, too little knowledge, too many wounds through their affections to their children, their brethren, their race.

Mankind becomes more clear-sighted as time unfolds the sequence of his hieroglyphic scroll; and a transition in the morals and manners of nations is an inevitable consequence, slow as men are in deciphering the picture-writing of the old teacher; unapt as men are in connecting picture with picture, so as to draw thence a truth, and in the truth, a prophecy. We must look to new or renovated communities to see how much has been really learned.

The savage chief, who has never heard the saying "he that would be chief among you, let him be your servant," feels himself covered with glory when he paces along in his saddle, gorgeous with wampum and feathers, while his squaw follows in the dust, bending under the weight of his shelter, his food, and his children. Wise men look upon him with all pity and no envy. Higher and higher in society, the right of the strongest is supposed to involve honour: and physical is placed above moral strength. The work of the limbs, wholly repulsive when separated from that of the head, is devolved upon the weaker, who cannot resist; and hence arises the disgrace of work, and the honour of being able to keep soul and body together, more or less luxuriously, without it. The barbaric conqueror makes his captives work for him. His descendants, who have no prisoners of war to make slaves of, carry off captives of a helpless nation, inferior even to themselves in civilisation. The servile class rises, by almost imperceptible degrees, as the dawn of reason brightens towards day. The classes by whom the hand-work of society is done, arrive at being cared for by those who do the head-work, or no work at all: then they are legislated for, but still as a common or inferior class, favoured, out of pure bounty, with laws, as with soup, which are pronounced "excellent for the poor:" then they begin to open their minds upon legislation for themselves; and a certain lip-honour is paid them, which would be rejected as insult if offered to those who nevertheless think themselves highly meritorious in vouchsafing it.

This is the critical period out of which must arise a new organisation of society. When it comes to this, a new promise blossoms under the feet of the lovers of truth. There are many of the hand-workers now who are on the very borders of the domain of head-work: and, as the encroachments of those who work not at all have, by this time, become seriously injurious to the rights of others, there are many thinkers and persons of learning who are driven over the line, and become hand-workers. There is no drowning the epithalamium with which these two classes celebrate the union of thought and handicraft. Multitudes press in, or are carried in to the marriage feast, and a new era of society has begun.

If the organisation of its society were a matter of will; if it had a disposable moral force, applicable to controllable circumstances, it is probable that the new nation would take after all old nations, and not dare to make, perhaps not dream of making, the explicit avowal, that that which had ever hitherto been a disgrace, except in the eyes of a very few prophets, had now come out to be a clear honour. Moral persuasions grow out of preceding circumstances, as institutions do; and conviction is not communicable where the evidence is not of a communicable kind. The advantage of the new nation over the old will be no more than that its individual members are more open to conviction, from being more accessible to evidence, less burdened with antique forms and institutions, and partial privileges, so called. The result will probably be that some members of the new society will follow the ancient fashion of considering work a humiliation; while, upon the whole, labour will be more honoured than it has ever been before.

America is in the singular position of being nearly equally divided between a low degree of the ancient bar-

barism in relation to labour, and a high degree of the
modern enlightenment. Wherever there is a servile class,
work is considered a disgrace, unless it bears some other
name, and is of an exclusive character. In the free States,
labour is more really and heartily honoured than, perhaps,
in any other part of the civilised world. The most extraordinary, and least pleasant circumstance in the case is that,
while the south ridicules and despises the north for what
is its very highest honour, the north feels somewhat uneasy
and sore under the contempt.

How do the two parties in reality spend their days?

In the north, the children all go to school, and work
there, more or less. As they grow up, they part off into
the greatest variety of employments. The youths must,
without exception, work hard; or they had better drown
themselves. Whether they are to be lawyers, or otherwise
professional; or merchants, manufacturers, farmers, or citizens, they have everything to do for themselves. A very
large proportion of them have, while learning their future
business, to earn the means of learning. There is much
manual labour in the country colleges; much teaching in
the vacations done by students. Many a great man in Congress was seen in his boyhood leading his father's horses
to water; and, in his youth, guiding the plough in his father's field. There is probably hardly a man in New England who cannot ride, drive, and tend his own horse.

There are a few young men, esteemed the least happy
members of the community, who inherit wealth. The time
will come, when the society is somewhat older, when it
will be understood that wealth need not preclude work:
but at present, there are no individuals so forlorn, in the
northern States, as young men of fortune. Men who have
shown energy and skill in working their way in society
are preferred for political representatives: there is no scientific or literary class, for such individuals to fall into:
all the world is busy around them, and they are reduced
to the predicament, unhappily the most dreaded of all in
the United States, of standing alone.

As for the women of the northern States, most have the
blessing of work, though not of the extent and variety

which will hereafter be seen to be necessary for the happiness of their lives. All married women, except the ladies of rich merchants and others, are liable to have their hands full of household occupation, from the uncertainty of domestic service; a topic to be referred to hereafter. Women who do not marry have, in many instances, to work for their support; and, as will be shown in another connexion, under peculiar disadvantages. Work, on the whole, may be considered the rule, and vacuity the exception.

What is life in the slave States, in respect of work?

There are two classes, the servile and the imperious, between whom there is a great gulf fixed. The servile class has not even the benefit of hearty toil. No solemn truths sink down into them, to cheer their hearts, stimulate their minds, and nerve their hands. Their wretched lives are passed between an utter debasement of the will, and a conflict of the will with external force.

The other class is in circumstances as unfavourable as the least happy order of persons in the old world. The means of educating children are so meagre that young people begin life under great disadvantages. The vicious fundamental principle of morals in a slave country, that labour is disgraceful, taints the infant mind with a stain which is as fatal in the world of spirits as the negro tinge is at present in the world of society. It made my heart ache to hear the little children unconsciously uttering thoughts with which no true religion, no true philosophy can coexist. "Do you think I shall work?" "O, you must not touch the poker here." "You must not do this or that for yourself: the negroes will be offended, and it won't do for a lady to do so." "Poor thing! she has to teach: if she had come here, she might have married a rich man, perhaps." "Mamma has so much a-year now, so we have not to do our work at home, or any trouble. 'Tis such a comfort!"— When children at school call everything that pleases them "gentlemanly," and pity all (but slaves) who have to work, and talk of marrying early for an establishment, it is all over with them. A more hopeless state of degradation can hardly be conceived of, however they may ride, and play the harp, and sing Italian, and teach their slaves what they call religion.

"Poor things!" may be said of such, in return. They know little, with their horror of work, of what awaits them. Theirs is destined to be, if their wish of an establishment is fulfilled, a life of toil, irksome and unhonoured. They escape the name; but they are doomed to undergo the worst of the reality. Their husbands are not to be envied, though they do ride on white horses, (the slave's highest conception of bliss,) lie down to repose in hot weather, and spend their hours between the discharge of hospitality and the superintendence of their estates; and the highly honourable and laborious charge of public affairs. But the wives of slave-holders are, as they and their husbands declare, as much slaves as their negroes. If they will not have everything go to rack and ruin around them, they must superintend every household operation, from the cellar to the garrets: for there is nothing that slaves can do well. While the slaves are perpetually at one's heels, lolling against the bed-posts before one rises in the morning, standing behind the chairs, leaning on the sofa, officiously undertaking, and invariably spoiling everything that one had rather do for one's-self, the smallest possible amount of real service is performed. The lady of the house carries her huge bunch of keys, (for every consumable thing must be locked up,) and has to give out, on incessant requests, whatever is wanted for the household. She is for ever superintending, and trying to keep things straight, without the slightest hope of attaining anything like leisure and comfort. What is there in retinue, in the reputation of ease and luxury, which can compensate for toils and cares of this nature?

Some few of these ladies are among the strongest-minded and most remarkable women I have ever known. There are great draw-backs, (as will be seen hereafter,) but their mental vigour is occasionally proportioned to their responsibility. Women who have to rule over a barbarous society, (small though it be,) to make and enforce laws, provide for all the physical wants, and regulate the entire habits of a number of persons who can in no respect take care of themselves, must be strong and strongly disciplined, if they in any degree discharge this duty. Those who shrink from it become perhaps the weakest women I have anywhere seen: selfishly timid, humblingly dependent, languid in body, and with minds of no reach at all. These two extremes are found in the slave States, in the most striking opposition.

There are a few unhappy persons in the slave States, too few, I believe, to be called a class, who strongly exemplify the consequences of such a principle of morals as that work is a disgrace. There are a few, called by the slaves "mean whites;" signifying whites who work with the hands. Where there is a coloured servile class, whose colour has become a disgrace through their servitude, two results are inevitable: that those who have the colour without the servitude are disgraced among the whites; and those who have the servitude without the colour are as deeply disgraced among the coloured. More intensely than white work-people are looked down upon at Port-au-Prince, are the "mean whites" despised by the slaves of the Carolinas. They make the most, of course, of the only opportunity they can ever have of doing what they see their superiors do,—despising their fellow-creatures. No inducement would be sufficient to bring honest, independent men into the constant presence of double-distilled hatred and contempt like this; and the general character of the "mean whites" may therefore be anticipated. They are usually men who have no prospect, no chance elsewhere; the lowest of the low.

MORALS OF SLAVERY

THIS title is not written down in a spirit of mockery; though there appears to be a mockery somewhere, when we contrast slavery with the principles and the rule which are the test of all American institutions:—the principles that all men are born free and equal; that rulers derive their just powers from the consent of the governed; and the rule of reciprocal justice. This discrepancy between principles and practice needs no more words. But the institution of slavery exists; and what we have to see is what the morals are of the society which is subject to it.

What social virtues are possible in a society of which injustice is the primary characteristic? in a society which is divided into two classes, the servile and the imperious?

The most obvious is Mercy. Nowhere, perhaps, can more touching exercises of mercy be seen than here. It must be remembered that the greater number of slave-holders have no other idea than of holding slaves. Their fathers did it: they themselves have never known the coloured race treated otherwise than as inferior beings, born to work for and to teaze the whites; helpless, improvident, open to no higher inducements than indulgence and praise; capable of nothing but entire dependence. The good affections of slave-holders like these show themselves in the form of mercy; which is as beautiful to witness as mercy, made a substitute for justice, can ever be. I saw endless manifestations of mercy, as well as of its opposite. The thoughtfulness of masters, mistresses, and their children about, not only the comforts, but the indulgences of their slaves, was a frequent subject of admiration with me. Kind masters are liberal in the expenditure of money, and (what is better) of thought, in gratifying the whims and fancies of their negroes. They make large sacrifices occasionally for the social or domestic advantage of their people; and use great forbearance in the exercise of the power conferred upon them by law and custom.

Nothing struck me more than the patience of slave-owners. In this virtue they probably surpass the whole christian world;—I mean in their patience with their slaves; for one cannot much praise their patience with the abolitionists, or with the tariff; or in some other cases of political vexation. When I considered how they love to be called "fiery southerners," I could not but marvel at their mild forbearance under the hourly provocations to which they are liable in their homes. It is found that such a degree of this virtue can be obtained only by long habit. Persons from New England, France, or England, becoming slave-holders, are found to be the most severe masters and mistresses, however good their tempers may always have appeared previously. They cannot, like the native proprietor, sit waiting half an hour for the second course, or see everything done in the worst possible manner; their rooms dirty, their property wasted, their plans frustrated, their infants slighted, themselves deluded by artifices,—they cannot, like the native proprietor, endure all this unruffled. It seems to me that every slave-holder's temper is subjected to a discipline which must either ruin or perfect it. While we know that many tempers are thus ruined, and must mourn for the unhappy creatures who cannot escape from their tyranny, it is evident, on the other hand, that many tempers are to be met with which should shame down and silence for ever the irritability of some whose daily life is passed under circumstances of comparative ease.

This mercy, indulgence, patience, was often pleaded to me in defence of the system, or in aggravation of the faults of intractable slaves. The fallacy of this is so gross as not to need exposure anywhere but on the spot. I was heart-sick of being told of the ingratitude of slaves, and weary of explaining that indulgence can never atone for injury: that the extremest pampering, for a life-time, is no equivalent for rights withheld, no reparation for irreparable injustice. What are the greatest possible amounts of finery, sweetmeats, dances, gratuities, and kind words and looks, in exchange for political, social, and domestic existence? for body and spirit? Is it not true that the life is more than meat, and the body than raiment?

This fallacious plea was urged upon me by three different persons, esteemed enlightened and religious, in relation to one case. The case was this. A lady of fortune carried into her husband's establishment, when she married, several slaves, and among them a girl two years younger than herself, who had been brought up under her, and who was employed as her own maid. The little slaves are accustomed to play freely with the children of the family—a practice which was lauded to me, but which never had any beauty in my eyes, seeing, as I did, the injury to the white children from unrestricted intercourse with the degraded race, and looking forward as I did to the time when they must separate into the servile and imperious. Mrs. —— had been unusually indulgent to this girl, having allowed her time and opportunity for religious and other instruction, and favoured her in every way. One night, when the girl was undressing her, the lady expressed her fondness for her, and said, among other things: "When I die you shall be free;"—a dangerous thing to say to a slave only two years younger than herself. In a short time the lady was taken ill,—with a strange, mysterious illness, which no doctor could alleviate. One of her friends, who suspected foul play, took the sufferer entirely under her own charge, when she seemed to be dying. She revived; and as soon as she was well enough to have a will of her own again, would be waited on by no one but her favourite slave. She grew worse. She alternated thus, for some time, according as she was under the care of this slave or of her friend. At last, the friend excluded from her chamber every one but the physicians: took in the medicines at the room door from the hands of the slave, and locked them up. They were all analysed by a physician, and arsenic found in every one of them. The lady partially recovered; but I was shocked at the traces of suffering in her whole appearance. The girl's guilt was brought clearly home to her. There never was a case of more cruel, deliberate intention to murder. If ever slave deserved the gallows, (which ought to be questionable to the most decided minds,) this girl did. What was done? The lady was tender-hearted, and could not bear to have her hanged. This was natural enough; but what did she therefore do? keep her under her own eye, that she might at least poison nobody else, and perhaps be touched and reclaimed by the clemency of the person she would have murdered? No. The lady sold her.

I was actually called upon to admire the lady's conduct; and was asked whether the ingratitude of the girl was not inconceivable, and her hypocrisy too; for she used to lecture her mistress and her mistress's friends for being so irreligious as to go to parties on Saturday nights, when they should have been preparing their minds for Sunday. Was not the hypocrisy of the girl inconceivable? and her ingratitude for her mistress's favours? No. The girl had no other idea of religion,—could have no other than that it consists in observances, and, wicked as she was, her wickedness could not be called ingratitude, for she was more injured than favoured, after all. All indulgences that could be heaped upon her were still less than her due, and her mistress remained infinitely her debtor.

Little can be said of the purity of manners of the whites of the south; but there is purity. Some few examples of domestic fidelity may be found: few enough, by the confession of residents on the spot; but those individuals who have resisted the contagion of the vice amidst which they dwell are pure. Every man who resides on his plantation may have his harem, and has every inducement of custom, and of pecuniary gain,* to tempt him to the common practice. Those who, notwithstanding, keep their homes undefiled may be considered as of incorruptible purity.

Here, alas! ends my catalogue of the virtues which are of possible exercise by slave-holders towards their labourers. The inherent injustice of the system extinguishes all others, and nourishes a whole harvest of false morals towards the rest of society.

The personal oppression of the negroes is the grossest vice which strikes a stranger in the country. It can never be otherwise when human beings are wholly subjected to the will of other human beings, who are under no other external control than the law which forbids killing and maiming;—a law which it is difficult to enforce in individual cases. A fine slave was walking about in Columbia, South Carolina, when I was there, nearly helpless and useless from the following causes. His master was fond of him, and the slave enjoyed the rare distinction of never having been flogged. One day, his master's child, supposed to be under his care at the time, fell down and hurt itself. The master flew into a passion, ordered the slave to be instantly flogged, and would not hear a single word the man had to say. As soon as the flogging was over, the slave went into the back yard, where there was an axe and a block, and

* The law declares that the children of slaves are to follow the fortunes of the mother. Hence the practice of planters selling and bequeathing their own children.

struck off the upper half of his right hand. He went and held up the bleeding hand before his master, saying, "You have mortified me, so I have made myself useless. Now you must maintain me as long as I live." It came out that the child had been under the charge of another person.

There are, as is well known throughout the country, houses in the free States which are open to fugitive slaves, and where they are concealed till the search for them is over. I know some of the secrets of such places; and can mention two cases, among many, of runaways, which show how horrible is the tyranny which the slave system authorises men to inflict on each other. A negro had found his way to one of these friendly houses; and had been so skilfully concealed, that repeated searches by his master, (who had followed for the purpose of recovering him,) and by constables, had been in vain. After three weeks of this seclusion, the negro became weary, and entreated of his host to be permitted to look out of the window. His host strongly advised him to keep quiet, as it was pretty certain that his master had not given him up. When the host had left him, however, the negro came out of his hiding-place, and went to the window. He met the eye of his master, who was looking up from the street. The poor slave was obliged to return to his bondage.

A young negress had escaped in like manner; was in like manner concealed; and was alarmed by constables, under the direction of her master, entering the house in pursuit of her, when she had had reason to believe that the search was over. She flew up stairs to her chamber in the third story, and drove a heavy article of furniture against the door. The constables pushed in, notwithstanding, and the girl leaped from the window into the paved street. Her master looked at her as she lay, declared she would never be good for anything again, and went back into the south. The poor creature, her body bruised, and her limbs fractured, was taken up, and kindly nursed; and she is now maintained in Boston, in her maimed condition, by the charity of some ladies there.

It is a common boast in the south that there is less vice in their cities than in those of the north. This can never, as a matter of fact, have been ascertained; as the proceedings of slave households are, or may be, a secret: and in the north, what licentiousness there is may be detected. But such comparisons are bad. Let any one look at the positive licentiousness of the south, and declare if, in such a state of society, there can be any security for domestic purity and peace. The Quadroon connexions in New Orleans are all but universal, as I was assured on the spot by ladies who cannot be mistaken. The history of such connexions is a melancholy one: but it ought to be made known while there are any who boast of the superior morals of New Orleans, on account of the decent quietness of the streets and theatres.

The Quadroon girls of New Orleans are brought up by their mothers to be what they have been; the mistresses of white gentlemen. The boys are some of them sent to France; some placed on land in the back of the State; and some are sold in the slave-market. They marry women of a somewhat darker colour than their own; the women of their own colour objecting to them, "ils sont si dégoutants!" The girls are highly educated, externally, and are, probably, as beautiful and accomplished a set of women as can be found. Every young man early selects one, and establishes her in one of those pretty and peculiar houses, whole rows of which may be seen in the Remparts. The connexion now and then lasts for life: usually for several years. In the latter case, when the time comes for the gentleman to take a white wife, the dreadful news reaches his Quadroon partner, either by a letter entitling her to call the house and furniture her own, or by the newspaper which announces his marriage. The Quadroon ladies are rarely or never known to form a second connexion. Many commit suicide: more die broken-hearted. Some men continue the connexion after marriage. Every Quadroon woman believes that her partner will prove an exception to the rule of desertion. Every white lady believes that her husband has been an exception to the rule of seduction.

What security for domestic purity and peace there can be where every man has had two connexions, one of which must be concealed; and two families, whose existence must not be known to each other; where the conjugal relation begins in treachery, and must be carried on with a heavy secret in the husband's breast, no words are needed to explain. If this is the system which is boasted of as a purer than ordinary state of morals, what is to be thought of the ordinary state? It can only be hoped that the boast is an empty one.

There is no occasion to explain the management of the female slaves on estates where the object is to rear as many as possible, like stock, for the southern market: nor to point out the boundless licentiousness caused by the practice: a practice which wrung from the wife of a planter, in the bitterness of her heart, the declaration that a planter's wife was only "the chief slave of the harem." Mr. Madison avowed that the licentiousness of Virginian plantations stopped just short of destruction; and that it was understood that the female slaves were to become mothers at fifteen.

A gentleman of the highest character, a southern planter, observed, in conversation with a friend, that little was known, out of bounds, of the reasons of the new laws by which emancipation was made so difficult as it is. He said that the very general connexion of white gentlemen with their female slaves introduced a mulatto race whose numbers would become dangerous, if the affections of their white parents were permitted to render them free. The liberty of emancipating them was therefore abolished, while that of selling them remained. There are persons who weakly trust to the force of the parental affection for putting an end to slavery, when the amalgamation of the races shall have gone so far as to involve a sufficient number! I actually heard this from the lips of a clergyman in the south. Yet these planters, who sell their own offspring to fill their purses, who have such offspring for the sake of filling their purses, dare to raise the cry of "amalgamation" against the abolitionists of the north, not one of whom has, as far as evidence can show, conceived the idea of a mixture of the races. It is from the south, where this mixture is hourly encouraged, that the canting and groundless reproach has come. I met with no candid southerner who was not full of shame at the monstrous hypocrisy.

It is well known that the most savage violences that are now heard of in the world take place in the southern and western States of America. Burning alive, cutting the heart out, and sticking it on the point of a knife, and other such diabolical deeds, the result of the deepest hatred of which the human heart is capable, are heard of only there. The frequency of such deeds is a matter of dispute, which time will settle.* The existence of such deeds is a matter of no dispute. Whether two or twenty such deeds take place in a year, their perpetration testifies to the existence of such hatred as alone could prompt them. There is no doubt in my mind as to the immediate causes of such outrages. They arise out of the licentiousness of manners. The negro is exasperated by being deprived of his wife,—by being sent out of the way that his master may take possession of his home. He stabs his master; or, if he cannot fulfil his desire of vengeance, he is a dangerous person, an object of vengeance in return, and destined to some cruel fate. If the negro attempts to retaliate, and defile the master's home, the faggots are set alight about him. Much that is dreadful ensues from the negro being subject to toil and the lash: but I am confident that the licentiousness of the masters is the proximate cause of society in the south and south-west being in such a state that nothing else is to be looked for than its being dissolved into its elements, if man does not soon cease to be called the property of man. This dissolution will never take place through the insurrection of the negroes; but by the natural operation of vice. But the process of demoralisation will be stopped, I have no doubt, before it reaches that point. There is no reason to apprehend serious insurrection; for the negroes are too degraded to act in concert, or to stand firm before the terrible face of the white man. Like all deeply-injured classes of persons, they are desperate and cruel, on occasion, kindly as their nature is; but as a class, they have no courage.

* I knew of the death of four men by summary burning alive, within thirteen months of my residence in the United States.

The voice of a white, even of a lady, if it were authoritative, would make a whole regiment of rebellious slaves throw down their arms and flee. Poison is the weapon that suits them best: then the knife, in moments of exasperation. They will never take the field, unless led on by free blacks. Desperate as the state of society is, it will be rectified, probably, without bloodshed.

It may be said that it is doing an injustice to cite extreme cases of vice as indications of the state of society. I do not think so, as long as such cases are so common as to strike the observation of a mere passing stranger; to say nothing of their incompatibility with a decent and orderly fulfilment of the social relations. Let us, however, see what is the very best state of things. Let us take the words and deeds of some of the most religious, refined, and amiable members of society. It was this aspect of affairs which grieved me more, if possible, than the stormier one which I have presented. The coarsening and hardening of mind and manners among the best; the blunting of the moral sense among the most conscientious, gave me more pain than the stabbing, poisoning, and burning. A few examples which will need no comment, will suffice.

Two ladies, the distinguishing ornaments of a very superior society in the south, are truly unhappy about slavery, and opened their hearts freely to me upon the grief which it caused them,—the perfect curse which they found it. They need no enlightening on this, nor any stimulus to acquit themselves as well as their unhappy circumstances allow. They one day pressed me for a declaration of what I should do in their situation. I replied that I would give up everything, go away with my slaves, settle them, and stay by them in some free place. I had said, among other things, that I dare not stay there,—on my own account,—from moral considerations. "What, not if you had no slaves?" "No." "Why?" "I could not trust myself to live where I must constantly witness the exercise of irresponsible power." They made no reply at the moment: but each found occasion to tell me, some days afterwards, that she had been struck to the heart by these words: the consideration I mentioned having never occurred to her before!

Madame Lalaurie, the person who was mobbed at New Orleans, on account of her fiendish cruelty to her slaves,—a cruelty so excessive as to compel the belief that she was mentally deranged, though her derangement could have taken such a direction nowhere but in a slave country;—this person was described to me as having been "very pleasant to whites."

A common question put to me by amiable ladies was, "Do not you find the slaves generally very happy?" They never seemed to have been asked, or to have asked themselves, the question with which I replied:—"Would you be happy with their means?"

One sultry morning, I was sitting with a friend, who was giving me all manner of information about her husband's slaves, both in the field and house; how she fed and clothed them; what indulgences they were allowed; what their respective capabilities were; and so forth. While we were talking, one of the house-slaves passed us. I observed that she appeared superior to all the rest; to which my friend assented. "She is A.'s wife?" said I. "We call her A.'s wife, but she has never been married to him. A. and she came to my husband, five years ago, and asked him to let them marry: but he could not allow it, because he had not made up his mind whether to sell A.; and he hates parting husband and wife." "How many children have they?" "Four." "And they are not married yet?" "No; my husband has never been able to let them marry. He certainly will not sell her: and he has not determined yet whether he shall sell A."

A southern lady, of fair reputation for refinement and cultivation, told the following story in the hearing of a company, among whom were some friends of mine. She spoke with obvious unconsciousness that she was saying anything remarkable: indeed such unconsciousness was proved by her telling the story at all. She had possessed a very pretty mulatto girl, of whom she declared herself fond. A young man came to stay at her house, and fell in love with the girl. "She came to me," said the lady, "for protection; which I gave her." The young man went away, but after some weeks, returned, saying he was so much in love with the girl that he could not live without her. "I pitied the young man," concluded the lady; "so I sold the girl to him for 1,500 dollars."

I repeatedly heard the preaching of a remarkably liberal man, of a free and kindly spirit, in the south. His last sermon, extempore, was from the text "Cast all your care upon him, for He careth for you." The preacher told us, among other things, that God cares for all,—for the meanest as well as the mightiest. "He cares for that coloured person," said he, pointing to the gallery where the people of colour sit,—"he cares for that coloured person as well as for the wisest and best of you whites." This was the most wanton insult I had ever seen offered to a human being; and it was with difficulty that I refrained from walking out of the church. Yet no one present to whom I afterwards spoke of it seemed able to comprehend the wrong. "Well!" said they: "does not God care for the coloured people?"

Of course, in a society where things like these are said and done by its choicest members, there is a prevalent unconsciousness of the existing wrong. The daily and hourly plea is of good intentions towards the slaves; of innocence under the aspersions of foreigners. They are as sincere in the belief that they are injured as their visitors are cordial in their detestation of the morals of slavery. Such unconsciousness of the milder degrees of impurity and injustice as enables ladies and clergymen of the highest character to speak and act as I have related, is a sufficient evidence of the prevalent grossness of morals. One remarkable indication of such blindness was the almost universal mention of the state of the Irish to me, as a worse case than American slavery. I never attempted, of course, to vindicate the state of Ireland: but I was surprised to find no one able, till put in the way, to see the distinction between political misgovernment and personal slavery: between exasperating a people by political insult, and possessing them, like brutes, for pecuniary profit. The unconsciousness of guilt is the worst of symptoms, where there are means of light to be had.

The degradation of the women is so obvious a consequence of the evils disclosed above, that the painful subject need not be enlarged on. By the degradation of women, I do not mean to imply any doubt of the purity of their manners. There are reasons, plain enough to the observer, why their manners should be even peculiarly pure. They are all married young, from their being out-numbered by the other sex: and there is ever present an unfortunate servile class of their own sex to serve the purposes of licentiousness, so as to leave them untempted. Their degradation arises, not from their own conduct, but from that of all other parties about them. Where the generality of men carry secrets which their wives must be the last to know; where the busiest and more engrossing concerns of life must wear one aspect to the one sex, and another to the other, there is an end to all wholesome confidence and sympathy, and woman sinks to be the ornament of her husband's house, the domestic manager of his establishment, instead of being his all-sufficient friend. I am speaking not only of what I suppose must necessarily be; but of what I have actually seen. I have seen, with heart-sorrow, the kind politeness, the gallantry, so insufficient to the loving heart, with which the wives of the south are treated by their husbands. I have seen the horror of a woman's having to work,—to exert the faculties which her Maker gave her;— the eagerness to ensure her unearned ease and rest; the deepest insult which can be offered to an intelligent and conscientious woman. I know the tone of conversation which is adopted towards women; different in its topics and its style from that which any man would dream of offering to any other man. I have heard the boast of the chivalrous consideration in which women are held throughout their woman's paradise; and seen something of the anguish of crushed pride, of the conflict of bitter feelings with which such boasts have been listened to by those whose aspirations teach them the hollowness of the system. The gentlemen are all the while unaware that women are not treated in the best possible manner among them: and they will remain thus blind as long as licentious intercourse with the lowest of the sex unfits them for appreciating the highest. A lady who, brought up elsewhere to use her own faculties, and employ them on such objects as she thinks proper, and who has more knowledge and more wisdom than perhaps any gentleman of her acquaintance, told me of the disgust with which she submits to the conversation which is addressed to her, under the idea of being fit for her; and how she solaces herself at home, after such provocation, with the silent sympathy of books. A father of promising young daughters, whom he sees likely to be crushed by the system, told me, in a tone of voice which I shall never forget, that women there might as well be turned into the street, for anything they are fit for. There are reasonable hopes that his children may prove an exception. One gentleman who declares himself much interested in the whole subject, expresses his horror of the employment of women in the northern States, for useful purposes. He told me that the same force of circumstances which, in the region he inhabits, makes men independent, increases the dependence of women, and will go on to increase it. Society is there, he declared, "always advancing towards orientalism."

Of course, the children suffer, perhaps the most fatally of all, under the slave system. What can be expected from little boys who are brought up to consider physical courage the highest attribute of manhood; pride of section and of caste its loftiest grace; the slavery of a part of society essential to the freedom of the rest; justice of less account than generosity; and humiliation in the eyes of men the most intolerable of evils? What is to be expected of little girls who boast of having got a negro flogged for being impertinent to them, and who are surprised at the "ungentlemanly" conduct of a master who maims his slave? Such lessons are not always taught expressly. Sometimes the reverse is expressly taught. But this is what the children in a slave country necessarily learn from what passes around them; just as the plainest girls in a school grow up to think personal beauty the most important of all endowments, in spite of daily assurances that the charms of the mind are all that are worth regarding.

The children of slave countries learn more and worse still. It is nearly impossible to keep them from close intercourse with the slaves; and the attempt is rarely made.

The generality of slaves are as gross as the total absence of domestic sanctity might be expected to render them. They do not dream of any reserves with children. The consequences are inevitable.

One of the absolutely inevitable results of slavery is a disregard of human rights; an inability even to comprehend them. Probably the southern gentry, who declare that the presence of slavery enhances the love of freedom; that freedom can be duly estimated only where a particular class can appropriate all social privileges; that, to use the words of one of them, "they know too much of slavery to be slaves themselves," are sincere enough in such declarations; and if so, it follows that they do not know what freedom is. They may have the benefit of the alternative,—of not knowing what freedom is, and being sincere; or of knowing what freedom is, and not being sincere. I am disposed to think that the first is the more common case.

One reason for my thinking so is, that I usually found in conversation in the south, that the idea of human rights was—sufficient subsistence in return for labour. This was assumed as the definition of human rights on which we were to argue the case of the slave.

Another of my reasons for supposing that the gentry of the south do not know what freedom is, is that many seem unconscious of the state of coercion in which they themselves are living; coercion, not only from the incessant fear of which I have before spoken,—a fear which haunts their homes, their business, and their recreations; coercion, not only from their fear, and from their being dependent for their hourly comforts upon the extinguished or estranged will of those whom they have injured; but coercion also from their own laws. The laws against the press are as peremptory as in the most despotic countries of Europe:* as may be seen in the small number and size, and

* No notice is taken of any occurrence, however remarkable, in which a person of colour, free or enslaved, has any share, for fear of the Acts which denounce death or imprisonment for life against those who shall write, print, publish, or distribute anything having a tendency to excite discontent or insubordination, &c.: or which doom to heavy fines those who shall use

poor quality, of the newspapers of the south. I never saw, in the rawest villages of the youngest States, newspapers so empty and poor as those of New Orleans. It is curious that, while the subject of the abolition of slavery in the British colonies was necessarily a very interesting one throughout the southern States, I met with planters who did not know that any compensation had been paid by the British nation to the West Indian proprietors. The miserable quality of the southern newspapers, and the omission from them of the subjects on which the people most require information, will go far to account for the people's delusions on their own affairs, as compared with those of the rest of the world, and for their boasts of freedom, which probably arise from their knowing of none which is superior. They see how much more free they are than their own slaves; but are not generally aware what liberty is where all are free. In 1834, the number of newspapers was, in the State of New York, 267; in Louisiana, 31; in Massachusetts, 108; in South Carolina, 19; in Pennsylvania, 220; in Georgia, 29.

What is to be thought of the freedom of gentlemen subject to the following law? "Any person or persons who shall attempt to teach any free person of colour, or slave, to spell, read, or write, shall, upon conviction thereof by indictment, be fined in a sum not less than two hundred and fifty dollars, nor more than five hundred dollars."*

What is to be thought of the freedom of gentlemen who cannot emancipate their own slaves, except by the consent of the legislature; and then only under very strict

---

or issue language which may disturb "the security of masters with their slaves, or diminish that respect which is commanded to free people of colour for the whites."

* Alabama Digest. In the same section occurs the following: "That no cruel or unusual punishment shall be inflicted on any slave within this territory. And any owner of slaves authorising or permitting the same, shall, on conviction thereof, before any court having cognizance, be fined according to the nature of the offence, and at the discretion of the court, in any sum not exceeding two hundred dollars."

Two hundred dollars' fine for torturing a slave: and five hundred for teaching him to read!

conditions, which make the deed almost impracticable? It has been mentioned that during a temporary suspension of the laws against emancipation in Virginia, 10,000 slaves were freed in nine years; and that, as the institution seemed in peril, the masters were again coerced. It is pleaded that the masters themselves were the repealers and re-enactors of these laws. True: and thus it appears that they thought it necessary to deprive each other of a liberty which a great number seem to have made use of themselves, while they could. No high degree of liberty, or of the love of it, is to be seen here. The laws which forbid emancipation are felt to be cruelly galling, throughout the south. I heard frequent bitter complaints of them. They are the invariable plea urged by individuals to excuse their continuing to hold slaves. Such individuals are either sincere in these complaints, or they are not. If they are not, they must be under some deplorable coercion which compels so large a multitude to hypocrisy. If they are sincere, they possess the common republican means of getting tyrannical laws repealed: and why do they not use them? If these laws are felt to be oppressive, why is no voice heard denouncing them in the legislatures? If men complainingly, but voluntarily, submit to laws which bind the conscience, little can be said of their love of liberty. If they submit involuntarily, nothing can be said for their possession of it.

What, again, is to be thought of the freedom of citizens who are liable to lose caste because they follow conscience in a case where the perversity of the laws places interest on the side of conscience, and public opinion against it? I will explain. In a southern city, I saw a gentleman who appeared to have all the outward requisites for commanding respect. He was very wealthy, had been governor of the State, and was an eminent and peculiar benefactor to the city. I found he did not stand well. As some pains were taken to impress me with this, I inquired the cause. His character was declared to be generally good. I soon got at the particular exception, which I was anxious to do only because I saw that it was somehow of public concern. While this gentleman was governor, there was an insurrection of slaves. His own slaves were accused. He did not believe them guilty, and refused to hang them. This was imputed to an unwillingness to sacrifice his property. He was thus in a predicament which no one can be placed in, except where man is held as property. He must either hang his slaves, believing them innocent, and keep his character; or he must, by saving their lives, lose his own character. How the case stood with this gentleman, is fully known only to his own heart. His conduct claims the most candid construction. But, this being accorded as his due, what can be thought of the freedom of a republican thus circumstanced?

Passing over the perils, physical and moral, in which those are involved who live in a society where recklessness of life is treated with leniency, and physical courage stands high in the list of virtues and graces,—perils which abridge a man's liberty of action and of speech in a way which would be felt to be intolerable if the restraint were not adorned by the false name of Honour,—it is only necessary to look at the treatment of the abolitionists by the south, by both legislatures and individuals, to see that no practical understanding of liberty exists there.

Upon a mere vague report, or bare suspicion, persons travelling through the south have been arrested, imprisoned, and, in some cases, flogged or otherwise tortured, on pretence that such persons desired to cause insurrection among the slaves. More than one innocent person has been hanged; and the device of terrorism has been so practised as to deprive the total number of persons who avowedly hold a certain set of opinions, of their constitutional liberty of traversing the whole country.

If it be said that these acts are attributable to the ignorant wrath of individuals only, it may be asked whence arose the Committees of Vigilance, which were last year sitting throughout the south and west, on the watch for any incautious person who might venture near them, with anti-slavery opinions in his mind? How came it that high official persons sat on these committees? How is it that some governors of southern States made formal application to governors of the northern States to procure the dispersion of anti-slavery societies, the repression of discussion, and the punishment of the promulgators of abolition opinions? How is it that the governor of South Carolina last year recommended the summary execution, without benefit of clergy, of all persons caught within the limits of the State, holding avowed anti-slavery opinions; and that every sentiment of the governor's was endorsed by a select committee of the legislature?

All this proceeds from an ignorance of the first principles of liberty. It cannot be from a mere hypocritical disregard of such principles; for proud men, who boast a peculiar love of liberty and aptitude for it, would not voluntarily make themselves so ridiculous as they appear by these outrageous proceedings. Such blustering is so hopeless, and, if not sincere, so purposeless, that no other supposition is left than that they have lost sight of the fundamental principles of both their federal and State constitutions, and do now actually suppose that their own freedom lies in crushing all opposition to their own will. No pretence of evidence has been offered of any further offence against them than the expression of obnoxious opinions. There is no plea that any of their laws have been violated, except those recently enacted to annihilate freedom of speech and the press: laws which can in no case be binding upon persons out of the limits of the States for which these new laws are made.

How fearfully have those who framed them degenerated in their comprehension and practice of liberty, violating both the spirit and the letter of their original Bill of Rights! They are not yet fully aware of this. In the calmer times which are to come, they will perceive it, and look back with amazement upon the period of desperation, when not a voice was heard, even in the legislatures, to plead for human rights; when, for the sake of one doomed institution, they forgot what their fathers had done, fettered their own presses, tied their own hands, robbed their fellow-citizens of their right of free travelling, and did all they could to deprive those same fellow-citizens of liberty and life, for the avowal and promulgation of opinions.

Meantime, it would be but decent to forbear all boasts of a superior knowledge and love of freedom.

Here I gladly break off my dark chapter on the Morals of Slavery.

MORALS OF MANUFACTURES

ONE remarkable effect of democratic institutions is the excellence of the work turned out by those who live under them. In a country where the whole course is open to every one; where, in theory, everything may be obtained by merit, men have the strongest stimulus to exert their powers, and try what they can achieve. I found master-workmen, who employ operatives of various nations, very sensible of this. Elsewhere, no artisan can possibly rise higher than to a certain point of dexterity, and amount of wages. In America, an artisan may attain to be governor of the State; member of Congress; even President. Instead of this possibility having the effect of turning his head, and making him unfit for business, (as some suppose, who seem to consider these opportunities as resembling the chances of a lottery,) it attaches him to his business and his master, to sober habits, and to intellectual cultivation.

The only apparent excess to which it leads is ill-considered enterprise. This is an evil sometimes to the individual, but not to society. A man who makes haste to be famous or rich by means of new inventions, may injure his own fortune or credit, but is usually a benefactor to society, by furnishing a new idea on which another may work with more success. Some of the most important improvements in the manufactures of the United States have been made by men who afterwards became insolvent. Where there is hasty enterprise, there is usually much conceit. The very haste seems to show that the man is thinking more of himself than of the subject on which he is employed.

The morals of the female factory population may be expected to be good when it is considered of what class it is composed. Many of the girls are in the factories because they have too much pride for domestic service. Girls who are too proud for domestic service as it is in America, can hardly be low enough for any gross immorality; or to need watching; or not to be trusted to avoid the contagion of evil example. To a stranger, their pride seems to take a mistaken direction, and they appear to deprive themselves of a respectable home and station, and many benefits, by their dislike of service: but this is altogether their own affair. They must choose for themselves their way of life. But the reasons of their choice indicate a state of mind superior to the grossest dangers of their position.

I saw a bill fixed up in the Waltham mill which bore a warning that no young lady who attended dancing-school that winter should be employed: and that the corporation had given directions to the overseer to dismiss any one who should be found to dance at the school. I asked the meaning of this; and the overseer's answer was, "Why, we had some trouble last winter about the dancing-school. It must, of course, be held in the evening, as the young folks are in the mill all day. They are very young, many of them; and they forget the time, and everything but the amusement, and dance away till two or three in the morning. Then they are unfit for their work the next day; or, if they get properly through their work, it is at the expense of their health. So we have forbidden the dancing-school; but, to make up for it, I have promised them that, as soon as the great new room at the hotel is finished, we will have a dance once a-fortnight. We shall meet and break up early; and my wife and I will dance; and we will all dance together."

I was sorry to see one bad and very unnecessary arrangement, in all the manufacturing establishments. In England, the best friends of the poor are accustomed to think it the crowning hardship of their condition that solitude is wholly forbidden to them. It is impossible that any human being should pass his life as well as he might do who is never alone,—who is not frequently alone. This is a weighty truth which can never be explained away. The silence, freedom and collectedness of solitude are absolutely essential to the health of the mind; and no substitute for this repose (or change of activity) is possible. In the dwellings of the English poor, parents and children are crowded into one room, for want of space and of furniture. All wise parents above the rank of poor, make it a primary consideration so to arrange their families as that each member may, at some hour, have some place where he may enter in, and shut his door, and feel himself alone. If possible, the sleeping places are so ordered. In America, where space is of far less consequence, where the houses are large, where the factory girls can build churches, and buy libraries, and educate brothers for learned professions, these same girls have no private apartments, and sometimes sleep six or eight in a room, and even three in a bed. This is very bad. It shows a want of inclination for solitude; an absence of that need of it which every healthy mind must feel, in a greater or less degree.

Now are the days when these gregarious habits should be broken through. New houses are being daily built: more parents are bringing their children to the factories. If the practice be now adopted, by the corporations, or by the parents who preside over separate establishments, of partitioning off the large sleeping apartments into small ones which shall hold each one occupant, the expense of partitions and windows and trouble will not be worth a moment's consideration in comparison with the improvement in intelligence, morals, and manners, which will be found to result from such an arrangement. If the change be not soon made, the American factory population, with all its advantages of education and of pecuniary sufficiency, will be found, as its numbers increase, to have been irreparably injured by its subjection to a grievance which is considered the very heaviest to which poverty exposes artisans in old countries. Man's own silent thoughts are his best safeguard and highest privilege. Of the full advantage of this safeguard, of the full enjoyment of this privilege, the innocent and industrious youth of a new country ought, by no mismanagement, to be deprived.

MORALS OF COMMERCE

It is said in the United States that Commerce and the Navy are patronised by the Federal party; as agriculture is, and the army would be, if there was one, by the Democratic party. This is true enough. The greater necessity for co-operation, and therefore for the partial sacrifice of independence, imposed by commercial pursuits, is more agreeable to the aristocratic portion of society than to its opposite. Yet, while commerce has been spreading and improving, Federalism has dwindled away; and most remarkably where commerce is carried on in its utmost activity: in Massachusetts. The Democracy are probably finding out that more is gained by the concentration of the popular will than is lost in the way of individual independence, by men being brought together for objects which require concession and mutual subordination. However this may be, the spirit of commerce in the United States is, on the whole, honourable to the people.

I shall have to speak hereafter of the regard to wealth, as the most important object in life, which extensively corrupts Americans as it does all other society. Here, I have to speak only of the spirit in which one method of procuring wealth is prosecuted.

The activity of the commercial spirit in America is represented abroad, and too often at home, as indicative of nothing but sordid love of gain: a making haste to be rich, a directly selfish desire of aggrandisement. This view of the case seems to me narrow and injurious. I believe that many desires, various energies, some nobler and some meaner, find in commerce a centre for their activity. I have studied with some care the minds and manners of a variety of merchants, and other persons engaged in commerce, and have certainly found a regard to money a more superficial and intermitting influence than various others.

The spirit of enterprise is very remarkable in the American merchants. Beginning life, as all Americans do, with the world all open before them, and only a head and a pair

of hands wherewith to gain it, a passionate desire to overcome difficulties arises in them. Being, (as I have before
declared my opinion,) the most imaginative people in the
world, the whole world rises fair before them, and they,
not believing in impossibilities, long to conquer it.

Then, there is the meaner love of distinction; meaner
than the love of enterprise, but higher than the desire of
gain. The distinction sought is not always that which at-
tends on superior wealth only; but on world-wide intercourses, on extensive affairs, on hospitality to a large variety of foreigners.

Again; there is the love of Art. Weak, immature, ignorant, perhaps, as this taste at present is, it exists: and indications of it which merit all respect, are to be found in
many abodes. There are other, though not perhaps such
lofty ways of pursuing art, than by embodying conceptions
in pictures, statues, operas, and buildings. The love of
Beauty and of the ways of Humanity may indicate and
gratify itself by other and simpler methods than those
which the high artists of the old world have sanctified. If
any one can witness the meeting of one kind of American
merchant with his supercargo, after a long, distant voyage,
hear the questioning and answering, and witness the delight with which new curiosities are examined, and new
theories of beauty and civilisation are put forth upon the
impulse of the moment, and still doubt the existence of a
love of art, still suppose the desire of gain the moving
spring of that man's mind,—may Heaven preserve the community from being pronounced upon by such an observer!
The critic with the stop-watch is magnanimous in comparison.

What are the facts? What are the manifestations of the
character of the American merchants? After their eager
money-getting, how do they spend it? How much do they
prize it?

Their benevolence is known throughout the world: not
only that benevolence which founds and endows charities,
and repairs to sufferers the mischief of accidents; but that
which establishes schools of a higher order than common,
and brings forward in life the most meritorious of those

who are educated there; the benevolence which watches over the condition of seamen on the ocean, and their safety at home; the benevolence which busies itself, with much expense of dollars and trouble, to provide for the improved civilisation of the whole of society. If the most liberal institutions in the northern States were examined into, it would be found how active the merchant class has been, beyond all others, in their establishment.

The bankruptcies in the United States are remarkably frequent and disgraceful,—disgraceful in their nature, though not sufficiently so in the eyes of society. A clergyman in a commercial city declares that almost every head of a family in his congregation has been a bankrupt since his settlement. In Philadelphia, from six to eight hundred persons annually take the benefit of the insolvent laws; and numerous compromises take place which are not heard of further than the parties concerned in them. On seeing the fine house of a man who was a bankrupt four years before, and who was then worth 100,000 dollars, I asked whether such cases were common, and was grieved to find they were. Some insolvents pay their old debts when they rise again; but the greater number do not. Few things are more disgraceful to American society than the carelessness with which speculators are allowed to game with other people's funds, and, after ruining those who put trust in them, to lift up their heads in all places, just as if they had, during their whole lives, rendered unto all their dues. Whatever may be the causes or the palliations of speculation; whatever may be pleaded about currency mistakes, and the temptations to young men to make fortunes by the public lands, one thing is clear; that no man, who, having failed, and afterwards having the means to pay his debts in full, does not pay them, can be regarded as an honest man, and ought to be received upon the same footing with honest men, whatever may be his accomplishments, or his subsequent fortune. What would be thought of any society which should cherish an escaped (not reformed) thief, because a large legacy had enabled him to set up his carriage? Yet how much difference is there in the two cases?

The gravest sin chargeable upon the merchants of the
United States is their conduct on the abolition question.
This charge is by no means general. There are instances of
a manly declaration of opinion on the side of freedom, and
also of a spirit of self-sacrifice in the cause, which can
hardly be surpassed for nobleness. There are merchants
who have thrown up their commerce with the south
when there was reason to believe that its gains were wrung
from the slave; and there are many who have freely poured
out their money, and risked their reputation, in defence of
the abolition cause, and of liberty of speech and the press.
But the reproach of the persecution of the abolitionists,
and of tampering with the fundamental liberties of the
people, rests mainly with the merchants of the northern
States.

It is worthy of remembrance that the Abolition movement originated from the sordid act of a merchant. While
Garrison was at Baltimore, studying the Colonisation
scheme, a ship belonging to a merchant of Newburyport,
Massachusetts, arrived at Baltimore to take freight for New
Orleans. There was some difficulty about the expected
cargo. The captain was offered a freight of slaves, wrote
to the merchant for leave, and received orders to carry
these slaves to New Orleans. Garrison poured out, in a
libel, (so called,) his indignation against this deed, committed by a man who, as a citizen of Massachusetts, thanks
God every Thanksgiving Day that the soil of his State is
untrod by the foot of a slave. Garrison was fined and imprisoned; and after his release, was warmly received in
New York, where he lectured upon Abolition; from which
time, the cause has gained strength so as to have now become unconquerable.

The spirit of this Newburyport merchant has dwelt in
too many of the same vocation. The Faneuil Hall meeting
was convened chiefly by merchants; and they have been
conspicuous in all the mobs. They have kept the clergy
dumb: they have overawed the colleges, given their cue
to the newspapers, and shown a spirit of contempt and
violence, equalling even that of the slave-holders, towards
those who, in acting upon their honest convictions, have

appeared likely to affect their sources of profit. At Cincinnati, they were chiefly merchants who met to destroy the right of discussion; and passed a resolution directly recommendatory of violence for this purpose. They were merchants who waited in deputation on the editor of the anti-slavery newspaper there, to intimidate him from the use of his constitutional liberty, and who made themselves by these acts answerable for the violences which followed. This was so clear, that they were actually taunted by their slave-holding neighbours, on the other side of the river, with their sordidness in attempting to extinguish the liberties of the republic for the sake of their own pecuniary gains.

The day will come when their eyes will be cleansed from the gold-dust which blinds them.

VIII.   Civilisation

"This country, which has given to the world the example of physical liberty, owes to it that of moral emancipation also; for as yet it is but nominal with us. The inquisition of public opinion overwhelms, in practice, the freedom asserted by the laws in theory."

Jefferson

THE degree of civilisation of any people corresponds with the exaltation of the idea which is the most prevalent among that people. The prominent idea of savages is the necessity of providing for the supply of the commonest bodily wants. The first steps in civilisation, therefore, are somewhat refined methods of treating the body. When, by combination of labour and other exercises of ingenuity, the wants of the body are supplied with regularity and comparative ease, the love of pleasure, the love of idleness, succeeds. Then comes the desire of wealth; and next, the regard to opinion. Further than this no nation has yet attained. Individuals there have been, probably in every nation under heaven, who have lived for a higher idea than any of these; and insulated customs and partial legislation have, among all communities, shown a tendency towards something loftier than the prevalent morality. The majesty of higher ideas is besides so irresistible, that an involuntary homage, purely inefficacious, has been offered to them from of old by the leaders of society.

"Earth is sick,
And Heaven is weary of the hollow words
Which States and Kingdoms utter when they talk
Of truth and justice."

Though, as yet, "profession mocks performance," the profession, from age to age, of the same lofty something not yet attained, may be taken as a clear prophecy of ultimate performance. It shows a perception, however dim, a regard, however feeble, from which endeavour and attainment cannot but follow, in course of time. But the time is not yet. In the old world, the transition is, in its most enlightened parts, only beginning to be made, from the few governing the many avowedly for the good of the few, to governing the many professedly for the good of the many.

The old world naturally looks with interest to the new, to see what point of civilisation it reaches under fresh circumstances. The interest may be undefined, and partly unconscious; but it is very eager. The many, who conceive of no other objects of general pursuit than the old ones of wealth, ease, and honour, look only to see under what forms these are pursued. The few, who lay the blame of the grovelling at home upon outward restrictions alone, look to America with extravagant expectations of a perfect reign of virtue and happiness, because the Americans live in outward freedom. What is the truth?

While the republics of North America are new, the ideas of the people are old. While these republics were colonies, they contained an old people, living under old institutions, in a new country. Now they are a mixed people, infant as a nation, with a constant accession of minds from old countries, living in a new country, under institutions newly combined out of old elements. It is a case so singular, that the old world may well have patience for some time, to see what will arise. The old world must have patience; for the Americans have no national character yet; nor can have, for a length of years. It matters not that they think they have: or it matters only so far as it shows to what they tend. Their veneration of Washington has led them to suppose that he is the type of their nation. Their

patriotic feelings are so far associated with him that they
conclude the nation is growing up in his likeness. If any
American were trusted by his countrymen to delineate what
they call their national character, it would infallibly come
out a perfect likeness of Washington. But there is a mistake here. There were influences prior to Washington, and
there are circumstances which have survived him, that
cause some images to lie deeper down in the hearts of
Americans than Washington himself. His character is a
grand and very prevalent idea among them: but there are
others which take the precedence, from being more general
still. Wealth and opinion were practically worshipped before Washington opened his eyes on the sun which was to
light him to his deeds; and the worship of Opinion is, at
this day, the established religion of the United States.

In a country where the will of the majority decides all
political affairs, there is a temptation to belong to the
majority, except where strong interests, or probabilities of
the speedy supremacy of the minority, countervail. The
minority, in such a case, must be possessed of a strong
will, to be a minority. A strong will is dreaded by the
weaker, who have so little faith as to believe that such a
will endangers the political equality which is the fundamental principle of their institutions. This dread occasions
persecution, or at least opprobrium: opprobrium becomes
a real danger; and, like all dangers, is much more feared
than it deserves, the longer it lasts, and the more it is dwelt
upon.

IX. Idea of Honour

"Talent and worth are the only eternal grounds of distinction. To these the Almighty has affixed his everlasting patent of nobility; and these it is which make the bright, 'the immortal names,' to which our children may aspire, as well as others. It will be our own fault if, in our own land, society as well as government is not organised upon a new foundation."

Miss Sedgwick

It is true that it is better to live for honour than for wealth: but how much better, depends upon the idea of honour. Where the honour is to be derived from present human opinion, there must be fear, ever present, and perpetually exciting to or withholding from action. In such a case, as painful a bondage is incurred as in the pursuit of wealth. If riches take to themselves wings, and fly away, so does popularity. If rich freights are in danger afar off from storms, and harvests at home from blights, so is reputation, from differences of opinion, and varieties of views and tempers. If all that moralists have written, and wise men have testified, about the vanity and misery of depending on human applause be true, there can be no true freedom in communities, any more than for individuals, who live to opinion. The time will come when the Americans also will testify to this, as a nation, as many individual members of their society have done already. The time will come when they will be astonished to discover how they

mar their own privileges by allowing themselves less liberty of speech and action than is enjoyed by the inhabitants of countries whose political servitude the Americans
justly compassionate and despise.

This regard to opinion shows itself under various forms
in different parts of the country, and under dissimilar social arrangements. In the south, where the labour itself is
capital, and labour cannot therefore be regarded with due
respect, there is much vanity of retinue, much extrava-
gance, from fear of the imputation of poverty which would
follow upon retrenchment; and great recklessness of life,
from fear of the imputation of cowardice which might follow upon forgiveness of injuries. Fear of imputation is here
the panic, under which men relinquish their freedom of
action and speech.

Not by any means as a fair specimen of society, but as
an example of what kind of honour may be enjoyed where
the fear of imputation is at its height, I give the description, as it was given me by a resident, of what a man may
do in an eminently duelling portion of the southern country.
"A man may kill another, and be no worse. He may be
shabby in his money transactions, but may not steal. He
may game, but not keep a gaming-house." It will not do
for the duellists of the south to drop in conversation, as
they do, that good manners can exist only where vengeance
is the penalty of bad. The fear of imputation and the dread
of vengeance are at least as contemptible as bad manners;
and unquestionably lower than the fear of opinion prevalent in the north.

In the north there can be little vanity of retinue, as
retinue is not to be had: but there is, instead of it, much
ostentation of wealth, in the commercial cities. It is here
that the aristocracy form and collect; and, as has been before said, the aristocratic is universally the fearing, while
the democratic is the hoping, party. The fear of opinion
takes many forms. There is fear of vulgarity, fear of responsibility; and above all, fear of singularity. There is something more displeasing, at the first view, in the caution of
the Yankees than in the recklessness of the cavalier race of
the south. Till the individual exceptions come out from the

mass; till the domestic frankness and generosity of the whole people are apparent, there is something little short of disgusting to the stranger who has been unused to witness such want of social confidence, in the caution which presents probably the strongest aspect of selfishness that he has ever seen.

The Americans of the northern States are, from education and habit, so accustomed to the caution of which I speak, as to be unaware of its extent and singularity. They think themselves injured by the remarks which strangers make upon it, and by the ridicule with which it is treated by their own countrymen who have travelled abroad. But the singularity is in themselves. They may travel over the world, and find no society but their own which will submit to the restraint of perpetual caution, and reference to the opinions of others. They may travel over the whole world, and find no country but their own where the very children beware of getting into scrapes, and talk of the effect of actions upon people's minds; where the youth of society determine in silence what opinions they shall bring forward, and what avow only in the family circle; where women write miserable letters, almost universally, because it is a settled matter that it is unsafe to commit oneself on paper; and where elderly people seem to lack almost universally that faith in principles which inspires a free expression of them at any time, and under all circumstances.

"Mrs. B.," said a child of eleven to a friend of mine, "what church do you go to?"—"To Mr. ——'s." "O, Mrs. B. are you a Unitarian?"—"No." "Then why do you go to that church?"—"Because I can worship best there." "O, but Mrs. B., think of the example,—the example, Mrs. B.!"

When I had been in the country some time, I remarked to one who knew well the society in which he lived, that I had not seen a good lady's letter since I landed; though the conversation of some of the writers was of a very superior kind. The letters were uniformly poor and guarded in expression, confined to common-places, and overloaded with flattery. "There are," replied he, "no good letters written in America. The force of public opinion is so strong, and the danger of publicity so great, that men do not write what they think, for fear of getting into bad hands: and this acts again upon the women, and makes their style artificial." It is not quite true that there are no good letters written in America: among my own circle of correspondents there, there are ladies and gentlemen whose letters would stand a comparison with any for frankness, grace, and epistolary beauty of every kind. But I am not aware of any medium between this excellence and the boarding-school insignificance which characterises the rest.

When the stranger has recovered a little from the first disagreeable impression of all this caution, he naturally asks what there can be to render it worth while. To this question, I never could discover a satisfactory answer. What harm the "force of public opinion," or "publicity," can do to any individual; what injury "bad hands" can inflict upon a good man or woman, which can be compared with the evil of living in perpetual caution, I cannot imagine. If men and women cannot bear blame, they had better hew out a space for themselves in the forest, and live there, as the only safe place. If they are afraid of observation and comment, they should withdraw from society altogether: for the interest which human beings take in each other is so deep and universal, that observation and comment are unavoidable wherever there are eyes to see, and hearts and minds to yearn and speculate. An honest man will not naturally fear this investigation. If he is not sure of his opinions on any matter, he will say so, and endeavour to gain light. If he is sure, he will speak them, and be ready to avow the grounds of them, as occasion arises. That there should be some who think his opinions false and dangerous is not pleasant; but it is an evil too trifling to be mentioned in comparison with the bondage of concealment, and the torment of fear. This bondage, this torment is worse than the worst that the "force of public opinion" can inflict, even if such force should close the prospect of political advancement, of professional eminence, and of the best of social privileges. There are some members of society in America who have found persecution, excommunication, and violence, more endurable than the concealment of their convictions.

Few persons really doubt this when the plain case is set down before them. They agree to it in church on Sundays, and in conversation by the fireside: and the reason why they are so backward as they are to act upon it in the world, is that habit and education are too strong for them. They have worn their chains so long that they feel them less than might be supposed. I doubt whether they can even conceive of a state of society, of its ease and comfort, where no man fears his neighbour, and it is no evil to be responsible for one's opinions: where men, knowing how undiscernible consequences are, and how harmless they must be to the upright, abide them without fear, and do not perplex themselves with calculating what is incalculable. Whenever the time shall come for the Americans to discover all this, to perceive how miserable a restraint they have imposed upon themselves by this servitude to opinion, they will see how it is that, while outwardly blessed beyond all parallel, they have been no happier than the rest of the world. I doubt whether, among the large "uneasy classes" of the Old World, there is so much heart-eating care, so much nervous anxiety, as among the dwellers in the towns of the northern States of America, from this cause alone. If I had to choose, I would rather endure the involuntary uneasiness of the Old World sufferers, than the self-imposed anxiety of those of the New: except that the self-imposed suffering may be shaken off at any moment. There are instances, few, but striking, of strong-minded persons who have discovered and are practising the true philosophy of ease; who have openly taken their stand upon principles, and are prepared for all consequences, meekly and cheerfully defying all possible inflictions of opinion. Though it does not enter into their calculations, such may possibly find that they are enjoying more, and suffering less from opinion, than those who most daintily court it.

There would be something amusing in observing the operation of this habit of caution, if it were not too serious a misfortune. When Dr. Channing's work on Slavery came out, the following conversation passed between a lady of Boston and myself. She began it with—

"Have you seen Dr. Channing's book?"

"Yes. Have you?"

"O no. Do not you think it very ill-timed?"

"No; I think it well-timed; as it did not come out sooner."

"But is it not wrong to increase the public excitement at such a time?"

"That depends upon the nature of the excitement. But this book seems to have a tranquillising effect: as the exhibition of true principles generally has."

"But Dr. Channing is not a practical man. He is only a retired student. He has no real interest in the matter."

"No worldly interest; and this, and his seclusion, enable him to see more clearly than others, in a case where principles enlighten men, and practice seems only to blind them."

"Well: I shall certainly read the book, as you like it so much."

"Pray don't, if that is your reason."

A reply to Dr. Channing's book soon appeared;—a pamphlet which savoured only of fear, dollars, and, consequently, insult. A gentleman of Boston, who had, on some important occasions, shown that he could exercise a high moral courage, made no mention of this reply for some time after it appeared. At length, on hearing another person speak of it as it deserved, he said, "Now people are so openly speaking of that reply, I have no objection to say what I think of it. I have held my tongue about it hitherto; but yesterday I heard —— speak of it as you do; and I no longer hesitate to declare that I think it an infamous production."

It may be said that such are remarkable cases. Be it so: they still testify to the habit of society, by the direction which the caution takes. Elsewhere, the parties might be quite as much afraid of something else; but they would not dream of refraining from a good book, or holding their tongues about the badness of a vicious pamphlet, till supported by the opinions of others.

How strong a contrast to all this the domestic life of the Americans presents will appear when I come to speak of

the spirit of intercourse. It is an individual, though prevalent, selfishness that I have now been lamenting.

The traveller should go into the west when he desires to
see universal freedom of manners. The people of the west
have a comfortable self-complacency, equally different
from the arrogance of the south, and the timidity of the
north. They seem to unite with this the hospitality which
distinguishes the whole country: so that they are, on the
whole, a very bewitching people. Their self-confidence
probably arises from their being really remarkably ener-
getic, and having testified this by the conquests over nature
which their mere settlement in the west evinces. They are
the freest people I saw in America: and accordingly one
enjoys among them a delightful exemption from the sorrow and indignation which worldly caution always inspires;
and from flattery. If the stranger finds himself flattered in
the west, he may pretty safely conclude that the person he
is talking with comes from New England. "We are apt to
think," said a westerner to me, "that however great and
good another person may be, we are just as great and
good." Accordingly, intercourse goes on without any reference whatever to the merits of the respective parties. In
the sunshine of complacency, their free thoughts ripen
into free deeds, and the world gains largely. There are,
naturally, instances of extreme conceit, here and there: but
I do not hesitate to avow that, prevalent as mock-mod-
esty and moral cowardice are in the present condition of
society, that degree of self-confidence which is commonly
called conceit grows in favour with me perpetually. An
over-estimate of self appears to me a far less hurtful and
disagreeable mistake than the idolatry of opinion. It is a
mistake which is sure to be rectified, sooner or later; and
very often, it proves to be no mistake where small critics
feel the most confident that they may safely ridicule it.
The event decides this matter of self-estimate, beyond all
question; and while the event remains undisclosed, it is
easy and pleasant to give men credit for as much as they
believe themselves to be capable of:—more easy and pleasant than to see men restricting their own powers by such
calculation of consequences as implies an equal want of

faith in others and in themselves. If John Milton were now here to avow his hope that he should produce that which "the world would not willingly let die," what a shout there would be of "the conceited fellow!" while, the declaration having been made venerable by the event, it is now cited as an instance of the noble self-confidence of genius.

The people of the west have a right to so much self-confidence as arises from an ascertainment of what they can actually achieve. They come from afar, with some qualities which have force enough to guide them into a new region. They subdue this region to their own purposes; and, if they do often forget that the world elsewhere is progressing; if they do suppose themselves as relatively great in present society as they were formerly in the wilderness, it should be remembered, on their behalf, that they have effectually asserted their manhood in the conquest of circumstances.

If we are not yet to see, except in individual instances, the exquisite union of fearlessness with modesty, of self-confidence with meekness;—if there must be either the love of being grand in one's own eyes, or the fear of being little in other people's,—the friends of the Americans would wish that their error should be that which is allied to too much, rather than too little freedom.

As for the anxiety about foreign opinions of America, I found it less striking than I expected. In the south, there is the keenest sensibility to the opinion of the world about slavery; and in New England, the veneration for England is greater than I think any one people ought to feel for any other. The love of the mother country, the filial pride in her ancient sages, are natural and honourable: and so, perhaps, is a somewhat exalted degree of deference for the existing dwellers upon the soil of that mother country, and on the spot where those sages lived and thought and spoke. But, as long as no civilised nation is, or can be ascertained to be, far superior or inferior to any other; as the human heart and human life are generally alike and equal, on this side barbarism, the excessive reverence with which England is regarded by the Americans seems to imply a deficiency of self-respect. This is an immeasurably higher and more healthy state of feeling than that which has been exhibited by a small portion of the English towards the Americans;—the contempt which, again, a sprinkling of Americans have striven to reciprocate. But the despisers in each nation, though so noisy as to produce some effect, are so few as to need no more than a passing allusion. If any English person can really see and know the Americans on their own ground, and fail to honour them as a nation, and love them as personal friends, he is no fair sample of the people whose name he bears; and is probably incapable of unperverted reverence: and if any American, having really seen and known the English on their own ground, does not reverence his own home exactly in proportion as he loves what is best in the English, he is unworthy of his home.

When I was on my voyage out, the Americans on board amused themselves with describing to me how incessantly I should be met by the question how I liked America. When we arrived within a few miles of New York, a steamboat met us, bringing the friends of some of the passengers. On board this steam-boat, the passengers went up to the city. It happened to be the smallest, dirtiest, and most clumsy steamer belonging to the port. A splashing rain drove us down into the cabin, where there was barely standing room for our company. We saw each other's faces by the dim light of a single shabby lamp. "Now, Miss M.," said some of the American passengers, "how do you like America?" This was the first time of my being asked the question which I have had to answer almost daily since. Yet I do not believe that many of my interrogators seriously cared any more for my answer than those who first put the question in the dirty cabin. I learned to regard it as a method of beginning conversation, like our meteorological observations in England; which are equally amusing to foreigners. My own impression is, that while the Americans have too exalted a notion of England, and too little self-respect as a nation, they are far less anxious about foreign opinions of themselves than the behaviour of American travellers in England would lead the English to suppose. The anxiety arises on English ground. At home, the generality of Americans seem to see clearly enough that it is yet truer with regard to nations than individuals that, though it is very pleasant to have the favourable opinion of one's neighbours, yet, if one is good and happy within oneself, the rest does not much matter. I met with a few who spoke with a disgusting affectation of candour, (some, as if they expected to please me thereby, and others under the influence of sectional prejudice,) of what they called the fairness of the gross slanders with which they have been insulted through the English press: but I was thankful to meet with more who did not acknowledge the jurisdiction of observers disqualified by prejudice, or by something worse, for passing judgment on a nation. The irritability of their vanity has been much exaggerated, partly to serve paltry purposes of authorship; and yet more from the ridiculous exhibitions of some Americans in England, who are no more to be taken as specimens of the nation to which they belong than a young Englishman who, when I was at New York, went up the Hudson in a drizzling rain, pronounced that West Point was not so pretty as Richmond; descended the river in the dark, and declared on his return that the Americans were wonderfully proud of scenery that was nothing particular in any way.

It will be well for the Americans, particularly those of the east and south, when their idea of honour becomes as exalted as that which inspired their revolutionary ancestors. Whenever they possess themselves of the idea of their democracy, as it was possessed by their statesmen of 1801, they will moderate their homage of human opinion, and enhance their worship of humanity. Not till then will they live up to their institutions, and enjoy that internal freedom and peace to which the external are but a part of the means. In such improvement, they will be much assisted by the increasing intercourse between Britain and America; for, however fascinating to Americans may be the luxury, conversational freedom, and high intellectual cultivation of some portions of English society, they cannot fail to be disgusted with the aristocratic insolence which is the vice of the whole. The puerile and barbaric spirit of contempt is scarcely known in America: the English insolence of class to class, of individuals towards each other, is not even conceived of, except in the one highly disgraceful instance of the treatment of the people of colour. Nothing in American civilisation struck me so forcibly and so pleasurably as the invariable respect paid to man, as man. Nothing since my return to England has given me so much pain as the contrast there. Perhaps no Englishman can become fully aware, without going to America, of the atmosphere of insolence in which he dwells; of the taint of contempt which infects all the intercourses of his world. He cannot imagine how all that he can say that is truest and best about the treatment of people of colour in America is neutralised on the spot, by its being understood how the same contempt is spread over the whole of society here, which is there concentrated upon the blacks.

CASTE

THIS word, at least its meaning, is no more likely to become obsolete in a republic than among the Hindoos themselves. The distinctive characteristics may vary; but there will be rank, and tenacity of rank, wherever there is society. As this is natural, inevitable, it is of course right. The question must be what is to entitle to rank.

As the feudal qualifications for rank are absolutely nonexistent in America, (except in the slave States, where there are two classes, without any minor distinctions,) it seems absurd that the feudal remains of rank in Europe should be imitated in America. Wherever the appearance of a conventional aristocracy exists in America, it must arise from wealth, as it cannot from birth. An aristocracy of mere wealth is vulgar everywhere. In a republic, it is vulgar in the extreme.

This is the only kind of vulgarity I saw in the United States. I imagine that the English who have complained the most copiously of the vulgarity of American manners, have done so from two causes: from using their own conventional notions as a standard of manners, (which is a vulgarism in themselves;) and also from their intercourses

with the Americans having been confined to those who consider themselves the aristocracy of the United States: the
wealthy and showy citizens of the Atlantic ports. Foreign
travellers are most hospitably received by this class of society; introduced to "the first people in Boston,"—"in New
York,"—"in Philadelphia;" and taught to view the country
with the eyes of their hosts. No harm is intended here: it
is very natural: but it is not the way for strangers to obtain an understanding of the country and the people. The
traveller who chooses industriously to see for himself, not
with European or aristocratic merely, but with human eyes,
will find the real aristocracy of the country, not only in
ball-rooms and bank-parlours, but also in fishing-boats, in
stores, in college chambers, and behind the plough. Till he
has seen all this, and studied the natural manners of the
natural aristocracy, he is no more justified in applying the
word "vulgar" to more than a class, than an American
would be who should call all the English vulgar, when he
had seen only the London alderman class.

I had the opportunity of perceiving what errors might
arise from this cause. I was told a great deal about "the
first people in Boston:" which is perhaps as aristocratic,
vain, and vulgar a city, as described by its own "first people," as any in the world. Boston is the headquarters of
Cant. Notwithstanding its superior intelligence, its large
provision of benevolent institutions, and its liberal hospitality, there is an extraordinary and most pernicious union, in
more than a few scattered instances, of profligacy and the
worst kind of infidelity, with a strict religious profession,
and an outward demeanour of remarkable propriety. The
profligacy and infidelity might, I fear, be found in all other
cities, on both sides the water; but nowhere, probably, in
absolute co-existence with ostensible piety. This is not the
connexion in which to speak of the religious aspect of the
matter; but, as regards the cant, I believe that it proceeds
chiefly from the spirit of caste which flourishes in a society
which on Sundays and holidays professes to have abjured
it. It is true that the people of New England have put
away duelling; but the feelings which used to vent themselves by the practice of duelling are cherished by the

members of the conventional aristocracy. This is revealed, not only by the presence of cant, but by the confessions of some who are bold enough not to pretend to be either republicans or christians. There are some few who openly desire a monarchy; and a few more who constantly insinuate the advantages of a monarchy, and the distastefulness of a republic. It is observable that such always argue on the supposition that if there were a monarchy, they should be the aristocracy: a point in which I imagine they would find themselves mistaken, if so impossible an event could happen at all. This class, or coterie, is a very small one, and not influential; though a gentleman of the kind once ventured to give utterance to his aspirations after monarchy in a fourth of July oration; and afterwards to print them. There is something venerable in his intrepidity, at least. The reproach of cant does not attach to him.

The children are such faithful reflectors of this spirit as to leave no doubt of its existence, even amidst the nicest operations of cant. Gentlemen may disguise their aristocratic aspirations under sighs for the depressed state of literature and science; supposing that wealth and leisure are the constituents of literature; and station the proximate cause of science; and committing the slight mistake of assuming that the natural aristocracy of England, her philosophers and poets, have been identical with, or originated by, her conventional aristocracy. The ladies may conceal their selfish pride of caste, even from themselves, under pretensions to superior delicacy and refinement. But the children use no such disguises. Out they come with what they learn at home. A school-girl told me what a delightful "set" she belonged to at her school: how comfortable they all were once, without any sets, till several grocers' daughters began to come in, as their fathers grew rich; and it became necessary for the higher girls to consider what they should do, and to form themselves into sets. She told me how the daughter of a lottery office-keeper came to the school; and no set would receive her; how unkindly she was treated, and how difficult it was for any individual to help her, because she had not spirit or temper enough to help herself. My informant went on to mention how anxious she and her set, of about sixty young people, were to visit exclusively among themselves, how "delightful" it would be to have no grocers' daughters among them; but that it was found to be impossible.

Here is an education to be going on in the middle of a republic! Much solace, however, lies in the last clause of the information above quoted. The Exclusives do find their aims 'impossible.' The chief effect of the aristocratic spirit in a democracy is to make those who are possessed by it exclusives in a double sense; in being excluded yet more than in excluding. The republic suffers no further than by having within it a small class acting upon anti-republican morals, and becoming thereby its perverse children, instead of its wise and useful friends and servants.

In Philadelphia, I was much in society. Some of my hospitable acquaintances lived in Chesnut Street, some in Arch Street, and many in other places. When I had been a few weeks in the city, I found to my surprise that some of the ladies who were my admiration had not only never seen or heard of other beautiful young ladies whom I admired quite as much, but never would see or hear of them. I inquired again and again for a solution of this mystery. One person told me that a stranger could not see into the usages of their society. This was just what I was feeling to be true; but it gave me no satisfaction. Another said that the mutual ignorance was from the fathers of the Arch Street ladies having made their fortunes, while the Chesnut Street ladies owed theirs to their grandfathers. Another, who was amused with a new fashion of curtseying, just introduced, declared it was from the Arch Street ladies rising twice on their toes before curtseying, while the Chesnut Street ladies rose thrice.

It is not to be supposed that the mere circumstance of living in a republic will ever eradicate that kind of self-love which takes the form of family pride. This species of exclusiveness exists wherever there are families.

No one will find fault with the pride of connexion in this stage. Supposing it to remain in its present state, it is harmless from its extreme smallness. In a city, under the stimulus of society, the same pride may be either perverted into the spirit of caste, or exalted into the affection of pure republican brotherhood. The alternative is significant as to the state of the republic, and all-important to the individual.

The extent and influence of the conventional aristocracy in the United States are significant of the state of the republic so far as that they afford an accurate measure of the anti-republican spirit which exists. Such an aristocracy must remain otherwise too insignificant to be dangerous. It cannot choose its own members, restrict its own numbers, or keep its gentility from contamination; for it must be perpetuated, not by hereditary transmission, but by accessions from below. Grocers grow rich, and mechanics become governors of States; and happily there is no law, nor reason, nor desire that it should be otherwise. This little cloud will always overhang the republic, like the perpetual vapour which hovers above Niagara, thrown up by the force and regularity of the movement below.

PROPERTY

I found it an admitted truth, throughout the United States, that enormous private wealth is inconsistent with the spirit of republicanism. Wealth is power; and large amounts of power ought not to rest in the hands of individuals.

Admitted truths are not complained of as hardships. I never met with any one who quarrelled with public opinion for its enmity to large fortunes: on the contrary, every one who spoke with me on the subject was of the same mind with everybody else. Amidst the prevalent desire of gain, against which divines are preaching, and moralists are writing in vain, there seems to be no desire to go beyond what public opinion approves. The desire of riches merges in a regard to opinion. There is more of the spirit of competition and of ostentation in it, than desire of accumulation.

The popular feeling is so strong against transmitting large estates, and favouring one child, that nobody attempts to do it. The rare endeavours made by persons of feudal prepossessions to perpetuate this vicious custom, have been all happily frustrated. Much ridicule was occasioned by the manœuvres of one such testator, who provided for the portions of a large estate reverting periodically; forgetting that the reversions were as saleable as anything else; and that, under a democracy, there can be no settling the private, any more than the public, affairs of future generations. The present Patroon of Albany, the story of whose hereditary wealth is universally known, intends to divide his property among his children,—in number, I believe, thirteen. Under him has probably expired the practice of favouring one child for the preservation of a large estate.

This remote approach to an equalisation of property is, as far as it goes, an improvement upon the state of affairs in the Old World, where the accumulation of wealth into masses, the consequent destitution of large portions of society, and the divisions which thus are established between class and class, between man and man, constitute a system too absurd and too barbarous to endure. The remote approach made by the Americans to an equalisation of wealth is yet more important as indicating the method by which society is to be eventually redeemed from its absurdity and barbarism in respect of property. This method is as yet perceived by only a few: but the many who imitate as far as they can the modes of the Old World, and cherish to the utmost its feudal prepossessions, will only for a time be able to resist the convictions which the working of republican principles will force upon them, that there is no way of securing perfect social liberty on democratic principles but by community of property.

There is, as there ought to be, as great a horror in America as everywhere else of the despotism that would equalise property arbitrarily. Such a despotism can never become more than the ghost of a fancy. The approach to equalisation now required by public opinion is that required by justice; it is required that no man should encroach on his neighbours for the sake of enriching himself; that no man should encroach on his younger children for the sake of enriching the eldest; that no man should encroach on the present generation for the sake of enriching a future one. All this is allowed and required. But by the same rule, and for the sake of the same principle, no one will ever be allowed to take from the industrious man the riches won by his industry, and give them to the idle: to take from the strong to give to the weak: to take from the wise to give to the foolish. Such aggression upon property can never take place, or be seriously apprehended in a republic where all, except drunkards and slaves, are proprietors, and where the Declaration of Independence claims for every one, with life and liberty, the pursuit of happiness in his own way. There will be no attacks on property in the United States.

But it appears to me inevitable that there will be a general agreement, sooner or later, on a better principle of property than that under which all are restless; under which the wisdom and peace of the community fall far below what their other circumstances would lead themselves and their well-wishers to anticipate.

Their moralists are dissatisfied. "Our present civilisation," says Dr. Channing, "is characterised and tainted by a devouring greediness of wealth; and a cause which asserts right against wealth, must stir up bitter opposition, especially in cities where this divinity is most adored." . . . . "The passion for gain is everywhere sapping pure and generous feeling, and everywhere raises up bitter foes against any reform which may threaten to turn aside a stream of wealth. I sometimes feel as if a great social revolution were necessary to break up our present mercenary civilisation, in order that Christianity, now repelled by the almost universal worldliness, may come into new contact with the soul, and may reconstruct society after its own pure and disinterested principles."* This is a prophecy. Men to whom truth and justice are not "hollow words" are the prophets of the times to come.

The scholars of America are dissatisfied. They complain of the superficial character of scholarship; of the depression, or rather of the non-existence, of literature. Some hope that matters will be better hereafter, merely from the na-

* Channing's Letter to Birney. 1837.

tion having grown older. The greater number ascribe the
mischief to men having to work at their employments; and
some few of these believe that America would have a literature if only she had a hereditary aristocracy; this being
supposed the only method of leaving to individuals the leisure and freedom of spirit necessary for literary pursuits.
It has been pointed out that this is a mistake. Nature and
social economy do not so agree as that genius is usually
given to those who have hereditary wealth. The capability
has so much more frequently shown itself among the busy
and poor than among the rich who have leisure, as to mock
the human presumption which would dictate from whose
lips the oracles of Heaven should issue. One needs but to
glance over the array of geniuses, of philosophers, of scientific men, and even of the far lower order of scholars, to
see how few of the best benefactors of mankind have issued from "classic shades," "learned leisure," "scientific retreats," &c., and how many more have sent up their
axioms, their song, their prophecy, their hallelujah, from
the very press of the toiling multitude. What tale is commoner than the poverty of poets; the need that philosophers have usually had of philosophy; the embarrassments
and destitution of inventors; the straits of scholars?

It is clearly a mistake that hereditary property, opportunity, leisure, and such things, will make a literature, or secure scholarship: as great a mistake as that of the American
newspaper editor who triumphantly anticipated an age of
statuary from there being an arrival at New York of a
statue by Canova, at the same time with a discovery of
marble quarries. It is true that the statue lies in the marble
quarry: but it is also true that it lies sepulchred in the far
deeper recesses of some one unfathomable human intellect:
and to bring the one right intellect to the quarry is the
problem which is not given to be solved by mortal skill,—
by devices of hereditary ease and scientific retreats. This
kind of guidance is just that which the supreme Artist does
not confide to created hands.

It is true, however, that though opportunity and leisure
are not everything; that without union with useful toil,
they are nothing,—yet, with this union they are something,

—much. The first attempt to advocate leisure as the birth-right of every human being was made now some half-century ago.* The plea then advanced is a sound one on behalf of other things besides philosophy, literature and scholarship. Leisure, some degree of it, is necessary to the health of every man's spirit. Not only intellectual produc-tion, but peace of mind cannot flourish without it. It may be had under the present system, but it is not. With com-munity of property, it would be secured to every one. The requisite amount of work would bear a very small propor-tion to that of disposable time. It would then be fairly seen how much literature may owe to leisure.

The professional men of America are dissatisfied. The best of them complain that professions rank lower than in Europe; and the reasons they assign for this are, that less education is required; and that every man who desires to get on must make himself a party man, in theology, science, or law. Professional service is not well paid in the United States, compared with other countries, and with other occupations on the spot. Very severe toil is neces-sary to maintain a respectable appearance, except to those who have climbed the heights of their profession; and to them it has been necessary. One of these last, a man whom the world supposes to be blessed in all conceivable re-spects, told me that he had followed a mistaken plan of life; and that if he could begin again, he would spend his life differently. He had chosen his occupation rightly enough, and been wholly satisfied with his domestic lot: but his life had been one of toil and care in the pursuit of what he now found would have done all it could for him in half the quantity. If he could set himself back twenty years, he would seek far less diligently for money and emi-nence, stipulate for leisure, and cultivate mirth. Though this gentleman cares for money only that he may have it to give away; though his generosity of spirit is the most remarkable feature of his character, he would gladly ex-change the means of gratifying his liberal affections, for

* Godwin's Inquirer.

more capacity for mirth, more repose of spirit. The present mercenary and competitive system does not suit him.

The merchants are dissatisfied. If money, if success, apart from the object, could give happiness, who would be so happy as the merchants of America? In comparison with merchants generally, they are happy: but in comparison with what men are made to be, they are shackled, careworn, and weary as the slave. I obtained many a glimpse into the condition of mind of this class; and, far superior as it is to what the state of large classes is in the Old World, it is yet full of toil and trouble. In New York, some friends, wishing to impress me with a conviction of the enviable lives of American ladies, told me how the rich merchants take handsome houses in the upper part of the city, and furnish them splendidly for their wives: how these gentlemen rise early, snatch their breakfasts, hurry off two or three miles to their counting-houses, bustle about in the heat and dust, noise and traffic of Pearl Street all the long summer's day, and come home in the evening, almost too wearied to eat or speak; while their wives, for whose sake they have thus been toiling after riches, have had the whole day to water their flowers, read the last English novel, visit their acquaintance, and amuse themselves at the milliner's; paying, perhaps, 100 dollars for the newest Paris bonnet. The representation had a different effect from what was expected. It appeared to me that if the ladies prefer their husbands' society to that of morning visitors and milliners, they are quite as much to be pitied as their husbands, that such a way of consuming life is considered necessary or honourable. If they would prefer to wear bonnets costing a dollar a-piece, and having some enjoyment of domestic life, their fate is mournful; if they prefer hundred dollar bonnets to the enjoyment of domestic life, their lot is the most mournful of all. In either case, they and their husbands cannot but be restless and dissatisfied.

I was at a ball in New York, the splendour of which equalled that of any entertainment I ever witnessed. A few days after, the lady who gave the ball asked me whether I did not disapprove of the show and luxury of their society. I replied, that of whatever was done for mere show, I did disapprove; but that I liked luxury, and approved of it, as long as the pleasures of some did not encroach on the rights of others.

"But," said she, "our husbands have to pay for it all. They work very hard."

"I suppose it is their own choice to do so. I should make a different choice, perhaps; but if they prefer hard work and plenty of money to indulge their families with, to moderate work and less money, I do not see how you can expect me to blame them."

"O, but we all live beyond our incomes."

In that case, your pleasures encroach on the rights of others, and I have no more to say."

If this be true, how should this class be otherwise than restless and dissatisfied?

Are the mechanic and farming classes satisfied? No: not even they: outwardly blessed as they are beyond any class that society has ever contained. They, too, are aware that life must be meant to be passed far otherwise than in providing the outward means of living. They must be aware that though, by great industry, they can obtain some portion of time for occupations which are not money-getting, there must be something wrong in the system which compels men to devote almost the whole of their waking hours to procure that which, under a different combination of labour, might be obtained at a saving of three-fourths of the time. They who best know the blessings inseparable from toil; who are aware that the inner life is nourished by the activity of the outer, yet perceive of what infinite consequence it is to their progress that this activity should be varied in its objects, and separated as far as possible from association with physical necessities, and selfish possession. The poor man is rightly instructed, in the present state of things, when he is told that it is his first duty to provide for his own wants. The lesson is at present true, because the only alternative is encroachment on the rights of others: but it is a very low lesson in comparison with that which will be taught in the days when mutual and self-perfection will be the prevalent idea which the civilisation of the time will express. No thinking man or woman, who reflects

on the amount of time, thought, and energy, which would
be set free by the pressure of competition and money-getting being removed,—time, thought, and energy now spent
in wearing out the body, and in partially stimulating and
partially wasting the mind, can be satisfied under the present system.

In England, the prevalent dissatisfaction must subsist a
long time before anything effectual can be done to relieve
it. The English are hampered with institutions in which
the rights of individual property are involved in almost
hopeless intricacy. Though clear-sighted persons perceive
that property is the great harbourage of crime and misery,
the adversary of knowledge, the corrupter of peace, the
extinguisher of faith and charity; though they perceive
that institutions for the regulation of outward affairs all
follow the same course, being first necessary, then useful,
then useless, pernicious, and finally intolerable,—that property is thus following the same course as slavery, which
was once necessary, and is now intolerable,—as monarchy,
which was once necessary, and is now useless, if not pernicious: though all this is clearly perceived by many far-
seeing persons in England, they can do nothing but wait
till the rest of society sees it too. Thus it is in England. In
America the process will be more rapid. The democratic
principles of their social arrangements, operating already to
such an equalisation of property as has never before been
witnessed, are favourable to changes which are indeed
necessary to the full carrying out of the principles adopted.
When the people become tired of their universal servitude
to worldly anxiety,—when they have fully meditated and
discussed the fact that ninety-nine hundredths of social
offences arise directly out of property; that the largest proportion of human faults bear a relation to selfish possession;
that the most formidable classes of diseases are caused by
over or under toil, and by anxiety of mind; they will be
ready for the inquiry whether this tremendous incubus be
indeed irremovable; and whether any difficulties attending
its removal can be comparable to the evils it inflicts. In
England, the people have not only to rectify the false principles of barbarous policy, but to surmount the accumula-

tion of abuses which they have given out: a work, perhaps, of ages. In America, the people have not much more to do (the will being once ripe) than to retrace the false steps which their imitation of the old world has led them to take. Their accumulation of abuses is too small to be a serious obstacle in the way of the united will of a nation.

It is objected that the majority of society in America would have a horror of any great change like that contemplated: and that, though in bondage to worldly anxiety, they are unconscious of their servitude, or reconciled to it. Well: as long as this is the case, they have no change to dread; for all such alteration must proceed from their own will. There is no power upon earth from which they have any compulsion to fear. Yet it may be allowed to their friends to speculate upon the better condition which is believed to await them. When we look at a caterpillar, we like to anticipate the bright day when it will be a butterfly. If we could talk about it with the caterpillar, it would probably be terrified at the idea, and plead the exceeding danger of being high up in the air. We do not desire or endeavour to force or hasten the process: yet the caterpillar becomes a butterfly, without any final objection on its own part.

The principal fear, expressed or concealed, of those who dislike the mere mention of the outgrowth of individual property is lest they should be deprived of their occupations, objects, and interests. But no such deprivation can take place till they will have arrived at preferring other interests than money, and at pursuing their favourite occupation with other views than of obtaining wealth. "O, what shall I ever do without my currant leaves?" might the caterpillar exclaim. "How shall I ever get rid of the day, if I must not crawl along the twigs any more?" By the time it has done with crawling, it finds a pair of wings unfolding, which make crawling appear despicable in comparison. It is conscious, also, of a taste for nectar, which is better than currant leaves, be they of the juiciest. Men may safely dismiss all care about the future gratification of their tastes under new circumstances, as long as it happens to be the change of tastes which brings about the change of circumstances, the incompatibility between the two being lessened at every transition.

As for the details of the future economy indicated, it will be time enough for them when the idea which now burns like a taper in scattered minds shall have caught, and spread, and lighted up all into an illumination sufficient to do the work by. Whenever a healthy hunger enables the popular mind to assimilate a great principle, there are always strong and skilful hands enough to do the requisite work.

INTERCOURSE

THE manners of the Americans (in America) are the best I ever saw: and these are seen to the greatest advantage in their homes, and as to the gentlemen, in travelling. But for the drawback of inferior health, I know of no such earthly paradise as some of the homes in which I have had the honour and blessing of spending portions of the two years of my absence. The hospitality of the country is celebrated; but I speak now of more than usually meets the eye of a stranger; of the family manners, which travellers have rarely leisure or opportunity to observe. If I am asked what is the peculiar charm, I reply with some hesitation: there are so many. But I believe it is not so much the outward plenty, or the mutual freedom, or the simplicity of manners, or the incessant play of humour, which characterise the whole people, as the sweet temper which is diffused like sunshine over the land. They have been called the most good-tempered people in the world: and I think they must be so. The effect of general example is here most remarkable. I met, of course, with persons of irritable temperament; with hot-tempered, and with fidgetty people; with some who were disposed to despotism, and others to contradiction: but it was delightful to see how persons thus afflicted were enabled to keep themselves in order; were so wrought upon by the general example of cheerful helpfulness as to be restrained from clouding their homes by their moods. I have often wondered what the Americans make of European works of fiction in which ailing tempers are exhibited. European fiction does not represent such in half the extent and variety in which they might be truly and profitably exhibited: but I have often wondered what the Americans make of them, such as they are. They possess the initiatory truth, in the variety of temperaments which exists among themselves, as everywhere else; and in the moods of children: but the expansion of deformed tempers in grown people must strike them as monstrous caricatures.

Of course, there must be some general influence which sweetens or restrains the temper of a whole nation, of the same Saxon race which is not everywhere so amiable. I imagine that the practice of forbearance requisite in a republic is answerable for this pleasant peculiarity. In a republic, no man can in theory overbear his neighbour; nor, as he values his own rights, can he do it much or long in practice. If the moral independence of some, of many, sinks under this equal pressure from all sides, it is no little set-off against such an evil that the outbreaks of domestic tyranny are thereby restrained; and that the respect for mutual rights which citizens have perpetually enforced upon them abroad, comes thence to be observed towards the weak and unresisting in the privacy of home.

Some may find it difficult to reconcile this prevalence of good temper with the amount of duelling in the United States; with the recklessness of life which is not confined to the semi-barbarous parts of the country. When it is understood that in New Orleans there were fought, in 1834, more duels than there are days in the year, fifteen on one Sunday morning; that in 1835, there were 102 duels fought in that city between the 1st of January and the end of April; and that no notice is taken of shooting in a quarrel; when the world remembers the duel between Clay and Randolph; that Hamilton fell in a duel; and several more such instances, there may be some wonder that a nation where such things happen, should be remarkably good-tempered. But New Orleans is no rule for any place but itself. The spirit of caste, and the fear of imputation, rage in that abode of heathen licentiousness. The duels there are, almost without exception, between boys for frivolous causes. All but one of the 102 were so. And even on the spot, there is some feeling of disgust and shame at the extent of the practice. A Court of Honour was instituted for the restraint of the practice; of course, without effectual result. Its function degenerated into choosing weapons for the combatants, so that it ended by sanctioning, instead of repressing, duelling. Those who fight the most frequently and fatally are the French creoles, who use small swords.

The extreme cases which afford the clearest reading of the folly and wickedness of the practice,—of the meanness of the fear which lies at the bottom of it,—are producing their effect. The young men who go into the west to be the founders of new societies are in some instances taking their responsibility to heart, and resolving to use well their great opportunity for substituting a true for a false, a moral for a physical courage. The dreadful affair at Philadelphia, never to be forgotten there, when a quiet, inoffensive young man, the only child of a widowed mother, was forced out into the field, against his strongest remonstrances, made to stand up, and shot through the heart, could not but produce its effect. One of the principal agents was degraded in the American navy, (but has been since reinstated,) and none of the parties concerned has ever stood as well with society as other men since. Hamilton's fall, again, has opened men's eyes to the philosophy of duelling, and is working to that purpose, more and more. At the time, it was pretty generally agreed that he could not help fighting; now, there are few who think so. His correspondence with his murderer, previous to the duel, is remarkable. Having been told, on my entrance into the country, that Hamilton had been its "greatest man," I was interested in seeing what a greater than Washington could say in excuse for risking his life in so paltry a way. I read his correspondence with Colonel Burr with pain. There is fear in every line of it; a complicated, disgraceful fear. He was obviously perishing between two fears—of losing his life, and of not being able to guard his own honour against the attacks of a ruffian. Between these two fears he fell. I was talking over the correspondence with a duelling gentleman, "O," said he, "Hamilton went out like a capuchin." So the "greatest man" did not obtain even that for which he threw away what he knew was considered the most valuable life in the country. This is as it should be. When contempt becomes the wages of slavery to a false idea of honour, it will cease to stand in the way of the true; and "greatest men" will not end their lives in littleness.

That such hubbub as this is occasioned by a false idea of honour, and not by fault of temper, is made clear by the amiability shown by Americans, in all cases where their idea of honour is not concerned. In circumstances of failure and disappointment, delay, difficulty, and other provocation, they show great self-command. In all cases that I witnessed, from the New York fire, and baffled legislation, down to the being "mired" in bad roads, they appeared to be proof against irritation. Sometimes this went further than I could quite understand.

While travelling in Virginia, we were anxious one day to push on, and waste no time. Our "exclusive extra" drew up before a single house, where we were to breakfast. We told the landlady that we were excessively hungry, and in some hurry, and that we should be obliged by her giving us anything she happened to have cooked, without waiting for the best she could do for us. The woman was the picture of laziness, of the most formal kind. She kept us waiting till we thought of going on without eating. When summoned to table, at length, we asked the driver to sit down with us, to save time. Never did I see a more ludicrous scene than that breakfast. The lady at the tea-tray, tossing the great bunch of peacocks' feathers, to keep off the flies, and as solemn as Rhadamanthus. So was our whole party, for fear of laughter from which we should not be able to recover. Everything on the table was sour; it seemed as if studiously so. The conflict between our appetites and the disgust of the food was ridiculous. We all presently gave up but the ravenous driver. He tried the bread, the coffee, the butter, and all were too sour for a second mouthful; so were the eggs, and the ham, and the steak. No one ate anything, and the charge was as preposterous as the delay; yet our paymaster made no objection to the way we were treated. When we were off again, I asked him why he had been so gracious as to appear satisfied.

"This is a newly-opened road," he replied; "the people do not know yet how the world lives. They have probably no idea that there is better food than they set before us."

"But do not you think it would be a kindness to inform them?"

"They did their best for us, and I should be sorry to hurt their feelings."

"Then you would have them go through life on bad food, and inflicting it on other people, lest their feelings should be hurt at their being told how to provide better. Do you suppose that all the travellers who come this way will be as tender of the lady's feelings?"

"Yes, I do. You see the driver took it very quietly."

When we were yet worse treated, however, just after, when spending a night at Woodstock, our paymaster did remonstrate, (though very tenderly,) and his remonstrance was received with great candour by the master of the house; his wife being the one most to blame.

With this forbearance is united the most cheerful and generous helpfulness. If a farmer is burned out, his neighbours collect, and never leave him till he is placed in a better house than the one he has lost. His barns, in like case, are filled with contributions from their crops. Though there is nothing that men prize there so much as time, there is nothing that they are more ready to give to the service of others. Their prevalent generosity in the giving of money is known, and sufficiently estimated, considering how plentiful wealth is in the country. The expenditure of time, thought, and ingenuity, is a far better test of the temper from which the helpfulness proceeds. I am sorry that it is impossible to describe what this temper is in America; its manifestations being too incessant and minute for description. If this great virtue could be exhibited as clearly as it is possible to exhibit their faults, the heart of society would warm towards the Americans more readily than it has ever been alienated from them by their own faults, or the ill-offices of strangers.

It seems to me that the Americans are generally un-aware how one bad habit of their own, springing out of this very temper, goes to aggravate the evil offices of strangers. It is to me the most prominent of their bad habits; but one so likely to be cured by their being made aware of it, that I cannot but wish that some of the English vituperation which has been expended upon tobacco and its effects had been directed upon the far more serious fault of flattery. It will be seen at once how the practice of flattery is almost a necessary result of the combination of a false idea of honour with kindliness of temper. Its prevalence is so great as to tempt one to call it a necessary result. There is no getting out of the way of it. A gentleman, who was a de-praved school-boy, a fiendish husband, father, and slave-owner, whose reputation for brutality was as extensive as the country, was eulogised in the newspapers at his death. Every book that comes out is exalted to the skies. The pub-lic orators flatter the people; the people flatter the orators. Clergymen praise their flocks; and the flocks stand amazed at the excellence of their clergymen. Sunday-school teach-ers admire their pupils; and the scholars magnify their teachers. As to guests, especially from abroad, hospitality requires that some dark corner should be provided in every room where they may look when their own praises are being told to their own faces. Even in families, where, if anywhere, it must be understood that love cannot be sweetened by praise, there is a deficiency of that modesty, "simplicity and godly sincerity," in regard to mutual esti-mate, which the highest fidelity of affection inspires.

Passing over the puerility and vulgarity of the practice, —I think, if the Americans were convinced of its selfishness, —of its being actually a breach of benevolence, they would exercise the same command over their tongues that they do over their tempers, and suppress painful praises, as they rise to the lips. It was pleaded to me that the admiration is real, the praise sincere. Be it so: but why are they to be expressed, more than any other real thoughts whose expression would give pain? Let the admiration by all means be enjoyed: but what a pity to destroy sympathy with the person admired, by talking on the very subject at which sympathy must cease! Is it not clear that if praise be not painful to the person praised, it must be injurious? If he be modest, it is torture: if not, it is poison.

If I am not much mistaken, society in the new world is wakening up, under the stimulus of the slave-question, to a sense of its want of practical freedom, owing to its too great regard to opinion. The examples of those who can and do assert and maintain their liberty in these times of fiery trial, are venerable and beautiful in the eyes of the young. Those in the cities who have grown old in the practice of mistrust are unconscious of the extent of their privations: but the free yeomanry, and the youth of the towns, have an eye for the right, and a heart for the true, amid the mists and subtleties in which truth and liberty have been of late involved. The young men of Boston, especially, seem to be roused: and it is all-important that they should be. Boston is looked to throughout the Union, as the superior city she believes herself to be: and nowhere is the entrance upon life more perilous to the honesty and consistency of young aspirants after the public service. Massachusetts is the head-quarters of Federalism. Federalism is receding before Democracy, even there; but that State has still a Federal majority. A Massachusetts man has little chance of success in public life, unless he starts a Federalist: and he has no chance of rising above a certain low point, unless, when he reaches that point, he makes a transition into Democracy. The trial is too great for the moral independence of most ambitious men: and it fixes the eyes of the world on the youth of Boston. They are watched, that it may be seen whether they who now burn with ardour for complete freedom will hereafter "reverence the dreams of their youth," or sink down into cowardice, apathy, and intolerance, as they reach the middle of life.

So much for the spirit of intercourse. As for the modes in which the spirit is manifested, their agreeableness, or the contrary, is a matter of taste. No nation can pretend to judge another's manners; for the plain reason that there is no standard to judge by: and if an individual attempts to pronounce upon them, his sentence amounts to nothing more than a declaration of his own particular taste. If such a declaration from an individual is of any consequence, I am ready to acknowledge that the American manners please me, on the whole, better than any that I have seen.

The circumstances which strike a stranger unpleasantly are the apparent coldness and indifference of persons in hotels and shops; the use of tobacco, and consequent spitting; the tone of voice, especially among the New England ladies; and at first, but not afterwards, the style of conversation. The great charm is the exquisite mutual respect and kindliness.

Of the tobacco and its consequences, I will say nothing but that the practice is at too bad a pass to leave hope that anything that could be said in books would work a cure. If the floors of boarding-houses, and the decks of steam-boats, and the carpets of the Capitol, do not sicken the Americans into a reform; if the warnings of physicians are of no avail, what remains to be said? I dismiss the nauseous subject.

The most common mode of conversation in America I should distinguish as prosy, but withal rich and droll. For some weeks, I found it difficult to keep awake during the entire reply to any question I happened to ask. The person questioned seemed to feel himself put upon his conscience to give a full, true, and particular reply; and so he went back as near to the Deluge as the subject would admit, and forward to the millennium, taking care to omit nothing of consequence in the interval. There was, of course, one here and there, as there is everywhere, to tell me precisely what I knew before, and omit what I most wanted: but this did not happen often: and I presently found the information I obtained in conversation so full, impartial, and accurate, and the shrewdness and drollery with which it was conveyed so amusing, that I became a great admirer of the American way of talking before six months were over. Previous to that time, a gentleman in the same house with me expressed pleasantly his surprise at my asking so few questions: saying that if he came to England, he should be asking questions all day long. I told him that there was no need of my seeking information as long as more was given me in the course of the day than my head would carry. I did not tell him that I had not power of attention sufficient for such information as came in answer to my own desire. I can scarcely believe now that I ever felt such a difficulty.

Yet there is an epigrammatic turn in the talk of those who have never heard of "the art of conversation" which is supposed to be studied by the English. A reverend divine, —no other than Dr. Channing,—was one day paying toll, when he perceived a notice of gin, rum, tobacco, &c., on a board which bore a strong resemblance to a grave-stone. "I am glad to see," said the Dr. to the girl who received the toll, "that you have been burying those things."—"And if we had," said the girl, "I don't doubt you would have gone chief mourner."

Some young men, travelling on horseback among the White Mountains, became inordinately thirsty, and stopped for milk at a house by the road-side. They emptied every basin that was offered, and still wanted more. The woman of the house at length brought an enormous bowl of milk, and set it down on the table, saying, "One would think, gentlemen, you had never been weaned."

Of the same kind was the reply made by a gentleman of Virginia to a silly question by a lady. "Who made the Natural Bridge?"—"God knows, madam."

I was struck with repeated instances of new versions, generally much improved, of old fables. I think the following an improvement upon Sour Grapes. Noah warned his neighbours of what was coming, and why he was building his ark; but nobody minded him. When people on the high grounds were up to their chins, an old acquaintance of Noah's was very eager to be taken into the ark: but Noah refused again and again. "Well," said the man, when he found it was in vain, "go, get along, you and your old ark! I don't believe we are going to have much of a shower." I tried to ascertain whether this story was American. I could trace it no further off than Plymouth, Massachusetts.

There cannot be a stronger contrast than between the fun and simplicity of the usual domestic talk of the United States, and the solemn pedantry of which the extremest examples are to be found there; exciting as much ridicule at home as they possibly can elsewhere. I was solemnly assured by a gentleman that I was quite wrong on some point, because I differed from him. Everybody laughed: when he went on, with the utmost gravity, to inform us that there had been a time when he believed, like other people, that he might be mistaken; but that experience had convinced him that he never was; and he had in consequence cast behind him the fear of error. I told him I was afraid the place he lived in must be terribly dull,—having an oracle in it to settle everything. He replied that the worst of it was, other people were not so convinced of his being always in the right as he was himself. There was no joke here. He is a literal and serious-minded man. Another gentleman solemnly remarked upon the weather of late having been "uncommonly mucilaginous." Another pointed out to me a gentleman on board a steam-boat as "a blue stocking of the first class." The mistakes of unconscious ignorance should be passed over with a silent smile: but affectation should be exposed, as a service to a young society.

As for the peculiarities of language of which so much has been made,—I am a bad judge: but the fact is, I should have passed through the country almost without observing any, if my attention had not been previously directed to them. Next to the well-known use of the word "sick," instead of "ill," (in which they are undoubtedly right,) none struck me so much as the few following. They use the word "handsome" much more extensively than we do: saying that Webster made a handsome speech in the Senate: that a lady talks handsomely, (eloquently:) that a book sells handsomely. A gentleman asked me on the Catskill Mountain, whether I thought the sun handsomer there than at New York. When they speak of a fine woman, they refer to mental or moral, not at all to physical superiority. The effect was strange, after being told, here and there, that I was about to see a very fine woman, to meet in such cases almost the only plain women I saw in the country. Another curious circumstance is, that this is almost the only connexion in which the word woman is used. This noble word, spirit-stirring as it passes over English ears, is in America banished, and "ladies" and "females" substituted: the one to English taste mawkish and vulgar; the other indistinctive and gross. So much for difference of taste.

A few other ludicrous expressions took me by surprise occasionally. A gentleman in the west, who had been discussing monarchy and republicanism in a somewhat original way, asked me if I would "swap" my king for his. We were often told that it was "a dreadful fine day;" and a girl at a hotel pronounced my trumpet to be "terrible handy."* In the back of Virginia these superlative expressions are the most rife. A man who was extremely ill, in agonizing pain, sent for a friend to come to him. Before the friend arrived, the pain was relieved, but the patient felt much reduced by it. "How do you find yourself?" inquired the friend. "I'm powerful weak; but cruel easy."

However much may be the fault of strangers, in regard to the coldness of manners which is complained of in those who serve travellers in America, and however soon it may be dissipated by a genial address on the part of the stranger, it certainly is very disagreeable at the first moment. We invariably found ourselves well-treated; and in no instance that I remember failed to dissipate the chill by showing that we were ready to help ourselves, and to be sociable. The instant we attacked the reserve, it gave way. But I do not wonder that strangers who are not prepared to make the concession, and especially gentlemen travelling from hotel to hotel, find the constraint extremely irksome. It should never be forgotten that it is usually a matter of necessity or of favour, seldom of choice, (except in the towns,) that the wife and daughters of American citizens render service to travellers. Such a breaking in

---

* This reminds me of a singular instance of confusion of ideas. The landlady of a hotel declared my trumpet to be the best invention she had ever seen: better than spectacles. Query, better for what?

upon their domestic quiet, such an exposure to the society
of casual travellers, must be so distasteful to them generally
as to excuse any apparent want of cordiality. Some American travellers, won by the *empressement* of European
waiters, declare themselves as willing to pay for civility as
for their dinner. I acknowledge a different taste. I had
rather have indifference than civility which bears a reference to the bill: but I prefer to either the cordiality which
brightens up at your offer to make your own bed, mend
your own fire, &c.—the cordiality which brings your hostess
into your parlour, to draw her chair, and be sociable, not
only by asking where you are going, but by telling you all
that interests her in her neighbourhood. A girl at a Meadville hotel, in Pennsylvania, urged us to change our route,
that we might visit some friends of hers,—"a beautiful
bachelor that had lately lost his wife, and his fine son"—to
whom she would give us a letter of introduction. At Mays-
ville, Kentucky, the landlady sent repeated apologies for
not being able to wait on us herself, her attendance being
necessary at the bedside of her sick child. On our expressing our concern that, in such circumstances, she should
trouble herself about us, her substitute said we were very
unlike the generality of travellers who came. The ladies
were usually offended if the landlady did not wait upon
them herself, and would not open or shut the window with
their own hands; but rang to have the landlady to do it
for them. Such persons have probably been accustomed to
be waited on by slaves; or, perhaps, not at all; so that they
like to make the most of the opportunity. Our landlady at
Nashville, Tennessee, treated us extremely well; and on
parting kissed the ladies of the party all round.

So much more has naturally been observed by travellers
of American manners in stages and steam-boats than in
private-houses, that all has been said, over and over again,
that the subject deserves. I need only testify that I do not
think the Americans eat faster than other people, on the
whole. The celerity at hotel-tables is remarkable; but so it
is in stage-coach travellers in England, who are allowed ten
minutes or a quarter of an hour for dining. In private
houses, I was never aware of being hurried. The cheerful,

unintermitting civility of all gentlemen travellers, throughout the country, is very striking to a stranger. The degree
of consideration shown to women is, in my opinion, greater
than is rational, or good for either party; but the manners
of an American stage-coach might afford a valuable lesson
and example to many classes of Europeans who have a
high opinion of their own civilisation. I do not think it
rational or fair that every gentleman, whether old or young,
sick or well, weary or untired, should, as a matter of
course, yield up the best places in the stage to any lady
passenger. I do not think it rational or fair that five gentlemen should ride on the top of the coach, (where there is
no accommodation for holding on, and no resting-place for
the feet,) for some hours of a July day in Virginia, that a
young lady, who was slightly delicate, might have room to
lay up her feet, and change her posture as she pleased.

The manners of the wealthy classes depend, of course,
upon the character of their objects and interests: but they
are not, on the whole, so agreeable as those of their less
opulent neighbours. The restless ostentation of such as live
for grandeur and show is vulgar;—as I have said, the only
vulgarity to be seen in the country. Nothing can exceed
the display of it at watering-places. At Rockaway, on Long
Island, I saw in one large room, while the company was
waiting for dinner, a number of groups which would have
made a good year's income for a clever caricaturist. If any
lady, with an eye and a pencil adequate to the occasion,
would sketch the phenomena of affectation that might be
seen in one day in the piazza and drawing-room at Rockaway, she might be a useful censor of manners. But the
task would be too full of sorrow and shame for any one
with the true republican spirit. For my own part, I felt bewildered in such company. It was as if I had been set
down on a kind of debatable land between the wholly
imaginary society of the so-called fashionable novels of
late years, and the broad sketches of citizen-life given by
Madame D'Arblay. It was like nothing real. When I saw
the young ladies tricked out in the most expensive finery,
flirting over the backgammon-board, tripping affectedly
across the room, languishing with a seventy-dollar cambric

handkerchief, starting up in ecstasy at the entrance of a baby; the mothers as busy with affectations of another kind; and the brothers sidling hither and thither, now with assiduity, and now with nonchalance; and no one imparting the refreshment of a natural countenance, movement, or tone, I almost doubted whether I was awake. The village scenes that I had witnessed rose up in strong contrast; —the mirthful wedding, the wagon-drives, the offerings of wild-flowers to the stranger; the unintermitting, simple courtesy of each to all;—and it was scarcely credible that these contrasting scenes could both be existing in the same republic.

The best sort of rich persons, those whose principles and spirit are democratic, their desires moderate, their pursuits rational, drop out of sight of the mind's eye in considering the manners of the rich. Their wealth becomes only a comparatively unimportant circumstance connected with them. They support more beneficent objects than others, and perhaps have houses and libraries that it is a luxury to go to: but these things are not associated with themselves in the minds of their friends, as long as they are not so in their own. They fall into the ranks of the honourable, independent, thorough-bred classes of the country, (its true glory,) just as if they were not rich. The next best order of rich people,—those who put their time and money to good uses, but who are not blessed with the true democratic spirit of faith, have manners,—infinitely better than the Rockaway style,—but not so good as those of more faithful republicans. They are above the vanity of show and the struggle for fashion: but they dread the ascendency of ignorance, and distrust the classes whom they do not know. They are readers: their imaginations live in the Old World; and they have insensibly adopted the old-world prejudice, that "the people" must be ignorant, passionate, and rapacious. The conversation of such gives utterance to an assumption, and their bearing betrays an uneasiness, which are highly unfavourable to good manners. This small class are so respectable in the main, and for some great objects so useful, that it is much to be desired that they could be referred back perpetually to the democratic principles which would relieve their anxiety, and give to their manners that cheerfulness which should belong to honest republicans who have everything to hope, and little to fear.

One of the most remarkable sights in the country is the President's levee. Nothing is easier than to laugh at it. There is probably no mode in which a number of human beings can assemble which may not be laughable from one point of view or another. The President's levee presents many facilities for ridicule. Men go there in plaid cloaks and leather belts, with all manner of wigs, and offer a large variety of obeisance to the chief magistrate. Women go in bonnets and shawls, talk about the company, stand upon chairs to look over people's heads, and stare at the large rooms. There was a story of two girls, thus dressed, being lifted up by their escorting gentlemen, and seated on the two ends of the mantel-piece, like lustres, where they could obtain a view of the company as they entered. To see such people mixed in with foreign ambassadors and their suites, to observe the small mutual knowledge of classes and persons who thus meet on terms of equality, is amusing enough. But, amidst much that was laughable, I certainly felt that I was seeing a fine spectacle. If the gentry of Washington desire to do away with the custom, they must be unaware of the dignity which resides in it, and which is apparent to the eye of a stranger, through any inconveniences which it may have. I am sorry that its recurrence is no longer annual. I am sorry that the practice of distributing refreshments is relinquished: though this is a matter of less importance and of more inconvenience. If the custom itself should ever be given up, the bad taste of such a surrender will be unquestionable. There should be some time and place where the chief magistrate and the people may meet to exchange their respects, all other business being out of the question: and I should like to see the occasion made annual again.

I saw no bad manners at the President's levee, except on the part of a silly, swaggering Englishman. All was quiet and orderly; and there was an air of gaiety which rather surprised me. The great people were amused at the aspect of the assembly: and the humbler at the novelties that were going on before their eyes. Our party went at eight o'clock. As we alighted from the carriage, I saw a number of women, well attended, going up the steps in the commonest morning walking-dress. In the hall, were parties of young men, exhibiting their graces in a walk from end to end: and ladies throwing off their shawls, and displaying the most splendid dresses. The President, with some members of his cabinet on either hand, stood in the middle of the first room, ready to bow to all the ladies, and shake hands with all the gentlemen who presented themselves. The company then passed on to the fire-place, where stood the ladies of the President's family, attended by the Vice-president, and the Secretary of the Treasury. From this point, the visitors dispersed themselves through the rooms, chatting in groups in the Blue-room, or joining the immense promenade in the great East-room. After two circuits there, I went back to the reception-room; by far the most interesting to an observer. I saw one ambassador after another enter with his suite; the Judges of the Supreme Court; the majority of the members of both Houses of Congress; and intermingled with these, the plainest farmers, storekeepers, and mechanics, with their primitive wives and simple daughters. Some looked merry; some looked busy; but none bashful. I believe there were three thousand persons present. There was one deficiency,—one drawback, as I felt at the time. There were no persons of colour. Whatever individuals or classes may choose to do about selecting their society according to rules of their own making, here there should be no distinction. I know the pleas that would be urged,—the levee being held in a slave district; the presence of slave-holders from the south; and many others; but such pleas will not stand before the plain fact that this levee is the appointed means by which citizens of the United States of all degrees may, once in a time, meet together, to pay their equal respects to their chief magistrate. Every man of colour who is a citizen of the United States has a right to as free an admission as any other man; and it would be a dignity added to the White House if such were seen there. It is not to its credit that there is any place in the country where its people are more free to meet on equal terms. There is such a place. In the Catholic cathedral in New Orleans, I saw persons of every shade of colour kneeling on the pavement, without separation or distinction. I would fain have seen also some one secular house where, by general consent, all kinds of men might meet as brethren. But not even in republican America is there yet such an one.

The Americans possess an advantage in regard to the teaching of manners which they do not yet appreciate. They have before their eyes, in the manners of the coloured race, a perpetual caricature of their own follies; a mirror of conventionalism from which they can never escape. The negroes are the most imitative set of people living. While they are in a degraded condition, with little principle, little knowledge, little independence, they copy the most successfully those things in their superiors which involve the least principle, knowledge, and independence; viz. their conventionalisms. They carry their mimicry far beyond any which is seen among the menials of the rich in Europe. The black footmen of the United States have tiptoe graces, stiff cravats, and eye-catching flourishes, like the footmen in London: but the imitation extends into more important matters. As the slaves of the south assume their masters' names and military titles, they assume their methods of conducting the courtesies and gaieties of life. I have in my possession a note of invitation to a ball, written on pink paper with gilt edges.* When the lady invited came to her mistress for the ticket which was necessary to authorise her being out after nine at night, she was dressed in satin with muslin over it, satin shoes, and white kid gloves:— but, the satin was faded, the muslin torn: the shoes were tied upon the extremities of her splay feet, and the white gloves dropping in tatters from her dark fingers. She was a caricature, instead of a fine lady. A friend of mine walked a mile or two in the dusk behind two black men and a woman whom they were courting. He told me that nothing

* "Mr. Richard Masey requests the pleasure of Mrs. Miken's, and Miss Arthur's company, on Saturday evening at seven o'clock, in Dr. Smith's long brick-store."

could be more admirable than the coyness of the lady, and the compliments of the gallant and his friend. It could not be very amusing to those who reflect that holy and constant love, free preference, and all that makes marriage a blessing instead of a curse, were here out of the question: but the resemblance in the mode of courtship to that adopted by whites, when meditating marriage of a not dissimilar virtue,—a marriage of barter,—could not be overlooked.

Even in their ultimate, funereal courtesies, the coloured race imitate the whites. An epitaph on a negro baby at Savannah begins, "Sweet blighted lily!"—They have few customs which are absolutely peculiar. One of these is refusing to eat before whites. When we went on long expeditions, carrying luncheon, or procuring it by the road-side, the slaves always retired with their share behind trees or large stones, or other hiding-places.

The Americans may be considered secure of good manners generally while intellect is so reverenced among them as it is, above all other claims to honour. Whatever follies and frivolities the would-be fashionable classes may perpetrate, they will never be able to degrade the national manners, or to make themselves the first people in the republic. Intellect carries all before it in social intercourse, and will continue to do so. I was struck by the fact that, in country villages, the most enlightened members of a family may be cultivated as acquaintance, without the rest. They may be invited to a superior party, and the others left for an inferior one. As for the cities, Washington, with its motley population in time of Session, is an exception to all rules; and I certainly saw some uncommonly foolish people treated with more attention, of a temporary kind, than some very wise ones. But in other cities I am not aware of having seen any great influence possessed by persons who had not sufficient intellectual desert. In the capitals of States, men rank according to their supposed intellect. Many mistakes are made in the estimate; and (far worse) many pernicious allowances are made for bad morals, for the sake of the superior intellect: but still the taste is a higher one, the gradation a more rational one, than is to be found elsewhere: and, where such a taste and a gradation subsist, the essentials of good manners can never be wanting. It is refreshing to witness the village homage paid to the author and the statesman, as to the highest of human beings. Whatever the author and the statesman may be, the homage is honourable to those who offer it. It is no less refreshing in the cities to see how the vainest fops and the most solid capitalists readily succumb before men and women who are distinguished for nothing but their minds. The worst of manners,—those which fly off the furthest from nature, and do the most violence to the affections—are such as arise from a surpassing regard to things outward and shadowy: the best are those which manifest a pursuit of things invisible and real. The Americans are better mannered than others, in as far as they reverence intellect more than wealth and fashion. It remains for them to enlarge their notions, and exalt their tests of intellect, till it shall identify itself with morals. National manners, national observances of rank graduated on such a principle would be no subject of controversy, but would command the admiration, and gradually form the taste, of the world.

Women

"The vale best discovereth the hill. There is little friendship in the world, and least of all between equals, which was wont to be magnified. That that is, is between superior and inferior, whose fortunes may comprehend the one the other."

Bacon

I<small>F</small> a test of civilisation be sought, none can be so sure as the condition of that half of society over which the other half has power,—from the exercise of the right of the strongest. Tried by this test, the American civilisation appears to be of a lower order than might have been expected from some other symptoms of its social state. The Americans have, in the treatment of women, fallen below, not only their own democratic principles, but the practice of some parts of the Old World.

The unconsciousness of both parties as to the injuries suffered by women at the hands of those who hold the power is a sufficient proof of the low degree of civilisation in this important particular at which they rest. While woman's intellect is confined, her morals crushed, her health ruined, her weaknesses encouraged, and her strength punished, she is told that her lot is cast in the paradise of women: and there is no country in the world where there is so much boasting of the "chivalrous" treatment she enjoys. That is to say,—she has the best place in stage-coaches: when there are not chairs enough for everybody, the gentlemen stand: she hears oratorical flourishes on public occasions about wives and home, and apostrophes to woman: her husband's hair stands on end at the idea of her working, and he toils to indulge her with money: she has liberty to get her brain turned by religious excitements, that her attention may be diverted from morals, politics, and philosophy; and, especially, her morals are guarded by the strictest observance of propriety in her presence. In short, indulgence is given her as a substitute for justice. Her case differs from that of the slave, as to the principle, just so far as this; that the indulgence is large and universal, instead of petty and capricious. In both cases, justice is denied on no better plea than the right of the strongest. In both cases, the acquiescence of the many, and the burning discontent of the few, of the oppressed, testify, the one to the actual degradation of the class, and the other to its fitness for the enjoyment of human rights.

The intellect of woman is confined by an unjustifiable restriction of both methods of education,—by express teaching, and by the discipline of circumstance. The former, though prior in the chronology of each individual, is a direct consequence of the latter, as regards the whole of the sex. As women have none of the objects in life for which an enlarged education is considered requisite, the education is not given. Female education in America is much what it is in England. There is a profession of some things being taught which are supposed necessary because everybody learns them. They serve to fill up time, to occupy attention harmlessly, to improve conversation, and to make women something like companions to their husbands, and able to teach their children somewhat. But what is given is, for the most part, passively received; and what is obtained is, chiefly, by means of the memory. There is rarely or never a careful ordering of influences for the promotion of clear intellectual activity. Such activity, when it exceeds that which is necessary to make the work of the teacher easy, is feared and repressed. This is natural enough, as long as women are excluded from the objects for which men are trained. While there are natural rights which women may not use, just claims which are not to be listened to, large objects which may not be approached, even in imagination, intellectual activity is dangerous: or, as the phrase is, unfit. Accordingly, marriage is the only object left open to woman. Philosophy she may pursue only fancifully, and under pain of ridicule: science only as a pastime, and under a similar penalty. Art is declared to be left open: but the necessary learning, and, yet more, the indispensable experience of reality, are denied to her. Literature is also said to be permitted: but under what penalties and restrictions? Nothing is thus left for women but marriage.—Yes; Religion, is the reply.—Religion is a temper, not a pursuit. It is the moral atmosphere in which human beings are to live and move. Men do not live to breathe: they breathe to live.

The morals of women are crushed. If there be any human power and business and privilege which is absolutely universal, it is the discovery and adoption of the principle and laws of duty. As every individual, whether man or woman, has a reason and a conscience, this is a work which each is thereby authorised to do for him or herself. But it is not only virtually prohibited to beings who, like the American women, have scarcely any objects in life proposed to them; but the whole apparatus of opinion is brought to bear offensively upon individuals among women who exercise freedom of mind in deciding upon what duty is, and the methods by which it is to be pursued. There is nothing extraordinary to the disinterested observer in women being so grieved at the case of slaves,—slave wives and mothers, as well as spirit-broken men,—as to wish to do what they could for their relief: there is nothing but what is natural in their being ashamed of the cowardice of such white slaves of the north as are deterred by intimidation from using their rights of speech and of the press, in behalf of the suffering race, and in their resolving not to do likewise: there is nothing but what is justifiable in their using their moral freedom, each for herself, in neglect of the threats of punishment: yet there were no bounds to the efforts made to crush the actions of women who thus used their human powers in the abolition question, and the convictions of those who looked on, and who

might possibly be warmed into free action by the beauty
of what they saw. It will be remembered that they were
women who asserted the right of meeting and of discussion, on the day when Garrison was mobbed in Boston.
Bills were posted about the city on this occasion, denouncing these women as casting off the refinement and delicacy
of their sex: the newspapers, which laud the exertions of
ladies in all other charities for the prosecution of which
they are wont to meet and speak, teemed with the most
disgusting reproaches and insinuations: and the pamphlets
which related to the question all presumed to censure the
act of duty which the women had performed in deciding
upon their duty for themselves.—One lady, of high talents
and character, whose books were very popular before she
did a deed greater than that of writing any book, in acting
upon an unusual conviction of duty, and becoming an
abolitionist, has been almost excommunicated since. A
family of ladies, whose talents and conscientiousness had
placed them high in the estimation of society as teachers,
have lost all their pupils since they declared their anti-
slavery opinions. The reproach in all the many similar cases
that I know is, not that the ladies hold anti-slavery opinions, but that they act upon them.

How fearfully the morals of woman are crushed, appears from the prevalent persuasion that there are virtues
which are peculiarly masculine, and others which are peculiarly feminine. It is not only that masculine and feminine
employments are supposed to be properly different. No one
in the world, I believe, questions this. But it is actually
supposed that what are called the hardy virtues are more
appropriate to men, and the gentler to women. As all virtues nourish each other, and can no otherwise be nourished,
the consequence of the admitted fallacy is that men are,
after all, not nearly so brave as they ought to be; nor
women so gentle. But what is the manly character till it
be gentle? The very word magnanimity cannot be thought
of in relation to it till it becomes mild—Christ-like. Again,
what can a woman be, or do, without bravery? While
woman is human, men should beware how they deprive
her of any of the strength which is all needed for the strife

and burden of humanity. Let them beware how they put her off her watch and defence, by promises which they cannot fulfil;—promises of a guardianship which can arise only from within; of support which can be derived only from the freest moral action,—from the self-reliance which can be generated by no other means.

But, it may be asked, how does society get on,—what does it do? for it acts on the supposition of there being masculine and feminine virtues,—upon the fallacy just exposed.

It does so; and the consequences are what might be looked for. Men are ungentle, tyrannical. They abuse the right of the strongest, however they may veil the abuse with indulgence. They want the magnanimity to discern woman's human rights; and they crush her morals rather than allow them. Women are, as might be anticipated, weak, ignorant and subservient, in as far as they exchange self-reliance for reliance on anything out of themselves. Those who will not submit to such a suspension of their moral functions, (for the work of self-perfection remains to be done, sooner or later,) have to suffer for their allegiance to duty. They have all the need of bravery that the few heroic men who assert the highest rights of women have of gentleness, to guard them from the encroachment to which power, custom, and education, incessantly conduce.

Such brave women and such just men there are in the United States, scattered among the multitude, whose false apprehension of rights leads to an enormous failure of duties. There are enough of such to commend the true understanding and practice to the simplest minds and most faithful hearts of the community, under whose testimony the right principle will spread and flourish. If it were not for the external prosperity of the country, the injured half of its society would probably obtain justice sooner than in any country of Europe. But the prosperity of America is a circumstance unfavourable to its women. It will be long before they are put to the proof as to what they are capable of thinking and doing: a proof to which hundreds, perhaps thousands of Englishwomen have been put by adversity, and the result of which is a remarkable improvement in their social condition, even within the space of ten years. Persecution for opinion, punishment for all manifestations of intellectual and moral strength, are still as common as women who have opinions and who manifest strength: but some things are easy, and many are possible of achievement, to women of ordinary powers, which it would have required genius to accomplish but a few years ago.

MARRIAGE

IF there is any country on earth where the course of true love may be expected to run smooth, it is America. It is a country where all can marry early, where there need be no anxiety about a worldly provision, and where the troubles arising from conventional considerations of rank and connexion ought to be entirely absent. It is difficult for a stranger to imagine beforehand why all should not love and marry naturally and freely, to the prevention of vice out of the marriage state, and of the common causes of unhappiness within it. The anticipations of the stranger are not, however, fulfilled: and they never can be while the one sex overbears the other. Marriage is in America more nearly universal, more safe, more tranquil, more fortunate than in England: but it is still subject to the troubles which arise from the inequality of the parties in mind and in occupation. It is more nearly universal, from the entire prosperity of the country: it is safer, from the greater freedom of divorce, and consequent discouragement of swindling, and other vicious marriages: it is more tranquil and fortunate from the marriage vows being made absolutely reciprocal; from the arrangements about property being generally far more favorable to the wife than in England; and from her not being made, as in England, to all intents and purposes the property of her husband. The outward requisites to happiness are nearly complete, and the institution is purified from the grossest of the scandals which degrade it in the Old World: but it is still the imperfect institution which it must remain while women continue to be ill-educated, passive, and subservient: or well-educated, vigorous, and free only upon sufferance.

The institution presents a different aspect in the various parts of the country. I have spoken of the early marriages of silly children in the south and west, where, owing to the disproportion of numbers, every woman is married before she well knows how serious a matter human life is. She has an advantage which very few women elsewhere are allowed: she has her own property to manage. It would be a rare sight elsewhere to see a woman of twenty-one in her second widowhood, managing her own farm or plantation; and managing it well, because it had been in her own hands during her marriage. In Louisiana, and also in Missouri, (and probably in other States,) a woman not only has half her husband's property by right at his death, but may always be considered as possessed of half his gains during his life; having at all times power to bequeath that amount. The husband interferes much less with his wife's property in the south, even through her voluntary relinquishment of it, than is at all usual where the cases of women having property during their marriage are rare. In the southern newspapers, advertisements may at any time be seen, running thus:—"Mrs. A, wife of Mr. A, will dispose of &c. &c." When Madame Lalaurie was mobbed in New Orleans, no one meddled with her husband or his possessions; as he was no more responsible for her management of her human property than anybody else. On the whole, the practice seems to be that the weakest and most ignorant women give up their property to their husbands; the husbands of such women being precisely the men most disposed to accept it: and that the strongest-minded and most conscientious women keep their property, and use their rights; the husbands of such women being precisely those who would refuse to deprive their wives of their social duties and privileges.

I have mentioned that divorce is more easily obtained in the United States than in England. In no country, I believe, are the marriage laws so iniquitous as in England, and the conjugal relation, in consequence, so impaired.

Whatever may be thought of the principles which are to enter into laws of divorce, whether it be held that pleas for divorce should be one, (as narrow interpreters of the New Testament would have it;) or two, (as the law of England has it;) or several, (as the Continental and United States' laws in many instances allow,) nobody, I believe, defends the arrangement by which, in England, divorce is obtainable only by the very rich. It will be seen at a glance how such an arrangement tends to vitiate marriage: how it offers impunity to adventurers, and encouragement to every kind of mercenary marriages: how absolute is its oppression of the injured party: and how, by vitiating marriage, it originates and aggravates licentiousness to an incalculable extent. To England alone belongs the disgrace of such a method of legislation.

Of the American States, I believe New York approaches nearest to England in its laws of divorce. It is less rigid, in as far as that more is comprehended under the term "cruelty." The husband is supposed to be liable to cruelty from the wife, as well as the wife from the husband. There is no practical distinction made between rich and poor by the process being rendered expensive: and the cause is more easily resumable after a reconciliation of the parties. In Massachusetts, the term "cruelty" is made so comprehensive, and the mode of sustaining the plea is so considerately devised, that divorces are obtainable with peculiar ease. The natural consequence follows: such a thing is never heard of. A long-established and very eminent lawyer of Boston told me that he had known of only one in all his experience. Thus it is wherever the law is relaxed, and, *cæteris paribus*, in proportion to its relaxation: for the obvious reason, that the protection offered by law to the injured party causes marriages to be entered into with fewer risks, and the conjugal relation carried on with more equality. Retribution is known to impend over violations of conjugal duty. When I was in North Carolina, the wife of a gamester there obtained a divorce without the slightest difficulty. When she had brought evidence of the danger to herself and her children,—danger pecuniary and moral,

—from her husband's gambling habits, the bill passed both Houses without a dissenting voice.

It is clear that the sole business which legislation has with marriage is with the arrangement of property; to guard the reciprocal rights of the children of the marriage and the community. There is no further pretence for the interference of the law, in any way. An advance towards the recognition of the true principle of legislative interference in marriage has been made in England, in the new law in which the agreement of marriage is made a civil contract, leaving the religious obligation to the conscience and taste of the parties. It will be probably next perceived that if the civil obligation is fulfilled, if the children of the marriage are legally and satisfactorily provided for by the parties, without the assistance of the legislature, the legislature has, in principle, nothing more to do with the matter.

It is assumed in America, particularly in New England, that the morals of society there are peculiarly pure. I am grieved to doubt the fact: but I do doubt it. Nothing like a comparison between one country and another in different circumstances can be instituted: nor would any one desire to enter upon such a comparison. The bottomless vice, the all-pervading corruption of European society cannot, by possibility, be yet paralleled in America: but neither is it true that any outward prosperity, any arrangement of circumstances, can keep a society pure while there is corruption in its social methods, and among its principles of individual action. Even in America, where every young man may, if he chooses, marry at twenty-one, and appropriate all the best comforts of domestic life, —even here there is vice. Men do not choose to marry early, because they have learned to think other things of more importance than the best comforts of domestic life.

I was struck with the great number of New England women whom I saw married to men old enough to be their fathers. One instance which perplexed me exceedingly, on my entrance into the country, was explained very little to my satisfaction. The girl had been engaged to a young man whom she was attached to: her mother broke off the engagement, and married her to a rich old man. This story was a real shock to me; so persuaded had I been that in America, at least, one might escape from the disgusting spectacle of mercenary marriages. But I saw only too many instances afterwards. The practice was as-cribed to the often-mentioned fact of the young men mi-grating westwards in large numbers, leaving those who should be their wives to marry widowers of double their age. The Auld Robin Gray story is a frequently enacted tragedy here.

The unavoidable consequence of such a mode of mar-rying is, that the sanctity of marriage is impaired, and that vice succeeds. Any one must see at a glance that if men and women marry those whom they do not love, they must love those whom they do not marry. There are sad tales in country villages, here and there, which attest this; and yet more in towns, in a rank of society where such things are seldom or never heard of in England. I rather think that married life is immeasurably purer in America than in England: but that there is not otherwise much superiority to boast of. I can only say, that I unavoidably knew of more cases of lapse in highly respectable families in one State than ever came to my knowledge at home; and that they were got over with a disgrace far more temporary and superficial than they could have been vis-ited with in England.

The ultimate and very strong impression on the mind of a stranger, pondering the morals of society in America, is that human nature is much the same everywhere, what-ever may be its environment of riches or poverty; and that it is justice to the human nature, and not improvement in fortunes, which must be looked to as the promise of a better time. Laws and customs may be creative of vice; and should be therefore perpetually under process of ob-servation and correction: but laws and customs cannot be creative of virtue: they may encourage and help to preserve it; but they cannot originate it.

OCCUPATION

THE greater number of American women have home and
its affairs, wherewith to occupy themselves. Wifely and
motherly occupation may be called the sole business of
woman there. If she has not that, she has nothing. The
only alternative, as I have said, is making an occupation
of either religion or dissipation; neither of which is fit to
be so used: the one being a state of mind; the other altogether a negation when not taken in alternation with
business.

It must happen that where all women have only one
serious object, many of them will be unfit for that object.
In the United States, as elsewhere, there are women no
more fit to be wives and mothers than to be statesmen
and generals; no more fit for any responsibility whatever,
than for the maximum of responsibility. There is no need
to describe such: they may be seen everywhere. I allude
to them only for the purpose of mentioning that many of
this class shirk some of their labours and cares, by taking
refuge in boarding-houses. It is a circumstance very unfavourable to the character of some American women,
that boarding-house life has been rendered compulsory
by the scarcity of labour,—the difficulty of obtaining domestic service. The more I saw of boarding-house life, the
worse I thought of it; though I saw none but the best.
Indeed, the degrees of merit in such establishments weigh
little in the consideration of the evil of their existence at
all. In the best it is something to be secure of respectable
company, of a good table, a well-mannered and courteous
hostess, and comfort in the private apartments: but the
mischiefs of the system throw all these objects into the
back-ground.

The study of the economy of domestic service was a
continual amusement to me. What I saw would fill a
volume. Many families are, and have for years been, as
well off for domestics as any family in England; and I
must say that among the loudest complainers there were

many who, from fault of either judgment or temper, deserved whatever difficulty they met with. This is remarkably the case with English ladies settled in America. They carry with them habits of command, and expectations of obedience; and when these are found utterly to fail, they grow afraid of their servants. Even when they have learned the theory that domestic service is a matter of contract, an exchange of service for recompense, the authority of the employer extending no further than to require the performance of the service promised,—when the ladies have learned to assent in words to this, they are still apt to be annoyed at things which in no way concern them. If one domestic chooses to wait at table with no cap over her scanty chevelure, and in spectacles,—if another goes to church on Sunday morning, dressed exactly like her mistress, the lady is in no way answerable for the bad taste of her domestics. But English residents often cannot learn to acquiesce in these things; nor in the servants doing their work in their own way; nor in their dividing their time as they please between their mistress's work and their own. The consequence is, that they soon find it impossible to get American help at all, and they are consigned to the tender mercies of the low Irish; and every one knows what kind of servants they commonly are. Some few of them are the best domestics in America: those who know how to value a respectable home, a steady sufficient income, the honour of being trusted, and the security of valuable friends for life: but too many of them are unsettled, reckless, slovenly; some dishonest, and some intemperate.

All American ladies should know how to clear-starch and iron: how to keep plate and glass: how to cook dainties: and, if they understand the making of bread and soup likewise, so much the better. The gentlemen usually charge themselves with the business of marketing; which is very fair. A lady, highly accomplished and very literary, told me that she had lately been left entirely without help, in a country village where there was little hope of being speedily able to procure any. She and her daughter made the bread, for six weeks, and entirely kept the house, which might vie with any nobleman's for true luxury; perfect sufficiency and neatness. She mentioned one good result from the necessity: that she should never again put up with bad bread. She could now testify that bread might always be good, notwithstanding changes of weather, and all the excuses commonly given. I heard an anecdote from this lady which struck me. She was in the habit of employing, when she wanted extra help, a poor woman of colour, to do kitchen-work. The domestics had always appeared on perfectly good terms with this woman till, one day, when there was to be an evening party, the upper domestic declined waiting on the company; giving as a reason that she was offended at being required to sit down to table with the coloured woman. Her mistress gently rebuked her pride, saying "If you are above waiting on my company, my family are not. You will see my daughter carry the tea-tray, and my niece the cake." The girl repented, and besought to be allowed to wait; but her assistance was declined; at which she cried heartily. The next day, she was very humble, and her mistress reasoned with her, quite successfully. The lady made one concession in silence. She had the coloured woman come after dinner, instead of before.

Many anecdotes are current about the manners of the young people who come down from the retired parts of the country to domestic service in Boston. A simple country girl obeyed her instructions exactly about putting the dinner upon the table, and then summoning the family. But they delayed a few minutes, from some cause; and they entered the dining-room, found the domestic seated and eating. She had helped herself from a fowl, thinking that "the folk were so long a-coming, the things would get cold." A young man from Vermont was hired by a family who were in extreme want of a footman. He was a most friendly personage, as willing as he was free and easy; but he knew nothing of life out of a small farmhouse. An evening or two after his arrival, there was a large party at the house. His mistress strove to impress upon him that all he had to do at tea-time was to follow, with the sugar and cream, the waiter who carried the tea; to see that every one had cream and sugar; and to hold his tongue. He did his part with an earnest face, stepping industriously from guest to guest. When he had made the circuit, and reached the door, a doubt struck him whether a group in the furthest part of the room had had the benefit of his attentions. He raised himself on his toes with, "I'll ask;" and shouted over the heads of the company, "I say, how are ye off for sweetenin' in that ere corner?"

These extreme cases sound ridiculously and uncomfortably enough: but it must be remembered that they are extreme cases. For my own part, I had rather suffer any inconvenience from having to work occasionally in chambers and kitchen, and from having little hospitable designs frustrated, than witness the subservience in which the menial class is held in Europe. In England, servants have been so long accustomed to this subservience; it is so completely the established custom for the mistress to regulate their manners, their clothes, their intercourse with their friends, and many other things which they ought to manage for themselves, that it has become difficult to treat them any better. Mistresses who abstain from such regulation find that they are spoiling their servants; and heads of families who would make friends of their domestics find them little fitted to reciprocate the duty. In America it is otherwise: and may it ever be so! All but those who care for their selfish gratification more than for the welfare of those about them will be glad to have intelligent and disinterested friends in the domestics whom they may be able to attach, though there may be difficulty at first in retaining them; and some eccentricities of manner and dress may remain to be borne with.

One of the pleasures of travelling through a democratic country is the seeing no liveries. No such badge of menial service is to be met with throughout the States, except in the houses of the foreign ambassadors at Washington. Of how much higher a character American domestic service is than any which would endure to be distinguished by a badge, the following instance will show. I spent an evening at the house of the president of Harvard University. The party was waited on at tea by a domestic of the president's, who is also Major of the Horse. On cavalry days, when guests are invited to dine with the regiment, the major, in his regimentals, takes the head of the table, and has the president on his right hand. He plays the host as freely as if no other relation existed between them. The toasts being all transacted, he goes home, doffs his regimentals, and waits on the president's guests at tea.

As for the occupations with which American ladies fill up their leisure; what has been already said will show that there is no great weight or diversity of occupation. Many are largely engaged in charities, doing good or harm according to the enlightenment of mind which is carried to the work. In New England, a vast deal of time is spent in attending preachings, and other religious meetings: and in paying visits, for religious purposes, to the poor and sorrowful. The same results follow from this practice that may be witnessed wherever it is much pursued. In as far as sympathy is kept up, and acquaintanceship between different classes in society is occasioned, the practice is good. In as far as it unsettles the minds of the visitors, encourages a false craving for religious excitement, tempts to spiritual interference on the one hand, and cant on the other, and humours or oppresses those who need such offices least, while it alienates those who want them most, the practice is bad. I am disposed to think that much good is done, and much harm: and that, whenever women have a greater charge of indispensable business on their hands, so as to do good and reciprocate religious sympathy by laying hold of opportunities, instead of by making occupation, more than the present good will be done, without any of the harm.

All American ladies are more or less literary: and some are so to excellent purpose: to the saving of their minds from vacuity. Readers are plentiful: thinkers are rare. I met with more intellectual activity, more general power, among many ladies who gave little time to books, than among those who are distinguished as being literary. Natural philosophy is not pursued to any extent by women. There is some pretension to mental and moral philosophy; but the less that is said on that head the better.

This is a sad account of things. It may tempt some to ask 'what then are the American women?' They are better educated by Providence than by men. The lot of humanity is theirs: they have labour, probation, joy, and sorrow. They are good wives; and, under the teaching of nature, good mothers. They have, within the range of their activity, good sense, good temper, and good manners. Their beauty is very remarkable; and, I think, their wit no less. Their charity is overflowing, if it were but more enlightened: and it may be supposed that they could not exist without religion. It appears to superabound; but it is not usually of a healthy character. It may seem harsh to say this: but is it not the fact that religion emanates from the nature, from the moral state of the individual? Is it not therefore true that unless the nature be completely exercised, the moral state harmonised, the religion cannot be healthy?

One consequence, mournful and injurious, of the 'chivalrous' taste and temper of a country with regard to its women is that it is difficult, where it is not impossible, for women to earn their bread. Where it is a boast that women do not labour, the encouragement and rewards of labour are not provided. It is so in America. In some parts, there are now so many women dependent on their own exertions for a maintenance, that the evil will give way before the force of circumstances. In the meantime, the lot of poor women is sad. Before the opening of the factories, there were but three resources; teaching, needle-work, and keeping boarding-houses or hotels. Now, there are the mills; and women are employed in printing-offices; as compositors, as well as folders and stitchers.

I dare not trust myself to do more than touch on this topic. There would be little use in dwelling upon it; for the mischief lies in the system by which women are depressed, so as to have the greater number of objects of pursuit placed beyond their reach, more than in any minor arrangements which might be rectified by an exposure of particular evils. I would only ask of philanthropists of all countries to inquire of physicians what is the state of health of sempstresses; and to judge thence whether it is not inconsistent with common humanity that women should depend for bread upon such employment. Let them inquire what is the recompense of this kind of labour, and then wonder if they can that the pleasures of the licentious are chiefly supplied from that class. Let them reverence the strength of such as keep their virtue, when the toil which they know is slowly and surely destroying them will barely afford them bread, while the wages of sin are luxury and idleness. During the present interval between the feudal age and the coming time, when life and its occupations will be freely thrown open to women as to men, the condition of the female working classes is such that if its sufferings were but made known, emotions of horror and shame would tremble through the whole of society.

For women who shrink from the lot of the needlewoman,—almost equally dreadful, from the fashionable milliner down to the humble stocking-darner,—for those who shrink through pride, or fear of sickness, poverty, or temptation, there is little resource but pretension to teach. Ladies who fully deserve the confidence of society may realise an independence in a few years by school-keeping in the north: but, on the whole, the scanty reward of female labour in America remains the reproach to the country which its philanthropists have for some years proclaimed it to be. I hope they will persevere in their proclamation, though special methods of charity will not avail to cure the evil. It lies deep; it lies in the subordination of the sex: and upon this the exposures and remonstrances of philanthropists may ultimately succeed in fixing the attention of society; particularly of women. The progression or emancipation of any class usually, if not always, takes place through the efforts of individuals of that class: and so it must be here. All women should inform themselves of the condition of their sex, and of their own position. It must necessarily follow that the noblest of them will, sooner or later, put forth a moral power which shall prostrate cant, and burst asunder the bonds, (silken to some, but cold iron to others,) of feudal prejudices and usages. In the meantime, is it to be understood that the principles of the Declaration of Independence bear no relation to half of the human race? If so, what is the ground of the limitation? If not so, how is the restricted and dependent state of women to be reconciled with the proclamation that "all are endowed by their Creator with certain inalienable rights; that among these are life, liberty, and the pursuit of happiness?"

XI. Children

An evidence and reprehension both
Of the mere schoolboy's lean and tardy growth.
Cowper

NOTHING less than an entire work would be required for
the discussion of the subject of education in any country.
I can only indicate here two or three peculiarities which
strike the stranger in the discipline of American children; of
those whose lot is cast in the northern States; for it needs
no further showing, that those who are reared among
slaves have not the ordinary chances of wisdom and peace.

The Americans, particularly those of New England, look
with a just complacency on the apparatus of education
furnished to their entire population. There are schools provided for the training of every individual, from the earliest
age; colleges to receive the élite of the schools; and ly-
ceums, and other such institutions, for the subsequent instruction of working men.

The instruction furnished is not good enough for the
youth of such a country, with such a responsibility and
such a destiny awaiting them as the working out the first
democratic organisation that the world has witnessed in
practice. But it must be remembered how young the society is; how far it has already gone beyond most other
countries; and how great is the certainty that the majority,

always ultimately in the right, will gradually exalt the character of the instruction which it has been already wise enough to provide. It must be remembered too, how much farther the same kind and degree of instruction goes in a democracy than elsewhere. The alphabet itself is of little or no value to a slave, while it is an inestimable treasure to a conscious young republican. One needs but go from a charity-school in an English county to a free-school in Massachusetts, to see how different the bare acquisition of reading and writing is to children who, if they look forward at all, do it languidly, and into a life of mechanical labour merely, and to young citizens who are aware that they have their share of the work of self-government to achieve. Elderly gentlemen in the country may smile, and foreigners of all ages may scoff at the self-confidence and complacency of young men who have just exercised the suffrage for the first time: but the being secure of the dignity, the certainty of being fully and efficaciously represented, the probability of sooner or later filling some responsible political office, are a stimulus which goes far to supply the deficiencies of the instruction imparted. It is much to be wished that this stimulus were as strong and as virtuous in one or two colleges whose inmates are on the very verge of the exercise of their political rights, as in some of even the primary schools. The aristocratic atmosphere of Harvard University, for instance, would be much purified by a few breezes of such democratic inspiration as issue from the school-houses of some of the country districts.

The early republican consciousness of which I have spoken, and the fact of the more important place which the children occupy in a society whose numbers are small in proportion to its resources, are the two circumstances which occasion that freedom of manners in children of which so much complaint has been made by observers, and on which so much remonstrance has been wasted;— I say "wasted," because remonstrance is of no avail against a necessary fact. Till the United States cease to be republican, and their vast area is fully peopled, the children there will continue as free and easy and as important as they are. For my own part, I delight in the American children.

There are instances, as there are everywhere, of spoiled, pert, and selfish children. Parents' hearts are pierced there, as elsewhere. But the independence and fearlessness of children were a perpetual charm in my eyes. To go no deeper, it is a constant amusement to see how the speculations of young minds issue, when they take their own way of thinking, and naturally say all they think. Some admirable specimens of active little minds were laid open to me at a juvenile ball at Baltimore. I could not have got at so much in a year in England. If I had at home gone in among eighty or a hundred little people, between the ages of eight and sixteen, I should have extracted little more than "Yes, ma'am," and "No, ma'am." At Baltimore, a dozen boys and girls at a time crowded round me, questioning, discussing, speculating, revealing in a way which enchanted me. In private houses, the comments slipped in at table by the children were often the most memorable, and generally the most amusing part of the conversation. Their aspirations all come out.

In conversing with a truly wise parent, one day, I remarked on the change of relation which takes place when the superior children of ordinary parents become guides and protectors to those who have kept their childhood restrained under a rigid rule. We talked over the difficulties of the transition here, (by far the hardest part of filial duty,) and speculated on what the case would be after death, supposing the parties to recognise each other in a new life of progression. My friend observed that the only thing to be done is to avoid to the utmost the exercise of authority, and to make children friends from the very beginning. He and many others have done this with gladdening success. They do not lay aside their democratic principles in this relation, more than in others, because they happen to have almost unlimited power in their own hands. They watch and guard: they remove stumbling-blocks: they manifest approbation and disapprobation: they express wishes, but, at the same time, study the wishes of their little people: they leave as much as possible to natural retribution: they impose no opinions, and quarrel with none: in short, they exercise the tenderest friendship

without presuming upon it. What is the consequence? I
had the pleasure of hearing this friend say, "There is nothing in the world so easy as managing children. You may
make them anything you please." In my own mind I
added, "with such hearts and minds to bring to the work
as the parents of your children have."—One reason of the
pleasure with which I regarded the freedom of American
children was that I took it as a sign that the most tremendous suffering perhaps of human life is probably lessened, if not obviated, there:—the misery of concealed
doubts and fears, and heavy solitary troubles,—the misery
which makes the early years of a shy child a fearful purgatory. Yet purgatory is not the word: for this misery
purges no sins, while it originates many. I have a strong
suspicion that the faults of temper so prevalent where
parental authority is strong, and where children are made
as insignificant as they can be made, and the excellence of
temper in America, are attributable to the different management of childhood in the one article of freedom. There
is no doubt that many children are irrecoverably depressed
and unnerved for want of being convinced that anybody
cares for them. They nourish doubts, they harbour fears
and suspicions, and carry within them prejudices and errors, for want of its occurring to them to ask questions;
and though they may outgrow these defects and errors,
they never recover from them. Unexplained and inexplicable obstacles are thrown in the way of their filial duty,—
obstacles which not even the strongest conscientiousness
can overcome with grace: the vigour of the spirit is pros-
trated, or perverted into wilfulness: the calmness of self-
respect is forfeited, and so is the repose of a loving faith
in others. In short, the temper is ruined, and the life is
spoiled; and all from the parents not having made friends
of their children from the beginning.—No one will suppose
that I mean to represent this mistake as general anywhere.
But I am confident it is very common at home: and that
it cannot, in the nature of things, ever become common in
America. I saw one or two melancholy instances of it: and
a few rare cases where parents attempted unjustifiably to
rule the proceedings of their grown up sons and daughters;

not by express command, but by pleas which, from a parent, are more irresistible than even commands. But these were remarkable, and remarked upon, as exceptions. I saw two extreme contrasting cases, in near neighbourhood, of girls brought up, the one in the spirit of love, the other in that of fear. Those two girls are the best teachers of moral philosophy that ever fell in my way. In point of birth, organisation, means of education, they were about equal. Both were made to be beautiful and intelligent. The one is pallid, indolent, (with the reputation of learning,) tasteless, timid, and triste, manifesting nothing but occasionally an intense selfishness, and a prudery beyond belief. The education of this girl has been the study of her anxious parents from the day of her birth: but they have omitted to let her know and feel that anybody loved her. The other, the darling of a large family, meeting love from all eyes, and hearing tenderness in every voice, is beautiful as a Hebe, and so free and joyous that her presence is like sunshine in a rainy day. She knows that she is beautiful and accomplished; but she is, as far as eye can see, absolutely devoid of vanity. She has been apprised, over and over again, that people think her a genius: she silently contradicts this, and settles with herself that she can acquire anything, but originate nothing. She studies with her whole being, as if she were coming out next year in a learned profession. She dances at balls as if nothing lay beyond the ball-room. She flits hither and thither, in rain or sunshine, walking, riding, or driving, on little errands of kindness; and bears the smallest interests of her friends in mind in the heights of her mirth and the depths of her studies. At dull evening parties, she can sit under the lamp, (little knowing how beautiful she looks) quietly amusing herself with prints, and not wanting notice: and she can speak out what she thinks and feels to a circle of admirers, as simply and earnestly as she would to her own mother. I have seen people shake their heads, and fear lest she should be spoiled; but my own conviction is that this young creature is unspoilable. She has had all the praise and admiration she can have: no watchfulness of parents can keep them from her. She does not want

SOCIETY IN AMERICA

praise and admiration. She has other interests and other desires: and my belief is, that if she were left alone to-morrow, the last of her family, she would be as safe, busy, and, in due time, happy, as she is now under their tender guardianship. She is the most complete example I ever witnessed of a being growing up in the light and warmth and perfect freedom of love; and she has left me very little toleration for authority, in education more than in anything else.

A question was asked me, oftener than once, which indicates the difference between family manners in England and America. I was asked whether it was possible that the Bennet family would act as they are represented in "Pride and Prejudice:" whether a foolish mother, with grown up daughters, would be allowed to spoil the two youngest, instead of the sensible daughters taking the case into their own hands. It is certainly true that in America the superior minds of the family would take the lead; while in England, however the domestic affairs might gradually arrange themselves, no person would be found breathing the suggestion of superseding the mother's authority. The most remarkable difference is, that in England the parents value the authority as a right, however lenient they may be in the use of it. In America, the parent disapproves of it, as a matter of reason: and, if he acts rationally, had rather not possess it. Little revelations of the state of the case were perpetually occurring, which excited my wonder at first, and my interest throughout. It appeared through the smallest circumstances; as, for instance, when a lady was describing to me the wedding-day of her eldest daughter. She mentioned that two or three of the children were not in the drawing-room at the time of the ceremony. Why? They were so angry at their brother-in-law for taking away their sister, that they kept out of the way till he had driven from the door with his bride. What children in England would have dreamed of absenting themselves in such a way?

XII.   Sufferers

"One of the universal sentiments which Christianity has deeply imbedded in the human heart is that of the *natural equality of men.* . . . . . It has produced the spectacle, which I believe to be peculiar to christian times, of one class uplifting another, the happy toiling for the miserable, the free vindicating the rights of the oppressed. With all the noble examples of disinterested friendship and patriotism, which ancient history affords, I can remember no approach to that *wholesale compassion,* that general action of one order of society on another, that system of *benevolent agitation* in behalf of powerless and forgotten suffering, which characterises the history of modern times."

Rationale of Religious Inquiry

THE idea of travelling in America was first suggested to me by a philanthropist's saying to me, "Whatever else may be true about the Americans, it is certain that they have got at principles of justice and mercy in the treatment of the least happy classes of society which we may be glad to learn from them. I wish you would go and see what they are." I did so; and the results of my investigation have not been reserved for this short chapter, but are spread over the whole of my book. The fundamental democratic principles on which American society is organised, are those "principles of justice and mercy" by which the guilty, the ignorant, the needy, and the infirm, are saved and blessed. The charity of a democratic society is heart-reviving to witness; for there is a security that no wholesale oppression is bearing down the million in one direction, while charity is lifting up the hundred in another. Generally speaking, the misery that is seen is all that exists: there is no paralysing sense of the hopelessness of setting up individual benevolence against social injustice. If the community has not yet arrived at the point at which all communities are destined to arrive, of perceiving guilt to be infirmity, of obviating punishment, ignorance, and want, still the Americans are more blessed than others, in the certainty that they have far less superinduced misery than societies abroad, and are using wiser methods than others for its alleviation. In a country where social equality is the great principle in which all acquiesce, and where, consequently, the golden rule is suggested by every collision between man and man, neglect of misery is almost as much out of the question as the oppression from which most misery springs.

In the treatment of the guilty, America is beyond the rest of the world, exactly in proportion to the superiority of her political principles. I was favoured with the confidence of a great number of the prisoners in the Philadelphia penitentiary where absolute seclusion is the principle of punishment. Every one of these prisoners, (none of them being aware of the existence of any other,) told me that he was under obligations to those who had the charge of him for treating him "with respect." The expression struck me much as being universally used by them. Some explained the contrast between this method of punishment and imprisonment in the old prisons, copied from those of Europe; where criminals are herded together, and treated like anything but men and citizens. Others said that though they had done a wrong thing, and were rightly sequestered on that ground, they ought not to have any further punishment inflicted upon them; and that it was the worst of punishments not to be treated with the respect due to men. In a community where criminals feel and speak thus, human rights cannot but be, at length, as much regarded in the infliction of punishment as in its other arrangements.

Much yet remains to be done, to this end. An enormous amount of wrong must remain in a society where the elaboration of a vast apparatus for the infliction of human misery, like that required by the system of solitary imprisonment, is yet a work of mercy. Milder and juster methods of treating moral infirmity will succeed when men shall have learned to obviate the largest possible amount of it. In the meantime, I am persuaded that this is the best method of punishment which has yet been tried. The grounds of preference were, that they could preserve their self-respect, in the first place; and, in the next, their chance in society on their release. They leave the prison with the recompense of their extra labour in their pockets, and without the fear of being waylaid by vicious old companions, or hunted from employment to employment by those whose interest it is to deprive them of a chance of establishing a character.

The pauperism of the United States is, to the observation of a stranger, nothing at all. To residents, it is an occasion for the exercise of their ever-ready charity. It is confined to the ports, emigrants making their way back into the country, the families of intemperate or disabled men, and unconnected women, who depend on their own exertions. The amount altogether is far from commensurate with the charity of the community; and it is to be hoped that the curse of a legal charity, at least to the able-bodied, will be avoided in a country where it certainly cannot become necessary within any assignable time.

In the south, I was rather amused at a boast which was made to me of the small amount of pauperism. As the plague distances all lesser diseases, so does slavery obviate pauperism. In a society of two classes, where the one class are all capitalists, and the other property, there can be no pauperism but through the vice or accidental disability of members of the first. But I was beset by many an anxious thought about the fate of disabled slaves. Masters are, of course, bound to take care of their slaves for life. There are doubtless many masters who guard the comfort of their helpless negroes all the more carefully from the sense of the entire dependence of the poor creatures upon their mercy: but, there are few human beings fit to be trusted with absolute power: and while there are

many who abuse the authority they have over slaves who
are not helpless, it is fearful to think what may be the
fate of those who are purely burdensome. At Columbia,
South Carolina, I was taken by a benevolent physician to
see the State Lunatic Asylum, which might be considered
his work; so diligent had he been in obtaining appropriations for the object from the legislature, and afterwards
in organising its plans, with great wisdom and humanity.
When we were looking out from the top of this building,
watching the patients in their airing grounds, I observed
that no people of colour were visible in any part of the
establishment. Where were they then?—It was some time
before I could get a clear answer to this: but my friend
the physician said, at length, that he had no doubt they
were kept in out-houses, chained to logs, to prevent their
doing harm. No member of society is charged with the
duty of investigating cases of disease and suffering among
slaves who cannot make their own state known. They are
wholly at the mercy of their owners. The physician told
me that it was his intention, now he had accomplished his
object of establishing a lunatic asylum for the whites, to
persevere no less strenuously till he obtained one for the
blacks. He will probably not find this a very difficult object
to effect; for the interest of masters, as well as their humanity, is concerned in having an asylum provided by the
State for their useless or mischievous negroes.

The Asylum for the Blind at Philadelphia was a young
institution at the time I saw it; but it pleased me more than
any I ever visited: more than the larger one at Boston;
whose institution and conduct are, however, honourable
to all concerned in it. The reason of my preference of the
Philadelphia one is that the pupils there were more active
and cheerful than those of Boston. The spirits of the inmates are the one infallible test of the management of
an institution for the blind. The fault of such in general
is that mirth is not sufficiently cultivated, and religion too
exclusively so.

It may be worth suggesting here that while some of the
thinkers of America, like many of the same classes in England, are mourning over the low state of the Philosophy

of Mind in their country, society is neglecting a most important means of obtaining the knowledge requisite for the acquisition of such philosophy. Scholars are embracing alternately the systems of Kant, of Fichte, of Spurzheim, of the Scotch school; or abusing or eulogising Locke, asking who Hartley was, or weaving a rainbow arch of transcendentalism, which is to comprehend the whole that lies within human vision, but sadly liable to be puffed away in dark vapour with the first breeze of reality; scholars are thus labouring at a system of mental philosophy on any but the experimental method, while the materials for experiment lie all around and within them. If they object, as is common, the difficulty of experimenting on their conscious selves, there is the mental pathology of their blind schools, and the asylums for the deaf and dumb. I am aware that they put away the phenomena of insanity as irrelevant; but the same objections do not pertain to the other two classes. Let the closet speculations be pursued with all vigour: but if there were joined with these a close and unwearied study of the phenomena of the minds of persons deficient in a sense, and especially of those precluded from the full use of language, the world might fairly look for an advance in the science of Mind equal to that which medical science owes to pathology. It will not probably lodge us in any final and total result, any more than medicine and anatomy promise to ascertain the vital principle: but it will doubtless yield us some points of certainty, in aid of the fluctuating speculations amidst which we are now tossed, while few can be found to agree even upon matters of so-called universal consciousness. I should like to see a few philosophers interested in ascertaining and recording the manifestations of some progressive minds, peculiar from infirmity, for a series of years. If any such in America, worthy to undertake the task, from having strength enough to put away theory and prejudice, and record only what is really manifested to them, should be disposed to take my hint, I hope they will not wait for a philosophical "class to fall into."

I was told at Washington, with a smile half satirical and half complacent, that "the people of New England do

good by mania." I watched accordingly for symptoms of
this second or third-rate method of putting benevolence
into practice. The result was, that I was convinced that
the people of New England, and of the whole country,
do good in all manner of ways; some better and some
worse, according to their light. I met with pious ladies
who make clothes for the poor, but who took work (her
means of bread) out of the hands of a sempstress, (who
had three children,) because her husband was in prison.
They told me it would be encouraging vice to have
anything to do with the families of persons who had committed offences: and when I asked how reformed offend-
ers were to put their reformation in practice, I was told
that if I would employ anybody who had been in prison,
I deserved the censure of society. The matter ended in the
sempstress (a good young woman) having to go home to
her father's house. I met with others, both men and women,
who make it the business of their lives, or of their leisure
from yet more pressing duties, to seek out the sinners of
society, and give them, not threats, nor scorn, nor lectures,
but sympathy and help. With regard to some methods of
charity, nothing could exceed the ingenuity, shrewdness,
forethought, and determination with which they were
managed: in others, I was reminded of what I had been
told about mania.

In regarding the Temperance movement, the word perpetually occurred to me. How the vice of intemperance
ever reached the pass it did in a country where there is
no excuse of want on the one hand, or of habits of con-
viviality on the other, was sometimes attempted to be explained to me; but never to my satisfaction. Much may be
said upon it, which cannot find a place here. Certain it is
that the vice threatened to poison society. It was as remarkable as licentiousness of other kinds ever was in Paris, or
at Vienna. Men who doubted the goodness of the principle
of Association in opposition to moral evil, were yet carried
away to countenance it by seeing nothing else that was to
be done. Some few of these foresaw that, as every man
must be virtuous in himself and by himself; as the principle
of temperance in a man is incommunicable; as no two

men's temptations are alike; and as, especially in this case, the temptations of the movers were immeasurably weaker than those of the mass to be wrought upon, there could be no radical truth, no pervading sincerity to rely upon. They foresaw what had happened; that there would be a vast quantity of perjury, of false and hasty promising, of lapse, and of secret, solitary drinking; that if some waverers were saved, others would be plunged into hypocrisy in addition to their intemperance; that schisms must arise out of the ignorance of bigots, which would cause as much scandal to good morals as intemperance itself; and that, worst of all, this method was the introduction of new and fatal perils to freedom of conscience. A few foresaw all this; but a very few had strength to resist the movement. A sort of reproach was cast upon those who refused to join, like that which is now visited upon such as adhere to the principle on which they first joined;—a kind of insinuation that their temperance is not thorough.—What have the consequences already been?

The amount of visible intemperance is actually lessened prodigiously; perhaps to the full extent anticipated by the originators of the movement. Spirit-shops have been shut up by hundreds; some few drunkards have been reformed; and very large numbers of young men, entering life, are now sober citizens, who seemed in danger of becoming a curse to society. The question is whether the causes of the preceding intemperance have been discovered and obviated. If not, there is every reason to expect that the control of opinion over them will be but temporary; and that the late sweeping and garnishing will give place to a state of things at least as bad as before.

My own convictions are that Associations, excellent as they are for mechanical objects, are not fit instruments for the achievement of moral aims: that there is yet no proof that the principle of self-restraint has been exalted and strengthened in the United States by the Temperance movement, while the already too great regard to opinion, and subservience to spiritual encroachment have been much increased: that, therefore, great as are the visible benefits of the institution, it may at length appear that they have been dearly purchased. I have reason to think that numbers of persons in the United States, especially enlightened physicians, (who have the best means of knowledge,) are of the same opinion. This is confirmed by the fact that there is a spreading dislike of Associations for moral, while there is a growing attachment to them for mechanical, objects. The majority will show to those who may be living at the time what is the right.

Though scarcely necessary, it may be well to indicate the distinction between Temperance and Abolition societies with regard to this principle. The bond of Temperance societies is a pledge or vow respecting the personal conduct of the pledger. The bond of the Abolitionists is agreement in a principle which is to be proposed and exhibited by mechanical means,—lecturing, printing, raising money for benevolent purposes. Nobody is bound in thought, word, or action. There have been a few Temperance societies which have avoided pledges, and confined their exertions to spreading knowledge on the pathology of intemperance, and its effects on the morals of the individual and of society. Associations confined to these objects are probably not only harmless, but highly useful.

XIII.   Utterance

"A country which has no national literature, or a literature too insignificant to force its way abroad, must always be, to its neighbours, at least in every important spiritual respect, an unknown and misestimated country. Its towns may figure on our maps; its revenues, population, manufactures, political connexions, may be recorded in statistical books: but the character of the people has no symbol and no voice; we cannot know them by speech and discourse, but only by mere sight and outward observation of their manners and procedure. Now, if both sight and speech, if both travellers and native literature, are found but ineffectual in this respect, how incalculably more so the former alone!"

Edinburgh Review.—Vol. xlvi. p. 309.

THERE is but one method by which most nations can express the general mind: by their literature. Popular books are the ideas of the people put into language by an individual. To a self-governing people there are two methods open: legislation is the expression of the popular mind, as well as literature.

The mind of a nation grows, like that of an individual; and its growth follows somewhat the same course. There may be in each a mind, vigorous and full of promise, unerring in the recognition of true principles, but apt to err in the application of them; ardent in admiration of all faithful and beautiful expression of mind by others; but not yet knowing how to utter itself. The youthful philoso-

pher or poet is commonly a metaphysician before he indicates what he is ultimately to become. In the age of vivid
consciousness, before he is twenty, the invisible and in-
tangible world of reality opens to him with a distinctness
and lustre which make him in after time almost envy himself his youthful years. In this bright spiritual world, much
is as indisputably revealed to him as material objects to
the bodily eye: principles in full prominence; and a long
perspective of certainties melting imperceptibly into probabilities; and lost at last in the haze of possibility, bright
with the meridian sun of faith. To him

"The primal duties shine aloft, like stars:
The charities that soothe and heal and bless
Lie scattered at the feet of man, like flowers."

But of all this he can, for some time, express nothing.
He burns with convictions, but can testify them to others
only by recognising the expression which others have obtained the power of affording. If he makes the attempt, he
is either unintelligible or trite.

This appears to me to be the stage at which the mind
of America has arrived. That the legislation of the country
is, on the whole, so noble, is owing to the happy circumstance (a natural one in the order of Providence, by which
great agents rise up when a great work has to be done)
that accomplished individuals were standing ready to help
the people to an expression of its first convictions. The earliest convictions of a nation so circumstanced are of their
fundamental and common rights: and the expression must
be legislation. This has been done so well by the Americans that there is every reason to anticipate that more will
follow; since principles are so linked together that it is
scarcely possible to grasp one without touching another.
Accordingly, though there is no contribution yet to the
Philosophy of Mind from America, many thinking men are
feeling after its principles amidst the accumulations of the
old world: though no light has been given to society from
the American press on the principles of politics, Americans
may be heard quoting Burke from end to end of the country, infallibly separating the democratic aspirations of his

genius from the aristocratic perversions of his temper and education: though America has yet witnessed no creation, either in literature or the arts, and cannot even distinguish a creation from a combination, imitation, or delineation, yet the power of admiration which she shows in hailing that which is far inferior to what she needs,—the vigour with which, after incessant disappointment, she applies herself to the produce of her press, to find the imperishable in what is just as transient as all that has gone before, —is a prophecy that a creator will arise. The faith that America is to have an artist of some order is universal: and such a faith is a sufficient guarantee of the event. Every ephemeron of a tale-writer, a dramatist, novelist, lyrist, and sonnetteer, has been taken by one or another for the man. But he has not come out of his silence yet; and it is likely that it may still be long before he does.

There is another reason, besides those which have been mentioned, why it would be highly unjust and injurious to conclude that there is nothing more in the nation's heart and brain than has come out before the eye. The American nation is made up of contributions from almost all other civilised nations: and, though the primary truths of God, and the universal characteristics of Man are common to them all, there are infinite diversities to be blended into unity before a national character can arise; before a national mind can be seen to actuate the mass of society. It is probable that the first great work of genius that appears will be the most powerful instrument for effecting this blending and reconciling: but the appearance of such a work is doubtless retarded in proportion to the checks and repression of social sympathy, caused by the diversity of influences under which society proceeds.

The best productions of American literature are, in my opinion, the tales and sketches in which the habits and manners of the people of the country are delineated, with exactness, with impartiality of temper, and without much regard to the picturesque. Such are the tales of Judge Hall of Cincinnati. Such are the tales by the author of Swallow Barn; where, however, there is the addition of a good deal of humour, and a subtraction of some of the truth.

Miss Sedgwick's tales are of the highest order of the three, from the moral beauty which they breathe. This moral beauty is of a much finer character than the *bonhommie* which is the charm of Irving's pictures of manners. She sympathises where he good-naturedly observes; she cheerily loves where he gently quizzes. Miss Sedgwick's novels have this moral beauty too; as has everything she touches: but they have great and irretrievable faults as works of art. Tale-writing is her forte: and in this vocation, no one who has observed her striking progression will venture to say what she may not achieve.

Among the host of tales which appear without the names of their authors are three, which strike me as excellent in their several ways: "Allen Prescott," containing the history of a New England boy, drawn to the life, and in a just and amiable spirit: "The New England Housekeeper," in which the *ménage* of a rising young lawyer, with its fresh joys and ludicrous perplexities, is humorously exhibited: and "Memoirs of a New England Village Choir," a sketch of even higher merit.

Irving's writings have had their meed. He has lived in the sunshine of fame for many years, and in the pleasant consciousness that he has been a benefactor to the present generation, by shedding some gentle, benignant, and beguiling influences on many intervals of their rough and busy lives. More than this he has probably not expected; and more than this he does not seem likely to achieve. If any of his works live, it will be his Columbus: and the later of his productions will be the first forgotten.

Cooper's novels have a very puny vitality. Some descriptions of scenery, and some insulated adventures, have great merit: but it is not human life that he presents. His female characters are far from human; and in his selections of the chances of mortal existence, he usually chooses the remotest. He has a vigour of perception and conception, which might have made him, with study and discipline, a great writer. As it is, he is, I believe, regarded as a muchregretted failure.

The Americans have a poet. Bryant has not done anything like what he can and will do: but he has done some things that will live. Those of his poems which are the best known, or the most quoted, are smooth, sweet, faithful descriptions of nature, such as his own imagination delights in. I shall always remember the voice and manner with which he took up a casual remark of mine, about sights to be seen in the pine-barrens. When the visitors had all departed, his question "And what of the pine-barrens?" revealed the spirit of the poet. Of his poems of this class, "The Evening Wind" is to me the most delicious. But others,—"The Past," and "Thanatopsis"—indicate another kind, and a higher degree of power. If he would live for his gifts, if his future years could be devoted to "clear poetical activity," "looking up," like the true artist, "to his dignity and his calling," that dignity and that calling may prove to be as lofty as they no doubt appeared in the reveries of his boyhood; and he may be listened to as lovingly over the expanse of future time, as he already is over that of the ocean.

The Americans have also a historian of promise. Mr. Bancroft's History of the United States is little more than begun: but the beginning is characterised by an impartial and benevolent spirit, and by the indications which it affords of the author's fidelity to democratic principles; the two primary requisites in a historian of the republic. The carrying on the work to a completion will be a task of great toil and anxiety: but it will be a most important benefit to society at large, if it fulfils its promise.

The periodical literature of the United States is of a very low order. I know of no review where anything like impartial, enlightened criticism is to be found. The North American Review had once some reputation in England; but it has sunk at home and abroad, less from want of talent than of principle. If it has any principle whatever at present, it seems to be to praise every book it mentions, and to fall in as dexterously as possible with popular prejudice. The American Quarterly, published at Philadelphia, is uninteresting from the triteness of its morals, and a general dearth of thought, amidst a good deal of cleverness. The Southern Review, published at Charleston,—sometime ago discontinued, but I believe lately renewed,—is the best

specimen of periodical literature that the country has afforded. After the large deductions rendered necessary by
the faults of southern temper, this Review maintains its
place above the rest; a rank which is, I believe, undisputed.

I met with one gem in American literature, where I
should have least expected it:—in the Knickerbocker; a
New York Monthly Magazine. Last spring, a set of papers
began to appear, called "Letters from Palmyra,"* six numbers of which had been issued when I left the country.
I have been hitherto unable to obtain the rest: but if they
answer to the early portions, there can be no doubt of
their being shortly in everybody's hands, in both countries.
These letters remain in my mind, after repeated readings,
as a fragment of lofty and tender beauty. Zenobia, Longi-
nus, and a long perspective of characters, live and move in
natural majesty; and the beauties of description and sentiment appear to me as remarkable as the strong conception
of character, and of the age. If this anonymous fragment
be not the work of a true artist,—if the work, when entire,
do not prove to be of a far higher order than anything
which has issued from the American press,—its early admirers will feel yet more surprise than regret.

It is continually said, on both sides of the water, and
with much truth, that the bad state of the laws of literary
property is answerable for some of the depression of American literature. It is true that the imperfection of these laws
inflicts various discouragements on American writers, while
it is disgracefully injurious to foreign authors. It is true
that American booksellers will not remunerate native authors while they can purloin the works of British writers:
and that the American public has a strong disposition to
listen to the utterance of the English in preference to the
prophets of their own country. It is true that in America,
where every man must work for his living, it is a discouragement to the pursuit of literature that a living cannot,
except in a few rare cases, be got by it. But all this is no

* "Letters of Lucius M. Piso, from Palmyra, to his friend
Marcus Curtius, at Rome: now first translated and published."
They present a picture of the state of the East in the reign of
Aurelian; and are to end, I suppose, with the fall of Palmyra.

solution of the fact of the nonexistence of literature in America: which fact is indeed no mystery. The present state of the law, by which the works of English authors are pirated, undefended against mutilation, and made to drive native works out of the market, is so conspicuously bad, that there is every prospect of a speedy alteration: but there is nothing in the abuse which can silence genius, if genius is wanting to speak. It ought by this time to be understood that there is no power on earth which can re-press mental force of the highest kinds; which can stifle the utterance of a thoroughly-moved spirit: certainly no power which is held by piratical booksellers under defec-tive laws. Such discouragement is unjust and harsh; but it cannot be fatal. If a native genius, of a far higher order than any English, had been existing in America for the last ten years, he would have made himself heard ere this, and won his way into the general mind and heart through a host of bookselling harpies, and a chaos of lawlessness: he would have done this, even if it had been necessary to give his dinner for paper, and sell his bed to pay the printer;—expedients which it is scarcely conceivable that any author in that thriving land should be driven to. The absence of protection to foreign literary property is injuri-ous enough, without its being made answerable for the de-ficiency of literary achievement. The causes lie deeper, and will not have ceased to operate till long after the law shall have been made just in this particular.

Some idea of the literary taste of the country may be arrived at through a mention of what appeared to me to be the comparative popularity of living or recent British authors.

I heard no name so often as Mrs. Hannah More's. She is much better known in the country than Shakspeare. This is, of course, an indication of the religious taste of the peo-ple; and the fact bears only a remote relation to literature. Scott is idolised; and so is Miss Edgeworth; but I think no one is so much read as Mr. Bulwer. I question whether it is possible to pass half a day in general society without hearing him mentioned. He is not worshipped with the dumb self-surrendering reverence with which Miss Edgeworth is regarded: but his books are in every house; his occasional democratic aspirations are in every one's mouth; and the morality of his books is a constant theme of discussion, from among the most sensitive of the clergy down to the "thinking, thoughtless school-boy" and his chum. The next name is, decidedly, Mrs. Jameson's. She is altogether a favourite; and her "Characteristics of Women" is the book which has made her so. At a considerable distance follows Mrs. Hemans. Byron is scarcely heard of. Wordsworth lies at the heart of the people. His name may not be so often spoken as some others; but I have little doubt that his influence is as powerful as that of any whom I have mentioned. It is less diffused, but stronger. His works are not to be had at every store; but within people's houses they lie under the pillow, or open on the workbox, or they peep out of the coat-pocket: they are marked, re-marked, and worn. Coleridge is the delight of a few. So is Lamb; regarded, however, with a more tender love. I heard Mr. Hallam's name seldom, but always in a tone of extraordinary respect, and from those whose respect is most valuable.

No living writer, however, exercises so enviable a sway, as far as it goes, as Mr. Carlyle. It is remarkable that an influence like his should have been gained through scattered articles of review and speculation, spread over a number of years and a variety of periodicals. The Americans have his "Life of Schiller;" but it was not that. His articles in the Edinburgh Review met the wants of several of the best minds in the society of New England; minds weary of cant, and mechanical morals, and seeking something truer to rest upon. The discipleship immediately instituted is honourable to both. Mr. Carlyle's remarkable work, "Sartor Resartus," issued piecemeal through Fraser's Magazine, has been republished in America, and is exerting an influence proportioned to the genuineness of the admiration it has excited. Perhaps this is the first instance of the Americans having taken to their hearts an English work which came to them anonymously, unsanctioned by any recommendation, and even absolutely neglected at home. The book is acting upon them with wonderful force.

It has regenerated the preaching of more than one of the clergy; and, I have reason to believe, the minds and lives of several of the laity. It came as a benefactor to meet a pressing want; how pressing, the benefited testify by the fervour of their gratitude.

I know of no method by which the Americans could be assisted to utter what they may have in them so good as one which has been proposed, but which is not yet, I believe, in course of trial. It has been proposed that a publication should be established, open to the perfectly full and free discussion of every side of every question, within a certain department of inquiry;—Social Morals, for instance. There are difficulties at present in the way of presenting the whole of any subject to the public mind; difficulties arising from the unprincipled partiality of the common run of newspapers, the cautious policy of reviewers, the fear of opinion entertained by individual writers, and the impediments thrown in the way of free publication by the state of the laws relating to literary property. A publication devoted to the object of presenting, without fear or favour, all that can be said on any subject, without any restriction, except in the use of personalities towards opponents, would be the best possible remedy, under the circumstances, for the inconveniences complained of; the finest stimulus to the ascertainment of truth; the best education in the art of free and distinct utterance.

XIV.   Religion

"Der Grund aller Democratie; die höchste Thatsache der Popularität."

Novalis

"The Christian Religion is the root of all democracy; the highest fact in the Rights of Man."

RELIGION is the highest fact in the Rights of Man from its being the most exclusively private and individual, while it is also a universal, concern, of any in which man is interested. Religion is, in its widest sense, "the tendency of human nature to the Infinite;" and its principle is manifested in the pursuit of perfection in any direction whatever. It is in this widest sense that some speculative atheists have been religious men; religious in their efforts after self-perfection; though unable to personify their conception of the Infinite. In a somewhat narrower sense, religion is the relation which the highest human sentiments bear towards an infinitely perfect Being.

There can be no further narrowing than this. Any account of religion which restricts it within the boundaries of any system, which connects it with any mode of belief, which implicates it with hope of reward or fear of punishment, is low and injurious, and debases religion into superstition.

The Christian religion is specified as being the highest

fact in the rights of man from its embodying (with all the rest) the principle of natural religion—that religion is at once an individual, an universal, and an equal concern. In it may be found a sanction of all just claims of political and social equality; for it proclaims, now in music and now in thunder,—it blazons, now in sunshine and now in lightning,—the fact of the natural equality of men. In giving forth this as its grand doctrine, it is indeed "the root of all democracy;" the root of the maxim (among others) that among the inalienable rights of all men are life, liberty, and the pursuit of happiness. The democracy of America is planted down deep into the christian religion; into its principles, which it has in common with natural religion, and which it vivifies and illumines, but does not alter.

How does the existing state of religion accord with the promise of its birth? In a country which professes to secure to every man the pursuit of happiness in his own way, what is the state of his liberty in the most private and individual of all concerns? How carefully are all men and women left free from interference in following up their own aspirations after the Infinite, in realising their own ideas of perfection, in bringing into harmonious action the functions of their spirits, as infinitely diversified as the expression of their features?

The absence of such diversity is the first striking fact which presents itself on the institution of such an inquiry. If there were no constraint,—no social reward or penalty,—such an approach to uniformity of profession could not exist as is seen in the United States. In a society where speculation and profession were left perfectly free, as included among the inalienable rights of man, there would be many speculative (though probably extremely few practical) atheists: there would be an adoption by many of the principles of natural religion, otherwise than in and through Christianity: and Christianity would be adopted in modes as various as the minds by which it would be recognised. Instead of this, we find laws framed against speculative atheists: opprobrium directed upon such as embrace natural religion otherwise than through Christianity. Truth is deprived of the irrefragable testimony which would be afforded by whatever agreement might arise amidst this diversity: religion is insulted and scandalised by nominal adherence and hypocritical advocacy. There are many ways of professing Christianity in the United States: but there are few, very few men, whether speculative or thoughtless, whether studious or ignorant, whether reverent or indifferent, whether sober or profligate, whether disinterested or worldly, who do not carefully profess Christianity, in some form or another. This, as men are made, is unnatural. Society presents no faithful mirror of the religious perspective of the human mind.

The almost universal profession in America of the adoption of Christianity,—this profession by many whose habits of thought, and others whose habits of living forbid the supposition that it is the religion of their individual intellects and affections, compels the inquiry what sort of Christianity it is that is professed, and how it is come by. There is no evading the conviction that it is to a vast extent a monstrous superstition that is thus embraced by the tyrant, the profligate, the worldling, the bigot, the coward, and the slave; a superstition which offers little molestation to their vices, little rectification to their errors; a superstition which is but the spurious offspring of that divine Christianity which "is the root of all democracy, the highest fact in the Rights of Man." That so many of the meek, pure, disinterested, free, and brave, make the same profession, proves only that they penetrate to religion through superstition; or that they cast away unconsciously the superstition with which their spirits have no affinity, and accept such truth as all superstition must include in order to live.

The only test by which religion and superstition can be ultimately tried is that with which they co-exist. "By their fruits ye shall know them."

I watched closely the preaching in the south,—that of all denominations,—to see what could be made of Christianity, "the highest fact in the Rights of Man," in such a region. I found the stricter religionists preaching reward and punishment in connexion with modes of belief, and hatred to the Catholics. I found the more philosophical

preaching for or against materialism, and diverging to
phrenology. I found the more quiet and "gentlemanly"
preaching harmless abstractions,—the four seasons, the attributes of the Deity, prosperity and adversity, &c. I heard
one clergyman, who always goes out of the room when
the subject of negro emancipation is mentioned, or when
slavery is found fault with, preach in a southern city
against following a multitude to do evil. I heard one noble
religious discourse from the Rev. Joel Parker, a Presbyterian clergyman, of New Orleans; but except that one, I
never heard any available reference made to the grand
truths of religion, or principles of morals. The great principles which regard the three relations to God, man, and
self,—striving after perfection, mutual justice and charity,
and christian liberty,—were never touched upon.—Meantime, the clergy were pretending to find express sanctions
of slavery in the Bible; and putting words to this purpose
into the mouths of public men, who do not profess to remember the existence of the Bible in any other connexion.
The hatred to the Catholics also approaches too nearly in
its irreligious character to the oppression of the negro. It
is pleaded by some who most mourn the persecution the
Catholics are at present undergoing in the United States,
that there is a very prevalent ignorance on the subject of
the Catholic religion; and that dreadful slanders are being
circulated by a very few wicked, which deceive a great
many weak, persons.

I was seriously told, by several persons in the south and
west, that the Catholics of America were employed by the
Pope, in league with the Emperor of Austria and the Irish,
to explode the Union. The vast and rapid spread of the
Catholic faith in the United States has excited observation,
which grew into this rumour. I believe the truth to be that,
in consequence of the Pope's wish to keep the Catholics of
America a colonial church, and the Catholics of the country thinking themselves now sufficiently numerous to be an
American Catholic church, a great stimulus has been given
to proselytism. This has awakened fear and persecution;
which last has, again, been favourable to the increase of

the sect. It is found so impossible to supply the demand
for priests, that the term of education has been shortened
by two years.—Those observers who have made themselves
familiar with the modes in which institutions, even of the
most definite character, adapt themselves to the wants of
the time, will not be made uneasy by the spread of a religion so flexible in its forms as the Catholic, among a people so intelligent as the Americans. The Catholic body is
Democratic in its politics, and made up from the more independent kind of occupations. The Catholic religion is
modified by the spirit of the time in America; and its professors are not a set of men who can be priest-ridden to
any fatal extent. If they are let alone, and treated on
genuine republican principles, they may show us how the
true, in any old form of religion, may be separated from
the false, till, the eye being made clear, the whole body
will be full of light. If they cannot do this, their form of
religion will decay, or at least remain harmless; for it is
assuredly too late now for a return of the dark ages. At
all events, every American is required by his democratic
principles to let every man alone about his religion. He
may do with the religion what seems to him good; study,
controvert, adopt, reject, speak, write, or preach, whatever he perceives and thinks about its doctrines and its
abuses: but with its professors he has nothing to do, further than religiously to observe his fraternal relation to
them; suffering no variance of opinion to seduce him into
a breach of the republican and christian brotherhood to
which he is pledged.

    There is in this respect a dreadful infringement on hu-
man rights throughout the north; though a better spirit is
being cherished and extended by a few who see how contrary to all christian and all democratic principles it is that
a man should be the worse for his opinions in society. I
have seen enough to know how little chance Christianity
has in consequence of this infringement. I know that very
large numbers of people are secretly disinclined to cherish
what is imposed upon them, with perpetual and unvarying
modes of observance, from their childhood up; and how

the disgust grows from the opprobrium with which unbelief is visited. I know that there are minds in New England, as everywhere else, which must, from their very structure, pass through a state of scepticism on their way to stability; and that such are surrounded with snares, such as no man should lay in his brother's path; with temptations to hypocrisy, to recklessness, to despair; and to an abdication of their human prerogative of reason, as well as conscience. I know how women, in whom the very foundations of belief have been ploughed up by the share of authority, go wearily to church, Sunday after Sunday, to hear what they do not believe; lie down at night full of self-reproach for a want of piety which they do not know how to attain; and rise up in the morning hopelessly, seeing nothing in the day before them but the misery of carrying their secret concealed from parents, husband, sisters, friends. I know how young men are driven into vice, by having only the alternative of conformity or opprobrium: feeling it impossible to believe what is offered them; feeling it to be no crime to disbelieve: but, seeing unbelief treated as crime, and themselves under suspicion of it, losing faith in others and in themselves, and falling in reality at last. All this, and very much more, I know to be happening. I was told of one and another, with an air of mystery, like that with which one is informed of any person being insane, or intemperate, or insolvent, that so and so was thought to be an unbeliever. I was always tempted to reply, "And so are you, in a thousand things, to which this neighbour of yours adds one."—An elderly, generally intelligent, benevolent gentleman told me that he wanted to see regulations made by which deists should be excluded from office, and moral men only admitted. Happily, the community is not nearly so far gone in tyranny and folly as to entertain such a project as this: but it must be a very superstitious society where such an idea could be deliberately expressed by a sane man.

One circumstance struck me throughout the country. Almost as often as the conversation between myself and any other person on religious subjects became intimate and

earnest, I was met by the supposition that I was a convert. It was the same in other instances: wherever there
was a strong interest in the christian religion, conversion
to a particular profession of it was confidently supposed.
This fact speaks volumes.

XV. Spirit of Religion

=====

"For God hath not given us the spirit of fear; but of power,
and of love, and of a sound mind."

Paul the Apostle

"Hands full of hearty labours: pains that pay
And prize themselves—do much that more they may.
No cruel guard of diligent cares, that keep
Crowned woes awake, as things too wise for sleep:
But reverend discipline, religious fear,
And soft obedience, find sweet biding here.
Silence, and sacred rest, peace and pure joys—
Kind loves keep house, lie close, and make no noise.
And room enough for monarchs, while none swells
Beyond the limits of contentful cells.
The self-remembering soul sweetly recovers
Her kindred with the stars: not basely hovers
Below—but meditates th' immortal way
Home to the source of light and intellectual day."

Crashaw

SOCIETY in America is as much in a transition state about
religion as France and England are about politics. The
people are in advance of the clergy in America, as the
English are in advance of such of their political institutions as are in dispute. Discouraging as the aspect of religious profession in America is on a superficial survey, a
closer study will satisfy the observer that all will be well;
that the most democratic of nations is religious at heart;

and that its superstitions and offences against the spirit of Christianity are owing to temporary influences.

In order to ascertain what the spirit of religion really is in the country, we must not judge by the periodicals. Religious periodicals are almost entirely in the hands of the clergy, who are in no country fair representatives of the religion of the people. These periodicals are, almost without exception, as far as my knowledge of them goes, extremely bad. A very few have some literary and scientific merit; and many advocate with zeal particular methods of charity, and certainly effect a wide and beneficent co-operation for mutual help which could not be otherwise so well secured. But arrogance and uncharitableness, cant, exclusiveness, and an utter absence of sympathy with human interests and affections, generally render this class of publications as distasteful as the corresponding organs of religious bodies in the Old World. They are too little human in their character, from the books of the Sunday School Union to the most important of the religious reviews, to be by any possibility a fair expression of the spiritual state of some millions of persons. The acts of the laity, and especially of those who are least under the influence of the clergy, must be looked to as the only true manifestations.

If religion springs from morals, the religion must be most faulty where the morals are so. The greatest fault in American morals is an excessive regard to opinion. This is the reason of the want of liberality of which unbelievers, and unusual believers, have so much reason to complain. But the spirit of religion is already bursting through sectarian restraints. Many powerful voices are raised, within the churches as well as out of them, and even from a few pulpits, against the mechanical adoption and practice of religion, and in favour of individuality of thought, and the consequent spontaneousness of speech and action.

I know also of one place, at least, and I believe there are now several, where the people of colour are welcome to worship with the whites,—actually intermingled with them, instead of being set apart in a gallery appropriated to them. This is the last possible test of the conviction of human equality entertained by the white worshippers. It is such a test of this, their christian conviction, as no persons of any rank in England are ever called upon to abide. I think it very probable that the course of action which is common in America will be followed in this instance. A battle for a principle is usually fought long, and under discouragement: but the sure fruition is almost instantaneous, when the principle is but once put into action. The people of colour do actually, in one or more religious assemblies, sit among the whites, in token that the principle of human brotherhood is fully admitted. It may be anticipated that the example will spread from church to church —in the rural districts of the north first, and then in the towns;* so that the clergy will soon find themselves released from the necessity of veiling, or qualifying, the most essential truth of the gospel, from the pastoral consideration for the passions and prejudices of the white portion of their flocks, which they at present plead in excuse of their compromise.

The noble beneficence of the whole community shows that the spirit of the gospel is in the midst of them, as it respects the condition of the poor, ignorant, and afflicted. Of the generosity of society there can be no question; and if it were only accompanied with the strict justice which the same principles of christian charity require; if there were as zealous a regard to the rights of intellect and conscience in all as to the wants and sufferings of the helpless, such a realisation of high morals would be seen as the world has not yet beheld.

* When I visited the New York House of Refuge for the reformation of juvenile delinquents, one of the officers showed me, with complacency, that children of colour were sitting among the whites, in both the boys' and girls' schools. On explaining to me afterwards the arrangements of the chapel, he pointed out the division appropriated to the pupils of colour. "Do you let them mix in school, and separate them at worship?" I asked. He replied, with no little sharpness, "We are not amalgamationists, madam." The absurdity of the sudden wrath, and of the fact of a distinction being made at worship (of all occasions) which was not made elsewhere, was so palpable, that the whole of our large party burst into irresistible laughter.

I was struck by the fact, that at the Jefferson University, at Charlottesville, Virginia, where no fundamental provision is made for worship, where not the slightest authority is exercised over the students with regard to religious observances, there is not only a most regular administration of religion, but the fullest attendance upon it. Every one knows what a burden and snare the public prayers are at our English Universities, where the attendance is compulsory. At Charlottesville, where the matter is left to the inclination of the students, the attendance is punctual, quiet, and absolutely universal.*

The ascetic proscription of amusements extends to the clergy throughout the country; and includes the whole of the religious world in New England. As to the clergy, the superstition can scarcely endure long, it is so destitute of all reason. I went to a large party at Philadelphia, with a clergyman and other friends. Dancing presently began. I was asked a question, which implied that my clerical friend had gone home. "There he is," I replied. "O, I concluded that he went away when the dancing began;" said the lady, in a tone which implied that she thought he ought to have gone home. It was observed of this gentleman, that he could not be a religious man, he was seen at so many parties during my visit to his house.

This ascetic practice of taking care of one another's morals has gone to such a length in Boston, as to excite the frequent satire of some of its wisest citizens. This indicates that it will be broken through. When there was talk of attempting to set up the Italian opera there, a gentleman observed that it would never do: people would be afraid of the very name. "O!" said another, "call it Lectures on Music, with illustrations, and everybody will come."

The way in which religion is made an occupation by women, testifies not only to the vacuity which must exist when such a mistake is fallen into, but to the vigour with which the religious sentiment would probably be carried

* Ministers of four denominations undertake the duty in rotation, in terms of a year each. The invitation, and the discharge of the duty, are as purely voluntary as the attendance upon the services.

into the great objects and occupations of life, if such were permitted. I was perpetually struck with this when I saw women braving hurricane, frost, and snow, to flit from preaching to preaching; and laying out the whole day among visits for prayer and religious excitement, among the poor and the sick. I was struck with this when I saw them labouring at their New Testament, reading super-stitiously a daily portion of that which was already too familiar to the ear to leave any genuine and lasting im-pression, thus read. Extraordinary instances met my knowl-edge of both clergymen and ladies making the grossest mistakes about conspicuous facts of the gospel history, while reading it in daily portions for ever. It is not sur-prising that such a method of perusal should obviate all real knowledge of the book: but it is astonishing that those who feel it to be so should not change their methods, and begin at length to learn that which they have all their lives been vainly trusting that they knew.

The morality and religion of the people of the United States have suffered much by their being, especially in New England, an ostensibly religious community. There will be less that is ostensible and more that is genuine, as they grow older. They are finding that it is the possession of the spirit, and not the profession of the form, which makes societies as well as individuals religious. All they have to do is to assert their birth-right of liberty; to be free and natural. They need have no fear of licence and irreligion. The spirit of their forefathers is strong in them: and, if it were not, the spirit of Humanity is in them; the very sanctum of religion. The idea of duty (perverted or unperverted) is before them in all their lives; and the love of their neighbour is in all their hearts. As surely then as they live and love, they will be religious. What they have to look to is that their religion be free and pure.

appearing to be true but not necessarily

XVI.   Administration of Religion

> "What will they then
> But force the spirit of grace itself, and bind
> His consort Liberty? what but unbuild
> His living temples, built by faith to stand,
> Their own faith, not another's?"
>
> *Milton*

> "Truth shall spring out of the earth;
> And righteousness shall look down from heaven."
>
> *85th Psalm*

THE inquiry concerning the working of the voluntary system in America,—the only country where it operates without an establishment by its side,—takes two directions. It is
asked, first, whether religion is administered sufficiently to
the people: and, secondly, what is the character of the
clergy.

The first question is easily answered. The eagerness for
religious instruction and the means of social worship are so
great that funds and buildings are provided wherever society exists. Though the clergy bear a larger proportion to
men of other occupations, I believe, than is the case anywhere, except perhaps in the Peninsula, they are too few
for the religious wants of the people. Men are wanting;
but churches and funds are sufficient. According to a gen-

eral summary of religious denominations,* made in 1835, the number of churches or congregations was 15,477; the population being, exclusive of the slaves, between fifteen and sixteen millions; and a not inconsiderable number being settlers scattered in places too remote for the formation of regular societies, with settled ministers. To these 15,477 churches there were only 12,130 ministers. If to these settled clergy, there are added the licentiates and candidates of the Presbyterian church, the local preachers of the Methodists, the theological students, and quaker administrators, it will be acknowledged that the number of religious teachers bears an unusually large proportion to the population. Yet the Baptist sect alone proclaims a want of above three thousand ministers to supply the existing churches. Every exertion is made to meet the religious wants of the people. The American Education Society has assisted largely in sending forth young ministers: the Mission and Bible Societies exhibit large results. In short, society in the United States offers every conceivable testimony that the religious instincts of the people may be trusted to supply their religious wants.

As to the other particular of the inquiry,—the character of the clergy,—more is to be said.

It is clear that there is no room under the voluntary system for some of the worst characteristics which have disgraced all christian priesthoods. In America, there can be no grasping after political power; no gambling in a lottery of church livings; no worldly pomp and state. These sins are precluded under a voluntary system, in the midst of a republic. Instead of these things, we find the protestant clergy generally belonging to the Federal party, when they open their lips upon politics at all. They belong to the apprehensive party; according to all precedent. It would be

* This summary does not pretend to be complete, but it is the nearest approximation to fact that can be obtained. According to it the Episcopalian Methodists are the most numerous sect: then the Catholics, Calvinistic Baptists, Presbyterians, Congregationalists, Christians, Episcopalians, and Quakers. The other denominations follow, down to the Tunkers and Shakers, which are the smallest.

called strange if it did not almost universally happen, that
(with the exception of the political churchmen of the Old
World) they who uphold a faith which shall remove mountains, who teach that men are not to fear "them that kill
the body, and afterwards have no more that they can do,"
are the most timid class of society; the most backward in
all great conflicts of principles.

The clergy in America are not, as a body, seekers of
wealth. It is so generally out of their reach, that the adoption of the clerical profession is usually an unequivocal testimony to their disinterestedness about money. But, as long
as the salaries of ministers are so moderate as they now
are, it cannot be otherwise than that the greater number
of clergy enter upon their profession in full view of a life
of labour, with small pecuniary recompense. There can, I
think, be no question that the vocation is adopted from
motives as pure as often actuate men; and that the dangers to which the clergy succumb arise afterwards out of
their disadvantageous position.

It is to be wished that some alteration could be made
in the mode of remunerating the clergy. At present, they
have usually small salaries and large presents. Nothing is
more natural than that grateful individuals or flocks should
like to testify their respect for their pastor by adding to his
comforts and luxuries: but, if all the consequences were
considered, I think the practice would be forborne, and
the salary increased instead. In the present state of morals,
it happens that instances are rare where one person can
give pecuniary benefit to another without injury to one or
both. Sympathy, help, may be given, with great mutual
profit; but rarely money or money's worth.* This arises
from the false associations which have been gathered round
wealth, and have implicated it too extensively with mental
and moral independence. Any one may answer for himself
the question whether it is often possible to regard a person

* "It is a mortifying truth, that two men in any rank of society could hardly be found virtuous enough to give money,
and to take it, as a necessary gift, without injury to the moral
entireness of one or both. But so stands the fact."
Edinburgh Review. xlviii, p. 303.

to whom he is under pecuniary obligation with precisely the same freedom, from first to last, which would otherwise exist. If among people of similar views, objects, and interests, this is felt as a difficulty, it is aggravated into a great moral danger when spiritual influences are to be dispensed by the aided and obliged party. I see no safety in anything short of a strict rule on the part of an honourable pastor to accept of no gift whatever. This would require some self-denial on the part of his friends; but they ought to be aware that giving gifts is the coarsest and lowest method of testifying respect and affection. Many ways are open to them: first by taking care that their pastor has such a fixed annual provision made for him as will secure him from the too heavy pressure of family cares; and then by yielding him that honest friendship, and plain-spoken sympathy, (without any religious peculiarity,) which may animate him in his studies and in his ministrations.

The American clergy being absolved from the common clerical vices of ambition and cupidity, it remains to be seen whether they are free also from that of the idolatry of opinion. They enter upon their office generally with pious and benevolent views. Do they retain their moral independence in it?—I cannot answer favourably.

The vices of any class are never to be imputed with the full force of disgraces to individuals. The vices of a class must evidently, from their extent, arise from some overpowering influences, under whose operation individuals should be respectfully compassionated, while the morbid influences are condemned. The American clergy are the most backward and timid class in the society in which they live; self-exiled from the great moral questions of the time; the least informed with true knowledge; the least efficient in virtuous action; the least conscious of that christian and republican freedom which, as the native atmosphere of piety and holiness, it is their prime duty to cherish and diffuse. The proximate causes of their degeneracy in this respect are easily recognised.

It is not merely that the living of the clergy depends on the opinion of those whom they serve. To all but the far and clear-sighted it appears that the usefulness of their function does so. Ordinary men may be excused for a willingness to seize on the precept about following after the things that make for peace, without too close an inquiry into the nature of that peace. Such a tendency may be excused, but not praised, in ordinary men. It must be blamed in all pastors who believe that they have grasped purer than ordinary principles of gospel freedom.

The first great mischief which arises from the disinclination of the clergy to bring what may be disturbing questions before their people, is that they themselves inevitably undergo a perversion of views about the nature of their pastoral office. To take the most striking instance now presented in the United States. The clergy have not yet begun to stir upon the Anti-Slavery question. A very few Presbyterian clergymen have nobly risked everything for it; some being members of Abolition societies; and some professors in the Oberlin Institute and its branches, where all prejudice of colour is discountenanced. But the bulk of the Presbyterian clergy are as fierce as the slave-holders against the abolitionists. I believe they would not object to have Mr. Breckinridge considered a sample of their body. The episcopalian clergy are generally silent on the subject of Human Rights, or give their influence against the Abolitionists. Not to go over the whole list of denominations, it is sufficient to mention that the ministers generally are understood to be opposed to abolition, from the circumstances of their silence in the pulpit, their conversation in society, and the conduct of those who are most under their influence. I pass on to the Unitarians, the religious body with which I am best acquainted, from my being a Unitarian myself. The Unitarians believe that they are not liable to many superstitions which cramp the minds and actions of other religionists. They profess a religion of greater freedom; and declare that Christianity, as they see it, has an affinity with all that is free, genial, intrepid, and true in the human mind; and that it is meant to be carried out into every social arrangement, every speculation of thought, every act of the life. Clergymen who preach this live in a crisis when a tremendous conflict of principles is taking place. On one side is the oppressor, struggling to keep his power for the sake of his gold; and with him the mercenary, the faithlessly timid, the ambitious, and the weak. On the other side are the friends of the slave; and with them those who, without possibility of recompense, are sacrificing their reputations, their fortunes, their quiet, and risking their lives, for the principle of freedom. What are the Unitarian clergy doing amidst this war which admits of neither peace nor truce, but which must end in the subjugation of the principle of freedom, or of oppression?

I believe Mr. May had the honour of being the first Unitarian pastor who sided with the right. Whether he has sacrificed to his intrepidity one christian grace; whether he has lost one charm of his piety, gentleness, and charity, amidst the trials of insult which he has had to undergo, I dare appeal to his worst enemy. Instead of this, his devotion to a most difficult duty has called forth in him a force of character, a strength of reason, of which his best friends were before unaware. It filled me with shame for the weakness of men, in their noblest offices, to hear the insolent compassion with which some of his priestly brethren spoke of a man whom they have not light and courage enough to follow through the thickets and deserts of duty, and upon whom they therefore bestow their scornful pity from out of their shady bowers of complacency.—Dr. Follen came next: and there is nothing in his power that he has not done and sacrificed in identifying himself with the cause of emancipation. I heard him, in a perilous time, pray in church for the "miserable, degraded, insulted slave; in chains of iron, and chains of gold." This is not the place in which to exhibit what his sacrifices have really been.— Dr. Channing's later services are well known. I know of two more of the Unitarian clergy who have made an open and dangerous avowal of the right: and of one or two who have in private resisted wrong in the cause. But this is all. As a body they must, though disapproving slavery, be ranked as the enemies of the abolitionists. Some have pleaded to me that it is a distasteful subject. Some think it sufficient that they can see faults in individual abolitionists. Some say that their pulpits are the property of their people, who are not therefore to have their minds disturbed by what they hear thence. Some say that the question is no business of theirs. Some urge that they should be turned out of their pulpits before the next Sunday, if they touched upon Human Rights. Some think the subject not spiritual enough. The greater number excuse themselves on the ground of a doctrine which, I cannot but think, has grown out of the circumstances; that the duty of the clergy is to decide on how much truth the people can bear, and to administer it accordingly.—So, while society is going through the greatest of moral revolutions, casting out its most vicious anomaly, and bringing its Christianity into its politics and its social conduct, the clergy, even the Unitarian clergy, are some pitying and some ridiculing the apostles of the revolution; preaching spiritualism, learning, speculation; advocating third and fourth-rate objects of human exertion and amelioration, and leaving it to the laity to carry out the first and pressing moral reform of the age. They are blind to their noble mission of enlightening and guiding the moral sentiment of society in its greatest crisis. They not only decline aiding the cause in weekdays by deed or pen, or spoken words; but they agree in private to avoid the subject of Human Rights in the pulpit till the crisis be past. No one asks them to harrow the feelings of their hearers by sermons on slavery: but they avoid offering those christian principles of faith and liberty with which slavery cannot co-exist.

Seeing what I have seen, I can come to no other conclusion than that the most guilty class of the community in regard to the slavery question at present is, not the slave-holding, nor even the mercantile, but the clerical: the most guilty, because not only are they not blinded by life-long custom and prejudice, nor by pecuniary interest, but they profess to spend their lives in the study of moral relations, and have pledged themselves to declare the whole counsel of God.—Whenever the day comes for the right principle to be established, let them not dare to glory in the glory of their country. Now, in its martyr-age, they shrink from being confessors. It will not be for them to march in to the triumph with the "glorious army." Yet, if the clergy of America follow the example of other rearguards of society, they will be the first to glory in the reformation which they have done their utmost to retard.

An extraordinary revelation of the state of the case between the clergy and the people was made to me, most unconsciously, by a minister who, by the way, acknowledges that he avoids, on principle, preaching on the subjects which interest him most: he thinks he serves his people best, by carrying into the pulpit subjects of secondary interest to himself. This gentleman, shocked with the tidings of some social tyranny on the anti-slavery question, exclaimed, "Such a revelation of the state of people's minds as this, is enough to make one leave one's pulpit, and set to work to mend society." What a volume do these few words disclose, as to the relation of the clergy to the people and the time!

What the effect would be of the clergy carrying religion into what is most practically important, and therefore most interesting, is shown as often as opportunity occurs; which is all too seldom. When Dr. Channing dropped, in a sermon last winter, that legislatures as well as individuals were bound to do the will of God, every head in the church was raised or turned; every eye waited upon him. When another minister preached on being 'alone,' and showed how the noblest benefactors of the race, the truest servants of God, must, in striking out into new regions of thought and action, pass beyond the circle of common human sympathies, and suffer accordingly, many a stout heart melted into tears; many a rigid face crimsoned with emotion; and the sermon was repeated and referred to, far and near, under the name of "the Garrison sermon;" a name given to it, not by the preacher, but by the consciences of some and the sympathies of others. Contrast with such an effect as this the influence of preaching, irrelevant to minds and seasons. If such sayings are admired or admitted at the moment, they are soon forgotten, or remembered only in the general. "Don't you think," said a gentleman to me, "that sermons are sadly useless things for the most part? admonitions strung like bird's eggs on a string; so that they tell pretty much the same, backwards or forwards, one way or another."

It appears to me that the one thing in which the clergy of every kind are fatally deficient is faith: that faith which would lead them, first, to appropriate all truth, fearlessly and unconditionally; and then to give it as freely as they have received it. They are fond of apostolic authority. What would Paul's ministry have been if he had preached on everything but idolatry at Ephesus, and licentiousness at Corinth? There were people whose silver shrines, whose prejudices, whose false moral principles were in danger. There were people who were as unconscious of the depth of their sin as the oppressors of the negro at the present day. How would Paul have then finished his course? Very like the American christian clergy of the nineteenth century.

The next great mischief that arises from the fear of opinion which makes the clergy keep aloof from the stirring questions of the time, is that they are deprived of that influence, (the highest kind of all,) that men exert by their individual characters and convictions. Their character is comparatively uninfluential from its being supposed professional; and their convictions, because they are concluded to be formed from imperfect materials. A clergyman's opinions on politics, and on other affairs of active life in which morals are most implicated, are attended to precisely in proportion as he is secular in his habits and pursuits. A minister preached, a few years ago, against discount, and high prices in times of scarcity. The merchants of his flock went away laughing: and the pastor has never got over it. The merchants speak of him as a very holy man, and esteem his services highly for keeping their wives, children, and domestics in strict religious order: but in preaching to themselves he has been preaching to the winds ever since that day. A liberal-minded, religious father of a family said to me, "Take care how you receive the uncorroborated statements of clergymen about that;" (a matter of social fact;) "they know nothing about it. They are not likely to know anything about it." "Why?" "Because there is nobody to tell them. You know the clergy are looked upon by all grown men as a sort of people between men and women." In a republic, where politics afford the discipline and means of expression of every man's morals, the clergy withdraw from, not only all party movements, but all political interests. Some barely vote: others do not even do this. Their plea is, as usual, that public opinion will not bear that the clergy should be upon the same footing as to worldly affairs as others. The statement should not, however, be taken on the word of the clergy alone; for they are very apt to think that the people cannot yet bear many things in which the flocks have already outstripped their pastors.

A third great mischief from the isolation of the clergy is that, while it deprives them of the highest kind of influence which is the prerogative of manhood, it gives them a lower kind:—an influence as strong as it is pernicious to others, and dangerous to themselves;—an influence confined to the weak members of society; women and superstitious men. By such they are called "faithful guardians." Guardians of what? A healthy person may guard a sick one: a sane man may guard a lunatic: a grown person may guard a child: and, for social purposes, an appointed watch may guard a criminal. But how can any man guard his equal in spiritual matters, the most absolutely individual of all? How can any man come between another's soul and the infinite to which it tends? If it is said that they are guardians of truth, and not of conscience, they may be asked for their warrant. God has given his truth for all. Each is to lay hold of what he can receive of it; and he sins if he devolves upon another the guardianship of what is given him for himself. As to the fitness of the clergy to be guardians, it is enough to mention what I know: that there is infidelity within the walls of their churches of which they do not dream; and profligacy among their flocks of which they will be the last to hear. Even in matters which are esteemed their peculiar business, the state of faith and morals, they are more in the dark than any other persons in society. Some of the most religious and moral persons in the community are among those who never enter their churches; while among the company who sit at the feet of the pastor while he refines upon abstractions, and builds a moral structure upon imperfect principles, or upon metaphysical impossibilities, there are some in whom the very capacity of stedfast belief has been cruelly destroyed; some who hide loose morals under a strict profession of religion; and some if possible more lost still, who have arrived at making their religion co-exist with their profligacy. Is there not here something like the blind leading the blind?

I cannot enlarge upon the disagreeable subject of the devotion of the ladies to the clergy. I believe there is no liberal-minded minister who does not see, and too sensibly feel, the evil of women being driven back upon religion as a resource against vacuity; and of there being a professional class to administer it. Some of the most sensible and religious elderly women I know in America speak, with a strength which evinces strong conviction, of the mischief to their sex of ministers entering the profession young and poor, and with a great enthusiasm for parochial visiting. There is no very wide difference between the auricular confession of the catholic church, and the spiritual confidence reposed in ministers the most devoted to visiting their flocks.

My final impression is, that religion is best administered in America by the personal character of the most virtuous members of society, out of the theological profession: and next, by the acts and preachings of the members of that profession who are the most secular in their habits of mind and life. The exclusively clerical are the worst enemies of Christianity, except the vicious.

XVII. Conclusion

My book must come to an end; but I offer no conclusion of my subject. I do not pretend to have formed any theory about American society or prospects to which a finishing hand can be put in the last page. American society itself constitutes but the first pages of a great book of events, into whose progress we can see but a little way; and that but dimly. It is too soon yet to theorise; much too soon to speak of conclusions even as to the present entire state of this great nation.

However the Americans may fall short, in practice, of the professed principles of their association, they have realised many things for which the rest of the civilised world is still struggling; and which some portions are only beginning to intend. They are, to all intents and purposes, self-governed. They have risen above all liability to a hereditary aristocracy, a connexion between religion and the State, a vicious or excessive taxation, and the irresponsibility of any class. Whatever evils may remain or may arise, in either the legislative or executive departments, the means of remedy are in the hands of the whole people: and those people are in possession of the glorious certainty that time and exertion will infallibly secure all wisely desired objects.

They have one tremendous anomaly to cast out; a deadly sin against their own principles to abjure. But they are doing this with an earnestness which proves that the national heart is sound. The progress of the Abolition question within three years, throughout the whole of the rural districts of the north, is a far stronger testimony to the virtue of the nation than the noisy clamour of a portion of the slave-holders of the south, and the merchant aristocracy of the north, with the silence of the clergy, are against it. The nation must not be judged of by that portion whose worldly interests are involved in the maintenance of the anomaly; nor yet by the eight hundred flourishing abolition societies of the north, with all the supporters they have in unassociated individuals. The nation must be judged of as to Slavery by neither of these parties; but by the aspect of the conflict between them. If it be found that the five abolitionists who first met in a little chamber five years ago, to measure their moral strength against this national enormity, have become a host beneath whose assaults the vicious institution is rocking to its foundations, it is time that slavery was ceasing to be a national reproach. Europe now owes to America the justice of regarding her as the country of abolitionism, quite as emphatically as the country of slavery.

The civilisation and the morals of the Americans fall far below their own principles. This is enough to say. It is better than contrasting or comparing them with European morals and civilisation: which contrast or comparison can answer no purpose, unless on the supposition, which I do not think a just one, that their morals and civilisation are derived from their political organisation. A host of other influences are at work, which must nullify all conclusions drawn from the politics of the Americans to their morals. Such conclusions will be somewhat less rash two centuries hence. Meantime, it will be the business of the world, as well as of America, to watch the course of republicanism and of national morals; to mark their mutual action, and humbly learn whatever the new experiment may give out. To the whole world, as well as to the Americans, it is important to ascertain whether the extraordinary mutual respect and kindness of the American people generally are attributable to their republicanism: and again, how far their republicanism is answerable for their greatest fault,— their deficiency of moral independence.

No peculiarity in them is more remarkable than their national contentment. If this were the result of apathy, it would be despicable: if it did not co-exist with an active principle of progress, it would be absurd. As it is, I can regard this national attribute with no other feeling than veneration. Entertaining, as I do, little doubt of the general safety of the American Union, and none of the moral progress of its people, it is clear to me that this national contentment will live down all contempt, and even all wonder; and come at length to be regarded with the same genial and universal emotion with which men recognise in an individual the equanimity of rational self-reverence.